MISSIONS AND MONEY

The American Society of Missiology Series, in collaboration with Orbis Books, seeks to publish scholarly works of high merit and wide interest on numerous aspects of missiology—the study of mission. Able presentations on new and creative approaches to the practice and understanding of mission will receive close attention.

Previously published in
The American Society of Missiology Series

American Society of Missiology Series, No. 15

MISSIONS AND MONEY

*Affluence as a Western
Missionary Problem*

Jonathan J. Bonk

ORBIS BOOKS

Maryknoll, New York 10545

Fourth Printing, April 1996

Copyright © 1991 by Orbis Books
Published by Orbis Books, Maryknoll, New York 10545
All rights reserved
Manufactured in the United States of America

All biblical citations are from the New International Version.

Library of Congress Cataloging-in-Publication Data

Bonk, Jon, 1945-
    Missions and money: affluence as a
western missionary problem / Jonathan J. Bonk.
        p.   cm. — (American Society of Missiology series; no. 15)
    Includes bibliographical references and index.
    ISBN 0-88344-718-5
    1. Missions—Theory.   2. Wealth—Religious aspects—Christianity.
3. Christianity and culture.   4. East and West.   5. Missions—
Controversial literature.   I. Title.   II. Series.
BV2063.B63   1990
266'.0231722—dc20   90-48231
                                                                      CIP

Contents

93828

Preface to the Series

The purpose of the ASM Series — now in existence since 1980 — is to publish, without regard for disciplinary, national, or denominational boundaries, scholarly works of high quality and wide interest on missiological themes from the entire spectrum of scholarly pursuits, e.g., biblical studies, theology, history, history of religions, cultural anthropology, linguistics, art, education, political science, economics, and development, to name only the major components. Always the focus will be on Christian mission.

By "mission" in this context is meant a passage over the boundary between faith in Jesus Christ and its absence. In this understanding of mission, the basic functions of Christian proclamation, dialogue, witness, service, worship, and nurture are of special concern. How does the transition from one cultural context to another influence the shape and interaction between these dynamic functions? Cultural and religious plurality are recognized as fundamental characteristics of the six-continent missionary context in East and West, North and South.

Missiologists know that they need the other disciplines. And those in other disciplines need missiology, perhaps more than they sometimes realize. Neither the insider's nor the outsider's view is complete in itself. The world Christian mission has through two millennia amassed a rich and well-documented body of experience to share with other disciplines. The complementary relation between missiology and other learned disciplines is a key of this Series, and interaction will be its hallmark.

The promotion of scholarly dialogue among missiologists may, at times, involve the publication of views and positions that other missiologists cannot accept, and with which members of the Editorial Committee do not agree. Manuscripts published in this series reflect the opinions of their authors and are not meant to represent the position of the American Society of Missiology or of the Editorial Committee for the ASM Series. The committee's selection of texts is guided by such criteria as intrinsic worth, readability, relative brevity, freedom from excessive scholarly apparatus, and accessibility to a broad range of interested persons and not merely to experts or specialists.

On behalf of the membership of the American Society of Missiology we express our deep thanks to the staff of Orbis Books, whose steadfast support over a decade for this joint publishing venture has enabled it to mature and bear scholarly fruit.

James A. Scherer, Chair
Mary Motte, FMM
Charles R. Taber
ASM Series Editorial Committee

Foreword

Missions and Foreign Money

Even though money and spirit are quite different realities, no one will claim that they have no relation to each other. Even Jesus used an apostle, Judas Iscariot, as "keeper of the funds" (John 12:6) — though admittedly Judas proved untrustworthy. The case of Judas, in fact, clearly illuminates the ambiguity of the relationship between money and the world of Christian spiritual ideals since earliest times.

As is the case with long-established churches, "mission" churches founded and supported by Northern churches in the South cannot exist without money; but neither do they necessarily thrive if money is available in abundance. Dramatically illustrating and calling attention to this problem, we have in our hands a penetrating discussion of missions and money by Jonathan Bonk, a Canadian Mennonite. A basic argument of this book is that an imbalance in the relative wealth of evangelizer-missionaries and those among whom they work distorts the transmission and inculturation of the Gospel. Professor Bonk makes a cogent argument for this thesis, chiefly as it applies to Protestant missions, and especially to those from North America. I commend his book to all persons interested in the spread of the whole Gospel in the whole world.

While the book discusses this question in its Protestant dimensions, it also has Roman Catholic aspects, which are too often passed over in embarrassed silence or are unacknowledged. I elaborated on this in several chapters in my book *The Coming of the Third Church*, (Maryknoll, N.Y.: Orbis Books, 1977). It is my belief that conclusions similar to those drawn by Jonathan Bonk for Protestant missions can also be reached concerning the Catholic church's mission work. But it is not the purpose of these few pages to draw these conclusions in any detail. Rather, a few general observations on this theme will be elaborated to insure that the issue is faced squarely.

It may be helpful to observe that the terminology surrounding "missions" is itself disturbing to us Catholics. Commonly, we understand the term missions to mean territories which Rome has assigned to various mission organizations in the system formerly known as the *jus commissionis*. Under

this system of entrusting territories, these mission organizations, usually
religious orders or clerical societies of apostolic life such as the Franciscans
or the Paris Foreign Mission Society, bore virtually complete responsibility
for administering "their" missions. Thus they sent missionaries to them,
collected the necessary funds for them, and endeavored to build up church
communities in their missions.

These organizations succeeded so well that, in great measure, almost
everywhere today we find Catholic parishes with native bishops, priests, and
religious. Vatican Council II recognized this and spoke not only of the "one,
holy, Catholic church," but began speaking of "the communion of many
local churches." As a result of this, in 1969 the *jus commissionis* system was
ended and these missions were raised to the status of dioceses, each with
its own bishop who had authority even over expatriate "missionaries" in
the service of the local church.

Thus it seems anachronistic to Catholics today to speak of missions and
for indigenous Christians in such local churches "missions" sounds a bit
patronizing. But the problems of missions and money and authentic inculturation of the Gospel are no less acute even if the terminology is somewhat
passé.

It would be a serious mistake for Roman Catholics to think that money
issues similar to those discussed by Professor Bonk have not in the past
distorted their mission activity, or that it does not today have an effect on
both the extensive and intensive growth of Southern churches. And facing
that problem may well be important for Northern churches to discover
deeper dimensions of Christian truth about the relationship of human communities and wealth.

For the independent Protestant churches described by Jonathan Bonk —
churches today sending thousands of young people into mission — the word
"mission" does not connote anything like "entrusted territories." For such
Protestants the term simply denotes a group of people who go out "on
mission" in the name of Jesus. But their great zeal for the Gospel does not
relieve them of the responsibility of reflecting upon the potential of money
to corrupt the inculturation of the message.

In his own day, Jesus is recalled as having had a simple solution to the
money problem for his apostle missionaries. His commissioning mandate
(see, for example, Luke 9:1-6 and 10:1-9 and parallels) is inherently fascinating in its idealism. It both engages one totally and portrays a life freeing
missionaries from every care for the sake of the Gospel of the arrival of
the Reign of God: "Take nothing for your journey, no staff, nor bag, nor
bread, nor money — not even an extra tunic" (Luke 9:1).

Down through the ages, that ideal was maintained as an ideal and even
physically approximated by missionaries in times when "sending churches"
and missionaries were not immeasurably wealthier and more powerful than
those to whom they were sent. For example, in 596 Pope Gregory the Great
sent St. Augustine and his band of Benedictine monks to England as mis-

sionaries. Sixth-century Irish-Scottish monks lived a life much like that of the apostles when they came as missionaries to the European continent. Similarly, St. Francis of Assisi (died, 1226), who was influenced by the ideals portrayed in the Lucan passages quoted above, lived in complete poverty and detachment. He sent his religious as missionaries to Morocco and Egypt with the admonition: "Cast your burden on the Lord; he will sustain you," echoing the spirituality of Psalm 55:23 and 1 Peter 5:7. Although it may verge on romanticizing the past to say so, one suspects that these earlier generations of missionaries knew that wealth was itself a problem. That insight has largely been lost in the modern age. Perhaps a postmodern age will be capable of recapturing the spiritual wisdom of the ancient insight, the tradition of which was kept by the early monks and mendicants.

With the European discovery of the New World and subsequently with the development of reliable means of transoceanic travel in the eighteenth century, this monastic and mendicant heritage of suspicion of money developed into something quite different. The dangerous memory of poor, itinerant heralds of the Gospel of the Founder of Christianity was almost totally domesticated. In addition, unlike the medieval Benedictine and Franciscan missionaries, modern missionaries — Protestant and Catholic — found themselves laboring under the burden of colonial and imperial systems. Perhaps more dangerously, psychologically they worked amongst peoples whose material culture most Europeans and North Americans looked down upon and whose spiritual culture few Westerners appreciated. Instead of sharing totally *as equals* in the life of their people in the Lucan spirit, modern missionaries created mini-European and American "stations" in exotic lands and often had their wives or cadres of dedicated religious sisters to provide a familiar hearth for them when they returned home from their day's exertions. Relative to standards of living in their homelands, such stations were modest; relative to standards among the peoples they sought to evangelize, these stations were often luxurious.

Simply "going there" was viewed as an immense sacrifice by the countrymen and relatives of these missionaries. No American or European, it was commonly thought, could live at the level of the "locals." But it was probably very seldom considered that if the missionary *could not* do so, that incapacity might cause serious disturbances in the evangelization and inculturation process.

The manner in which money is raised in the North for missions in the South is not a question of purely theoretical relevance. Vatican Council II raised it in a way that was easily forgotten, even though it forthrightly criticized the begging system heretofore used in mission fundraising. In the Conciliar Document on Missions (*Ad Gentes*) the bishops observed that missionary activity, "the greatest and holiest work of the Church" (art. 29), should be financed by having a set portion of the budget of all local churches directed to missionary activity (art. 38). The goal of the Council's directives was that the financing of evangelization efforts needed to be planned. The wisdom of that directive is clear, but it does not go to the heart of the matter in the way Jonathan Bonk points us: to ask even more basic questions about the affluence of Northern-based missionaries in the South. Going one step further, remembering the monks and early mendicants, one might ask if money in mission is so important and open to so many abuses that it needs careful attention lest its gathering and dispersing corrupt the message, the messenger, and reception of the Gospel. It must be admitted that the Council itself thought only of greater efficiency and providing *more* material resources for missions, not of the deeper questions. Indeed, this entire issue has been dealt with nowhere as thoroughly and painstakingly — in regard to to its deeper ramifications — as we find it treated in Professor Bonk's book.

It is not too radical, I think, to ask: Is the flow of large amounts of money from North to South still needed? Should the status of the young church remain humble and its growth proceed only as local economies grow? Would such a step lead local Christians to exert greater efforts toward socio-political and economic development and liberation than they do when, for example, they seek all the funds for a new pastoral ministry training center abroad rather than raise half or even more locally?

While not wanting to attack the notion of international Christian solidarity, the practical ambiguity of Northern financial support of Southern evangelization efforts simply must not be passed over in silence. We have the historical examples of an untold number of schools, churches, and hospitals founded and built by both Catholics and Protestants in their missions. Without question they did a lot of good, but they also created the impression that the mission/evangelization enterprise is performed by a mighty transnational religious corporation. The Christian missionaries of India became known as managers of schools and hospitals, yet not as masters of the spiritual life. Here one must think of Jesus who did not let himself be impressed by the magnificence of buildings in the Holy City. Consider his reply to the disciple's exclamation: "Look, Teacher, what large stones, what buildings!" The reaction of Jesus was: "Not one stone here will be left upon another; all will be thrown down" (Mark 13:1-2).

Reflecting on the challenges contained in the person and message of Jesus is as difficult for Catholics as it is for Evangelicals. No one needs to cast a stone at anyone else, but perhaps we can help one another understand the particular nature of the problems we face individually as churches. Jonathan Bonk is immensely helpful in this.

The extremes of poverty and wealth in today's world are a real scandal. "Scandal," in the weak sense of the word's common use means "shocking." What needs consideration is whether the scandal may be *real scandal* in the classic sense — leading people astray and corrupting them even if unconsciously. Put in the form of a question that flows naturally from Professor Bonk's book: "Does money today so obfuscate interchurch relations as to distort the Gospel? For both members of long established and younger churches?"

We Christians know we are called to work toward a climate where a reasonable contentment with a more modest living standard must become the norm. But when our very evangelization efforts—moving from the North to the South—involve us in funding church projects and development projects that undoubtedly benefit people, questions still need to be raised: Do not *even the best* of such projects run the risk of undesirable consequences?

The church, we easily say, does not exist for itself, but is founded as a sign of hope for the world. And we know that Christians did not receive the command to construct buildings but to invite peoples to discover their fellowship as forgiven, Spirit-enlivened believers under God in Jesus as the Christ. This is the task of God's people, that all may live more worthily in the sight of God and their fellow human beings.

Money is and will always be important and necessary for the life of churches. Nevertheless, it must be allocated in the right proportions and with full knowledge that—under present world conditions—it is not merely neutral, but dangerously liable to corrupt the evangelization process. Until a short time ago it was a one-way street between Western churches and the Southern missions. In the North was the rich, charitable, teaching church; in the South were the poor, needy recipients of Northern Christian largesse. In the past twenty-five years that relationship has been transformed into a highway with two-way traffic. We are no longer dealing with one-sided mission help, but with a need for a frank and critical exchange of insights between churches that can and should occur on several levels. That process receives an extremely insightful assist in the work of Professor Bonk. I only hope that the entire church will have the wisdom and courage to take up his invitation to reflect seriously on this important question.

Walbert Bühlmann, O.F.M. Cap.

Foreword

Wealthy Missionaries: An African Viewpoint

I grew up near a mission station where for many years I interacted and rubbed shoulders with missionaries. At that time, missionaries were the only people who had good and decent houses, clean piped water, telephones, electricity, and serviceable automobiles. They were able to employ quite a number of people in the neighborhood as cooks, ayahs, gardeners, messengers, and menials of various kinds who did many of the more tedious household chores for them. There was no doubt that they were privileged ones, envied by less lavishly endowed neighbors who would have embraced Christianity at once had they been assured that such immense affluence and wealth was part of the package. What brought about disillusionment and resentment to a young Christian community was the feeling that they had been conjured into believing that, by becoming Christians, their material and social statuses would dramatically improve. The missionary was, by local standards, a very wealthy person. People could not understand why, with so much wealth, the missionary seemed unwilling to share with those who were poverty stricken.

In *The Gospel and Frontier Peoples*, John Mbiti describes African converts as beggars of Christian spirituality, ideas, cash, and personnel. As he puts it:

> African Christians still regard the missionary or his home church overseas as "omniscient" in all matters pertaining to Christian faith; as the "omnipotent" in money and wealth.[1]

What Mbiti means is that African Christians expected so much from rich missionaries because they could see the rich baggage of a missionary who was arriving for a new appointment. They wondered why on earth should a single person have so much while most people lived in deprivation. Even chiefs, considered wealthy by local standards, would visit a missionary for the purpose of acquiring a part of his astonishing wealth. Such affluence gave the missionary leverage and power in the community. Reflecting on this phenomena, Jean-Marc Ela wonders how the Church can evangelize without being an incarnational institution sharing the life of the people, since that is the locus par excellence of the mediation of scripture, the fertile ground of all experience of prayer, and the celebration of salvation in Jesus Christ.[2]

The witness of self-denial, lived out in authentic imitation of Christ, places us at the very heart of the gospel. It locates us at a pivotal point where we are able to proclaim the saving power of God in a credible manner. The mere possession of a creed and articles of faith does not break down the wall of separation between poor and rich, slave and free; nor does orthodoxy ensure the operation of the Spirit in relationships between rich and poor within the Church. Together, excessive affluence and obsessive orthodoxy produce spiritual neuroticism.

Missionaries have been stunned and astonished to discover that their resources, job security and Western lifestyle elevate them to the ranks of the rich in most communities. The stark contrast with those among whom they serve—who are often poverty-stricken and have little hope of improving their lot—hits them like a bombshell. Because of innate human egocentrism, it is only discerning missionaries who are able to realize the degree to which their lifestyle contradicts the biblical message. The effectiveness of the gospel is hindered by insensitive affluence that makes social relationships not only difficult but embarrassing; for as long as there is an economic gap between missionaries and their converts, fraternal fellowship is difficult to maintain. In the end, the gospel that the missionary tries to proclaim is watered down, not intentionally but watered down nonetheless.

Traditionally, Christian missions in the developing countries were undertaken from positions of power and affluence. Missionaries appeared as heroes among their own people; religious literature and missionary pamphlets bolstered interest in a missionary "vogue" which was not only heroic but fascinating. This literature, with its fantasies of far away lands where exceptional persons performed mighty deeds, attracted many to the missionary vocation. As Adrian Hastings observes, at the beginning, the Baptists were not numerically or socially a powerful community. Their numerical growth, however, coincided with the growth of American neo-colonial interest in Africa and the rise of Baptist social status in the U.S.A. While at the beginning they were concerned about the poor, they have now "lost that objective status of disinterestedness and, perhaps, sympathy with the underdog which they previously possessed."[3]

In *Missions and Money: The Role of Affluence in the Christian Missionary Enterprise from the West*, Dr. Bonk addresses himself to an extremely important concern in mission work. As he most articulately shows, the *modus operandi* of Western missionaries reflects the increasing prosperity of their homelands in a world where the gap between rich and poor is widening.

Such affluence cataclysmically isolates missionaries from the "cutting edge" of missionary endeavors, rendering their efforts futile.

Dr. Bonk writes from a vantage point within the inner circle of missionary engagement, being a son of missionaries with whom he lived in Ethiopia for many years, and as a missionary in his own right, faithfully witnessing to the saving power of Jesus Christ and reflecting this in his own life. The sincerity with which he writes is genuine and endearing not only to evangelicals but to all Christians whose concern it is to share the truth of the gospel. The reader will be attracted not only by the lucid and vivid nature of this book, but also by its radically Biblical orientation and down-to-earth illustrations. The book challenges us not to resignation, but, through the enabling power of the Holy Spirit, to struggle to remove a dangerous contradiction from Western missionary endeavors. Dr. Bonk encourages us to adopt the incarnational model of mission, rejecting the easy power and prestige of affluence by an act of deliberate self-emptying. This book is a must for all people interested in doing Christian mission in a Christian way.

Zablon Nthamburi

Introduction

To speak of the affluence of missionaries in the context of a North American society that has become obsessed with consumption and with the mad pursuit of an ever higher standard of living may seem oddly incongruous. If there are any North American Christians who have consistently exemplified the path of discipleship described by Jesus following his encounter with the rich young man recorded in Matthew 19:16-30, they are our foreign missionaries. Who more than missionaries have literally "left houses or brothers or sisters or father or mother or children or fields" for Jesus' sake? In the popular mind, the North American missionary is a living thesaurus on the word sacrifice! And for good reason, too. The sacrifices made by missionaries going abroad from the shores of the wealthy nations have been real.

But here we have a paradox. Missionaries who bid farewell to the good life in North America and Europe have frequently, upon arrival in the country of their destination, found themselves regarded as rich! Their personal resources, employment security, benefits, and lifestyle choices combine to make them the envy of those among whom they serve — whose life circumstances make them relatively poverty stricken, and whose lifestyle options are severely limited by their lack of resources.

Several years ago, I tentatively explored some of the positive and negative implications of such disparity in a series of lectures and in articles appearing in two journals widely read by missionaries around the world.[1] The letter response confirmed to me the fact that the relative affluence of missionaries sent out from North American churches is of sufficient significance to warrant further investigation of the negative and positive, overt and covert, effects of the resulting economic and social disparity upon the accomplishing of the missionary task.

Often, after I have lectured on this subject, missionary reaction has been understandably defensive. But inevitably, as the discussion of the issue continues, missionaries have related personal anecdotes, reinforcing the central thesis that the relative affluence and security of our Western missionaries frequently constitutes a serious obstacle to the furtherance of the Gospel.

Surprisingly, a number of missionaries have chided me for not making the case against missionary affluence strong enough. Typical was the letter from W.E.C. missionary Patrick Johnstone, author of *Operation World*. "I have just been reading your article on the Achilles' Heel of modern missions. . . . Make it stronger; we want courageous missionaries who will battle through to a simpler lifestyle, and even to a Henry Martyn 'My love shall wait' commitment!"[2]

A church planter with Churches of Christ in Uruguay wrote commending me for "hitting the nail on the head." Affluence, he said, "has been the overwhelmingly greatest hindrance to my work in Montevideo."[3]

A researcher in Evangelism with the Presbyterian Church in Canada Board of Congregational Life pointed out that the issue of economic disparity was "a very important area for home missions as well as our foreign missions," and gave illustrations from her denomination's experience with inner city populations.[4]

After eight years in Irian Jaya, a missionary couple, in a letter to the Alumni Director of the institution where I teach, wrote:

> The greatest challenge we face in ministry in Irian is the day to day struggle against our far superior standard of living, the status and wealth we have, in comparison to the primitive people God has given us to minister to. They clearly are aware of the "gulf between" and desire to attain to that standard of power and wealth they see in us. We sought to cut back, and live more simply than most missionaries in Irian Jaya. But the struggle remains. So opposite of the example of Incarnation given us by Christ. But also easy to justify. Missionaries do it every day.[5]

Some will be disappointed to discover that this is not a "how-to" book. There are no easy answers to the perplexing and sometimes ministry-destroying effects of missionary affluence. But to deny that the problem exists is to manifest a willful myopia verging on blindness. And to refuse to confront an issue simply because it is too complicated to permit easy analysis or resolution is the height of folly. One well known academic— once a missionary in West Africa—told me that his affluence had been no problem, since an African neighbor owned a color television superior to his own! As I hope to demonstrate in the first three chapters, Western missionaries have seldom been unaware of the relative economic and material advantages which they clearly enjoy when abroad. Furthermore, many have selflessly put both themselves and their means at the disposal of those less fortunate than themselves. Some—though not many—have manifested quite remarkably the gracious spirit of their Lord, for the sake of others making themselves poor, that these through their poverty might be made rich (2 Cor. 8:9).

But missionaries sent into all the world by the affluent churches of the West usually do not—in any literal or deliberate sense—make this their *modus operandi.* Western missionaries reflect the increasing prosperity of their homelands in a world where the gulf between rich and poor is widening, where the rich are becoming proportionately fewer, and where the material prospects of the majority of peoples are dismal indeed. Missionaries from North American Churches in particular have attained a level of prosperity unimaginable to the vast majority of the peoples among whom they serve. It will be the argument of this book that this insular prosperity, while enabling the Western Church to engage in numerous expensive, efficient, and even useful activities overseas, has an inherent tendency to isolate missionaries from the cutting edge of missionary endeavor, rendering much of their effort either unproductive or counterproductive, or sometimes both.

This book has not been an easy one to write. As the son of missionaries who spent the best part of their lives in service to the people of Ethiopia; as one whose closest friends include numerous missionaries; and as one devoted to the task of sharing with the world the good news of Jesus as Savior and Lord; it is with a deep sense of personal humility and unworthiness that I write, for I am well aware of the deep and often sacrificial commitment to service characterizing many missionaries.

Nor should my criticism be interpreted as disloyalty to the cause. Those who speak or write are frequently tempted to say what people want to hear, instead of what needs to be said. Those seeking advice often manifest a marked preference for advisors whose words echo their own opinions. One man recently explained that he preferred the Unitarian Church over others he had tried because it was openminded, and made no awkward religious demands on him. It is an all too human tendency. Most of us—even missiologists and ecclesiastics—prefer the soothing optimism of possibility thinking to the discouraging pessimism of the prophet who declares that unless there is repentance, there is no hope (cf. Isaiah 30:9-11). American psychologists, having "proven that positive people outperform pessimists," have linked forces with business to find or create "supersalesmen."[6] This preference for positive thinkers is by no means restricted to the business world.

In ancient times, as now, the powerful frequently found it convenient to kill or otherwise dispose of those who spoke the truth, and would willingly listen to the counsel only of those whose opinions were in striking and flattering agreement with their own! Thus, Balak, the king of Moab, hired Balaam to curse the Israelites (Numbers 22); Ahab and Jezebel, smarting from the words of the prophets of Yahweh, attempted to obliterate them—somehow imagining that ignorance of the truth would change the facts (1 Kings 18-22). The men of Anathoth tried to destroy Jeremiah, in this instance the one through whom the Lord revealed His immensely unpopular will (Jeremiah 11:18-23; cf. 6:13-15; 8:14-16; 38); and Pashhur, the chief officer in the temple of the Lord, had Jeremiah beaten and placed in stocks for speaking words given to him by God Himself (Jeremiah 20). Our Savior was killed because the truth he lived and proclaimed was too threatening to the vested interests of both the religious establishment and the political radicals of his day. Paul and the other apostles met similar fates, as the truth which they spoke came into conflict with powerful political, economic or religious "powers that be," who stood to lose a great deal if the truth were to prevail.

Such behavior is not the exclusive prerogative of the mighty. Even we ordinary folk, with our modest but intensely personal stock in the status quo, are reticent to give our attention to those who speak of the need for repentance — *our* repentance. The human inclination, attested to by the sorry record of history, is to gather around us "a great number of teachers to say what our itching ears want to hear . . . to suit [our] own desires" (2 Timothy 4:4). As members of the Body of Christ, sent into the world to do and to be all that God sent Christ into the world to do and to be, our response to God's message should not be to do away with the medium. Rather — like David, as the shatteringly painful truth of Nathan's message came home to him — we should respond in a constructively repentant way to what God is saying to us. Any other course of action is more than deliberate disobedience; it is spiritual suicide.

It is my intention to speak the truth, insofar as I am able to discern it. This book is an attempt to explore, however inadequately, one aspect of Western missionary life and ministry which has, for a variety of reasons, been virtually ignored in the writing and teaching of most contemporary missiologists. The conscience, someone once said, is like a sundial. The person who shines his flashlight on it in the middle of the night can get it to tell him any time he wants. But when the sun shines on the dial, it can only tell the truth. That our consciences have been infected by the highly contagious hedonism characterizing Western societies cannot be denied. It remains to be seen whether the infection is lethal.

The argument of the book will evolve along the following lines: Beginning with a description of the nature, scale and context of missionary affluence, it will be argued that the sense of entitlement with which Western missionaries regard their personal material and economic advantage can be traced to the very beginnings of the modern missionary era and remains deeply embedded — for good and for ill — at the very core of Western missionary thinking, strategy and policy. Some of the varied consequences — foreseen and unforeseen, deliberate and accidental, profound and incidental, positive and negative — of this disparity will be explored. An examination of some of the relational, communicatory, and theological challenges facing the rich missionary will then follow. And finally, an attempt will be made to point to the narrow way out of the mire of personal affluence — a difficult way, certainly — but a hopeful way that has been and is being followed by tens of thousands of missionaries . . . some of these Western.

Despite Jesus' insistence that "no prophet is accepted in his home town" (Luke 4:24), in this book, I speak as an evangelical, primarily to evangelicals. Others of the household of faith are welcome to listen and are invited to contribute, of course. But if the language and the agenda of this book seem sometimes strange and unfamiliar, I beg you to bear with a fellow disciple.

Made possible by the cheerful support of my dearest and most loyal sojourners—Jean, Susie, and Jimmy; by the salaried sabbatical leave granted me by my school, Winnipeg Bible College and Winnipeg Theological Seminary; by the generous financial support of the Earhart Foundation; by the hospitality of the Overseas Ministries Study Center; and by the vast libraries and their helpful personnel at Yale University; this book is dedicated to those who read their sundials by the Son who is the true Light of the world, rather than by the lights of the world.

PART I

THE CONTEXT OF WESTERN MISSIONARY AFFLUENCE

In an economic variation of the David and Goliath theme so dear to the Christian heart, the last two hundred years have witnessed David (Western missionaries) wearing Saul's armor and carrying Saul's weapons, marching against a Goliath (the mission field) clad in a skin and armed with only a few stones and a sling. The economic might has been on the side of missionaries from the West — in some instances representing multinational mission agencies whose annual budgets exceed those of the host governments themselves and constituting those countries' most significant source of foreign exchange.

Part one of this book, comprised of chapters one through three, attempts to show that neither missionary affluence itself nor missionary thinking about affluence takes place within a vacuum. Historical, cultural, and rational influences have changed and continue to exert a powerful effect on that Western missionary theory and practice which touches upon the personal stewardship of money and possessions in the context of poverty. In chapter one the fact and the scale of Western missionary affluence are briefly outlined. Chapter two shows how each succeeding generation of Western missionaries is culturally conditioned to redefine personal material "needs" according to a continually escalating standard that most of the world's population can only regard as wildly inflated. Chapter three demonstrates that missionaries are rational creatures, making quite deliberate economic choices for the best of personal and strategic reasons.

1

The Fact and the Extent of Western Missionary Affluence

The wealth of the rich is their fortified city, but poverty is the ruin of the poor.

Solomon

Western missionary awareness and acknowledgement of relative personal affluence is nothing new. Indeed, even a cursory study of missions history reveals as commonplace a self-conscious sense of superiority on the part of missionaries, deriving from and proven by the fact of—it was thought, providential—economic advantage.

One hundred and forty-five years ago, in an essay which won its author two hundred guineas, missionary weal was accepted as a natural concomitant of British material prosperity, the climax of a slow but steady evolution from days when the nation had been "as obscure among the nations . . . as Africans [then were]." But now, Robert Moffat modestly continued,

> We have become rich in a variety of acquirements, favoured above measure in the gifts of Providence, unrivalled in Commerce, preeminent in arts, foremost in the pursuits of philosophy and science, and in all the blessings of civil society.[1]

Twenty years later, the Donnellan lecturer at the University of Dublin echoed Moffat. Though doubtless well read, Mr. Walsh confessed that he could not think of another nation "since the days of Israel" so highly favored as Britain.[2]

On the American side, somewhat later but no less confident than his British counterpart, the general secretary of the Evangelical Alliance was only one prominent voice among many at that time proclaiming the inauguration of the final age in world history. An unabashed racist,[3] Josiah Strong could foresee a time in the near future when, he said, the mighty centrifugal tendency inherent in [the Anglo-Saxon race] and strengthened in the United States [would]. . . [with its] unequalled energy, with all the majesty of numbers and the might of wealth behind it . . . spread itself over the earth.[4]

The strategies and the outcomes of Western Christian missionary endeavours for the past two hundred years are impossible to understand apart from the massive economic and material superiority enjoyed by missionaries, vis-à-vis the majority of the people inhabiting those countries popularly designated "mission fields."

Fifteen years in Egypt (1954-1969) with the United Presbyterian Church of North America convinced missionary Bernard Quick of this fact. A further five years of wide-ranging research on the subject confirmed that the *modus operandi* and the *modus vivendi* of American missions in Egypt was not an isolated case. To the contrary, in Quick's own words,

Economic power is still the most crucial power factor in the western missionary movement. It is still the most important way that the western missionary expresses his concept of what it means to "preach the gospel."[5]

Missiologist Harvie Conn, addressing delegates to the joint meeting of the American Association of Bible Colleges (AABC) and the Association of Evangelical Professors of Mission (AEPM) held in Chicago in October of 1985, argued that the most significant of four pressing issues confronting modern mission endeavours was the growing disparity between shrinking rich populations and the burgeoning poor. He wondered how, as partakers of the wealth and security enjoyed by the relatively few, Western missionaries could sit where the majority of this world's peoples sit—poor or absolutely poor, with no prospects beyond destitution.[6]

The statistical dimensions of this economic disparity—though not their tragic incarnation in suffering human flesh—are not difficult to document. A variety of resources, each in its own way, reveals the breathtaking scale of the economic rift separating the populations of rich nations from those of the poor.

The most commonly used indicator of international economic comparison is Gross National Product (GNP), which measures the total market value of goods and services produced in a country in one year. Comparing the GNP of one country with another requires use of a common currency, usually the U.S. dollar. An obviously crude and often misleading standard for comparison,[7] GNP is nevertheless the dark glass through which economists have to peer. And however dim and imprecise the view, it is clear enough to indicate something of the awesome gap between rich nations and poor nations in our time. Arranged by groups of countries, per capita

GNP and population figures based upon World Bank data released in 1986 appear in Table 1 below.[8]

In 1984, the last year for which there are comparative figures available, the relative affluence of a sampling of rich and poor countries – utilizing GNP as the basis of comparison – is indicated by the figures in Table 2 on page 6.[9]

Of course, there are richer nations in which North American missionaries serve in great numbers: Japan, France, and West Germany together host nearly three thousand. But there are poorer nations as well: Burkino Faso, Ethiopia, and Mali in Africa; Honduras, Nicaragua, and El Salvador in Central America; Bolivia and Guyana in South America; Bangladesh and Pakistan in Asia.

The fact that fully 78 per cent of all North American Protestant missionaries serve in some part of Africa, Latin America, or Oceania[10] – precisely those parts of our globe where most of the world's poor reside – suggests that most missionaries enjoy incredible economic and material superiority in the social contexts in which they have chosen to carry out their mandate. What the consequences of this disparity might be is the subject of later chapters.

GNP being the unsatisfactory indicator of comparative wealth that it is, the United Nations established in the mid-1960s its International Comparison Project (ICP), with a mandate to develop measures of real gross domestic product on an internationally comparable scale by using purchasing power parities rather than exchange rates as conversion factors.[11] Even using the more sophisticated ICP criteria of measurement, with the United States dollar as the standard (100) of purchasing power against which the relative purchasing power of each country is measured, one is driven to conclude that the economic distance between North Americans and the peoples of many of the countries in which North American missionaries

TABLE 1

Per Capita Gross National Products
According to Types of Economy

Country Group	Population (million)	Per Capita GNP (1984 dollars)	Average Annual Growth Rate of Per Capita GNP, 1965-84 (per cent)
Low-income Economies (excl. China, India)	611	190	0.9
China and India	1,778	290	3.3
Lower Middle-income Economies	691	740	3.0
Upper Middle-income Economies	497	1,950	3.3
High-income Oil Exporters	19	11,250	3.2
Industrial Market Economies	733	11,430	2.4

TABLE 2

**1984 Comparative Gross National Products (GNP) of Select
"Missionary Sending" Countries and "Missionary Receiving" Countries**

1984 Gross National Product of Select Rich Missionary Sending Countries

Country	GNP Per Capita ($U.S.)
Switzerland	15,990
United States	15,490
Norway	13,750
Canada	13,140
Australia	11,890
Germany	11,090
United Kingdom	8,350
New Zealand	7,240

1984 Gross National Products of Select Poor Missionary Receiving Countries

Country	GNP Per Capita ($U.S.)
Zaire	140
India	260
Kenya	300
Haiti	320
Bolivia	410
Indonesia	540
Philippines	660
Papua New Guinea	760
Nigeria	770
Thailand	850
Peru	980

work is virtually infinite. While figures at the time of this writing were not available for all of the poorer countries whose GNPs appear in the table above, those provided in *The World Development Report 1987* (see Table 3 on page 7[12]) are sufficient to confirm that economic disparity is a fact.

When it is remembered that such studies of relative national wealth, no matter how sophisticated the methodology, do not reflect the inequitable distribution of this wealth within the country itself,[13] and that missionaries as a rule have tended to concentrate on people in the lower social and economic echelons of society, it will be readily seen that the disparity between Western missionaries and the people among whom they work is often much greater than aggregate statistics indicate.

Not surprisingly, financial figures provided by North American Protestant agencies simply serve to accentuate the overwhelming scale of personal affluence enjoyed by North Americans—including missionaries.[14] While there are, as the figures below will indicate, considerable differences in per missionary expenditure within the ranks of North American agencies, on

TABLE 3

**1985 Purchasing Power Parities Per Capita of Select Nations by
International Comparison Product (ICP) Methods**

Country	ICP/PPP	GNP per capita ($U.S.)
United States	100.00	$16,160
Canada	99.8	16,128
United Kingdom	72.3	11,640
Norway	101.5	16,402
Ethiopia	2.0	323
Kenya	4.8	776
Nigeria	5.2	840
India	5.4	873
Honduras	8.7	1,404
Bolivia	9.5	1,535
Indonesia	9.6	1,551
Mali	9.8	1,584
El Salvador	9.8	1,584
Philippines	12.1	1,955

the whole missionaries from North America must be considered rich by most of the peoples among whom they serve.

On the basis of information provided by North American mission agencies themselves, total overseas income will be divided by the total number of missionaries to determine per missionary expenditure—first at the level of Mission Associations,[15] then at the level of specific, randomly chosen mission agencies.[16] A perusal of Table 4 on page 8 will make two things readily apparent: (1) Mission done in the North American way is exceedingly costly; and (2) some agencies—usually of the independent, ultraconservative variety—operate far more efficiently on a per missionary basis than do others.

Obviously, the wide differences between the per missionary overseas incomes of the associations cannot be attributed simply to disparate salary levels between missionaries employed by different agencies—although this is in many cases a significant factor. The Canadian Council of Churches-Commission on World Concerns (CCC-CWC), for example, serves as the channel through which the Canadian churches provide support for ecumenical projects overseas. Similarly, the Division of Overseas Ministries-National Council of Churches U.S.A. (DOM-NCCUSA), in addition to supporting American missionaries abroad, finances a number of specialized ministries focusing on agricultural, medical, and human rights concerns. Other associations, such as those listed in Table 5[17] on page 9, can, although to a lesser degree, similarly account for their relatively high per missionary expenditures.

Of course, such figures do not represent missionary salaries. As a general

TABLE 4

Per Missionary Per Year Financial Analysis by Association
(1985 figures)

Mission Associations	Number of Overseas Personnel	Total Overseas Income	Cost per Missionary
The Associated Missions-International Christian Council (TAM-ICC)	40	$550,000	$13,750
Evangelical Foreign Missions Association (EFMA)	11,817	379,513,652	32,116
Fellowship of Missions (FOM)	1,424	20,625,301	14,484
Interdenominational Foreign Missions Association (IFMA)	8,398	148,381,713	17,669
Division of Overseas Ministries-National Council of Churches United States of America (DOM-NCCUSA)	5,073	268,107,516	52,850
Canadian Council of Churches-Commission on World Concerns (CCC-CWC)	254	13,197,813	51,960

rule, mission agencies are involved in a variety of overseas programs, including medicine, education, community development, agricultural assistance, aid and relief, literature production, support of nationals and national churches, and technical assistance of various kinds.[18] Nevertheless, such data do indicate to a considerable degree the resources which—in the eyes of host peoples—missionaries represent, to some degree control, and apparently benefit from personally.

A better indicator of the personal financial resources of Western missionaries may be found in the support schedules established by mission agencies. Here, once again, salary or suggested missionary support levels vary considerably from agency to agency. The figures in Table 6 on page 10 indicate either the salary or the recommended support levels of an adult missionary in 1985.[19]

It is clear that the United States and Canada are rich nations. It is also clear that the missionaries sent from these nations, regardless of their personal resources relative to each other, are rich by the standards of most of the world's peoples. However misleading the figures cited in the tables above might be, the fact remains that most of the peoples among whom North American missionaries work would gladly trade economic places with a missionary; and conversely, few indeed are those North American mis-

TABLE 5

Per Missionary Per Year Financial Analysis by Agency
(1985 figures)

Agency	Number of Overseas Personnel	Total Overseas Income	Cost per Missionary
Southern Baptist Convention	3,346	$136,473,351	$40,738
Wycliffe Bible Translators	3,022	36,815,000	12,182
New Tribes Mission	1,438	10,181,937	7,080
Assemblies of God	1,237	56,799,964	45,917
General Conference Seventh Day Adventist	1,052	70,155,000	66,687
The Evangelical Alliance Mission	929	16,597,341	17,865
Christian and Missionary Alliance	874	12,416,451	14,206
SIM International	654	15,106,000	23,097
Baptist Mid-Missions	636	16,800,000	26,415
Campus Crusade for Christ	574	20,000,000	34,843
Conservative Baptist Foreign Mission Society	525	12,307,902	23,444
Africa Inland Mission	433	5,265,278	12,160
Gospel Missionary Union	391	6,035,541	15,436
UFM International	338	3,956,504	11,705
CAM International	212	3,081,133	14,533
Evangelical Free Church of America	209	5,270,189	25,216
Overseas Missionary Fellowship	166	2,238,932	13,487
General Conference Mennonite Church	162	3,350,000	20,679
Africa Evangelical Fellowship	160	1,668,144	10,435
Mennonite Brethren Missions/Services	149	2,923,275	25,372
SEND International	136	2,354,138	17,309
WEC International	132	797,087	6,038
World Baptist Fellowship	126	2,606,984	20,690
South America Mission	113	1,631,114	14,434
Eastern Mennonite	108	2,085,069	19,306
RBMU	103	879,952	8,543
Baptist General Conference	101	2,840,036	28,119
Child Evangelism Fellowship	100	2,178,957	21,179
Mennonite Board of Missions	90	1,830,000	20,333
Africa Inter-Mennonite Mission	80	1,396,858	17,460
Brethren in Christ Mission	38	1,591,232	41,874
Conservative Mennonite Board of Missions	21	217,197	10,342

TABLE 6

**Annual Actual or Recommended Per Missionary Salary/Support
Levels of Select North American Agencies**

Agency	Annual Salary	
AEF International	$ 3,600	
CAM International	9,408	
Conservative Baptist Foreign Mission Society	15,500	
Evangelical Free Church of America	15,373	(Zaire)
Gospel Missionary Union	11,460	
Mennonite Brethren	10,450	
New Tribes Mission	4,200 (minimum);	9,600 (maximum)
Overseas Missionary Fellowship	12,240	
SEND International	16,200	
SIM International	13,140	
The Evangelical Alliance Mission	10,524	
UFM International	7,740	
Child Evangelism Fellowship	5,880 (minimum);	9,360 (maximum)
Southern Baptist Convention Foreign Mission Board	9,390	

sionaries who would willingly trade places with the peoples among whom they work. For a missionary—even a very young missionary—can take for granted the material accoutrements, security, lifestyle, and future options that are beyond most people's wildest dreams. Members and missionaries of the North American Church are, beyond doubt, a "People of Plenty."[20]

Just what this means will be the subject of later chapters. But one thing is certain: neither the direct effects nor the indirect side effects of missionary affluence have ever been entirely positive. With the weal comes also the woe. As we shall discuss in chapters 4 through 6, outside observers have been generous, even lavish, in their criticism of missionary lifestyles abroad. Nor have missionaries themselves been blind to the Hydra-headed, complex nature of the problems attendant upon the possession and enjoyment of luxury by those who claim to speak for God. David Picton Jones, one of the very few early missionaries of the London Missionary Society to survive the rigors of East African life long enough to learn the local language well, interpreted his failure to win any converts to Christianity as an unintended side effect of his personal lifestyle. "Our life," he wrote to the Secretary of the London Missionary Society (LMS), "is far above them, and we are surrounded by things entirely beyond their reach. The consequence is, that they . . . *cannot* follow us. . . ."[21]

A contemporary of Jones working with the same agency in China, James Gilmour lay the blame for the general impotence of foreign missionary effort on their expensive, European style of life.[22]

These lonely voices were joined by a small but vocal chorus of more official missionary voices as the twentieth century progressed and as some of the unforseen and unwelcome side effects of economic disparity became increasingly manifest. One result of the 1928 World Conference at Jerusalem was the establishment (in 1930) by the International Missionary Council of the Department of Social and Economic Research and Counsel, under the direction of J. Merle Davis. Its mandate was, in the words of the director, "to collect and distribute information on the economic and social developments which challenge the Gospel of Christ and limit the growth of His Kingdom among the younger churches."[23]

Energetic pursuit of this mandate resulted in the completion of a series of studies which constituted a significant part of the agenda for the Tambaram Conference of 1938. "Economic Disparities on the Mission Field" was the title of the first chapter of Davis's report. "Economics create an immediate source of misunderstanding in the relationship of the missionary with his people," Davis wrote, explaining that

> The missionary comes from a world where salaries and expenditure are immensely greater than those prevailing in his new field of work. He is looked upon as the representative of a wealthy and powerful organisation. On arrival in his field the missionary puts into operation a new standard of economic values. ... To the average national the missionary appeared not so much as the exponent of a new religion or way of life as a possible source of personal economic improvement.[24]

Although the aim of these studies was to gather information which would enable younger churches to become self-governing, self-supporting, and self-propagating, the problem of missionary affluence was never far from the surface and warranted a short chapter in the Department's official report to the International Missionary Council in 1938.[25]

Excerpts from an editorial which appeared in the Calcutta-based *Baptist Missionary Review* spelled out the essence of the problem unambiguously:

> A village congregation growing up in the shadow of a mission station's foreign-built domes and towers is impressed from the beginning with its own economic weakness and develops a feeling of helplessness and futility.[26]

Nevertheless, the fundamental thrust of the conclusions and recommendations of the studies had little to say about the personal affluence of Western missionaries; nor does there appear to have been any suggestion that the West might be overdeveloped. The goal appears to have been simply to place national churches on an independent financial footing.

It was Daniel Johnson Fleming, Professor of Missions at Union Theological Seminary in New York, who seems to have spoken for those missionaries who saw missionary affluence as more than simply an awkward obstruction in the way of national church independence. In a book entitled *Ventures in Simpler Living*, written in acknowledgment of those ministry and credibility dilemmas which are a fact of life for Western missionaries whose material and economic resources are excessive by indigenous standards, Fleming chronicled and assessed a variety of practical missionary responses to the issue.[27]

Two years later, Fleming argued that "Differences in Standards of Living" was one of the great ethical issues facing world Christians,[28] a theme which he more fully elaborated in his book *Living as Comrades*, published in 1950.[29]

The message of these books seems to have sunk without a trace. Following World War II, with the swelling of North American missionary ranks from fewer than 19,000 missionaries in 1953 to over 39,000 in 1985, the item has virtually disappeared from missiological agendas.[30] This is due at least in part to the fact that the largest proportion of the new missionaries were associated with agencies that were either new and unaware of the mission tradition and experience of the Confessional church agencies or which looked upon all churches, mission agencies, and missionaries associated with the Ecumenical Movement with suspicion and ignored their collective experience. Whatever the reasons, economic and material disparity has not been high on the agendas of either independent evangelical agencies or those agencies associated with the Interdenominational Foreign Mission Association (IFMA), the Evangelical Foreign Mission Association (EFMA), or the Fellowship of Missions (FOM).

Desultory references to missionary affluence continue to appear in both academic and popular missiological writings from time to time. Professor Harry F. Wolcott, having closely observed the behaviour of American missionaries in one part of Africa in the course of a sabbatical year 1970-1971, observed:

> Problems related to money plague and obsess many urban missionaries. They always have too much of it, and they never have enough. Their standard of living makes them seem wealthy wherever they go and results in constant conflict for them when they hold back so much of what they have for themselves. An anthropologist critical of missionaries recalled the old saw that they set out to do "good" and often end up doing "well."[31]

Wolcott was certainly not hostile to the Christian missionary enterprise and made his observations while under the auspices of a mission agency himself. This concern with money had little to do with any profligacy on the missionaries' part. On the contrary, their material and economic resources were seldom, if ever, adequate—and often scarce; their possessions were meager; and their spending habits with regard to food and clothing frugal to a fault.[32] Missionary self-consciousness about their resources and lifestyles derived from the obvious fact of relative affluence in the African context—a state of affairs with which as Christians they were intuitively uncomfortable.

Members of the Mini-Consultation on Reaching the Urban Poor met in Pattaya, Thailand, from June 16-27 in 1980, under the Chairmanship of Rev. Jim Punton. The resulting report, *Christian Witness to the Urban Poor*,[33] is one indication that Evangelical missionaries are neither unaware of nor unconcerned for the world's poor. So far, however, there is little evidence that evangelical mission agencies have been able to make the implementation of the report's excellent recommendations a priority. It may be simply a case of willing spirits but inadequate flesh. Powerful mission agencies and the Westerners who comprise the rank and file of their missionaries have been either unwilling or unable to pay the price. It continues to be the Catholics who work in the world's worst slums.

Dana Jones has captured the feelings of anguished guilt and helplessness experienced by many Western missionaries in the context of poverty. The daughter of missionaries (linguists) to Mexico who had returned to the United States several years earlier, Dana returned to Mexico City at the age of 16, where she hoped to renew contact with Celia, her closest Mexican childhood friend—now married and the mother of a child. The story, written shortly after Dana's graduation from grade 12, needs to be told in her own words:

As we rounded a curve in the road, I spotted Celia's house and my heart sank. The entire house was the size of my bedroom. The walls were made of cariso (a type of wild cane that resembles bamboo) and held together with strips of tree bark. The roof was thatched with maguey plant leaves, and an old beer crate served as the door.

I approached the dark little doorway and called Celia's name. In a few seconds she emerged. I had grown so much in the years since I had seen her that I towered above her now and had to bend down to hug her. She was a little shy, but was glad to see me. Her eyes looked tired, and her shoulders sagged. I heard a baby cry inside and she went back in to see what was the matter.

I ducked my head and started to follow Celia until something made me change my mind. When my eyes adjusted to the semi-darkness, I could make out her husband lying on a straw mat on the dirt floor ... obviously drunk. The smell of cactus liquor permeated the air. I quickly stepped back out into the sunlight and stood there blinking and feeling embarrassed. Then, Celia reappeared, carrying her baby son.

His little nose was streaming, and she wiped at it with her blouse. His diapers consisted of a strip of a cast-off shirt. Not that Celia wasn't a good mother, but being clean was a luxury for her family. The closest well was half a mile away, and the water had to be carried in buckets. She offered me her only little chair, but I insisted she use it instead. My heart went out to Celia as I realized how our differences had become so obvious over the years. Her life had become so desolate and mine so full of potential. . . .

Suddenly, my perspective was changed. I realized how blessed I was and how thankful I should be. I thanked God for education, good nutrition, health, clothing, and for living in America. . . .

I deeply wanted to help Celia, but I felt powerless. I turned and looked at Diago, my little guide, and wondered what his life would be like. Then I realized that God could help me to make a difference. More than anything, these people need the hope that God can give them, and I want to deliver this message to people like Celia. . . .

Knowing Christ may not improve living conditions for this group of people, but Jesus can surely help them through difficult times and help them rise above their circumstances. . . .

The next morning, I took a bag of baby clothes to Celia's house. No one was home, but I left them there — along with a promise.[34]

While the combination of outrage and guilt, pity and relief, helplessness and optimism conveyed in this story are common to any Westerner who has lived in proximity to the poor, and while missiologists write endlessly about the subject of poverty and development, the subject of missionary affluence in the context of disparity — and of its impact upon the effectiveness of Western strategies — is not on the agenda of most, if any, of the North American agencies committed to fulfilling the Great Commission.

As a consequence, Western missionaries, although growing numerically and thriving financially, are increasingly finding themselves at a loss in relating the Good News to the swelling numbers of this world's absolutely poor — those, for example, who inhabit the slums of the great cities of Asia and Latin America. Despite all the talk of reaching the unreached, it is not North Americans who are doing the actual reaching. That task — as has perhaps ever been the case — is being carried out by the missionaries of poorer churches who demonstrate in their own lives the truth that Jesus is the way, the truth and the life for the poor, the destitute, and the hopeless — and not just for the rich.

These poorer missionaries are seldom acknowledged as missionaries in the West. Since they are not associated with any agency other than their sending churches and since their crosscultural missionary endeavours are restricted by the bounds of their own countries, they are referred to as national evangelists. But it is they who are on the cutting edge of the expansion of the Kingdom today. While missionaries from the affluent West get on with the expensive and complicated process of living comfortable and secure lives in a Third World context, their national counterparts take the Word and make it flesh, dwelling among peoples who see in their frail flesh the glory of a living Savior full of grace and truth.

In summary, the affluence of Western missionaries is a fact. Furthermore, the economic and material gulf between Western missionaries and the rest of the world is widening, not narrowing. Finally, although there have been many who throughout most of the period referred to as the "William Carey Era" in missions have acknowledged the fact of disparity—and there have been some who have regarded this disparity as an often significant obstacle in the accomplishing of Christian missionary objectives—scarcely any North American Protestant agencies, and very few North American missionaries, have made rectification of this problem a priority in their missiological agendas. The following chapters constitute a modest attempt to begin the process of redressing this lack.

2

The Historical and Cultural Context of Missionary Affluence

Whoever loves money never has money enough; whoever loves wealth is never satisfied with his income.

Solomon

He had a great respect for money and much overrated its value as a means of doing even what he called good: religious people generally do.
George MacDonald

And whatever happens began in the past and presses hard on the future.
T. S. Eliot

Material and economic abundance has been a hallmark of the *modus operandi* of Western missionaries throughout the past two centuries. In sharp contrast to their apostolic counterparts of the first century, portrayed by St. Paul as being "on display at the end of the procession, like men condemned to die in the arena" (1 Cor. 4:9), missionaries from Europe and the Americas have—with some notable exceptions—increasingly manifested a level of affluence and material security beyond even the dreams of the vast majority of the world's population.

Furthermore (as I hope to show in chapter five), Western missionary strategies have become increasingly reliant upon and preoccupied with expensive technologies which, while contributing to the speed and the comfort of Western missionaries, do not seem to contribute significantly to the numerical growth or the spiritual health of the church worldwide. Indeed, reminiscent of the seven churches described by St. John in the first three chapters of his Revelation, the church seems to be most vigorous among those peoples where Western affluence is most conspicuous by its absence.

That the Western missionary enterprise should today be so dependent upon the accoutrements of affluence is hardly surprising, given the cultural and religious "womb" in which it was conceived, and the social and historical environment in which it was nurtured. Born and bred in the economic abundance of the West, the character, outlook, values, preoccupations, and strategies of missionaries have naturally been deeply affected. For as missionaries would be the first to acknowledge, "the system of values which are maintained by a society have a profound effect upon the character of the individual members of the society."[1] Material plenty, as a basic condition of American life, "has had a pervasive influence upon the American people,"[2] including American missionaries.

Missionaries have tended to feel uncomfortable whenever they have been on the "rich" side of invidious economic comparisons. But the varied effects which their relative affluence has had upon the theory and practice of missions, and its impact upon those who have seen, heard, and responded to their comfortably incarnated Gospel, have not gone unnoticed. "It is not a coincidence that the greatest mission-sending nations have also been the nations possessing the greatest store of material resources and the highest standards of living," concluded the man commissioned by the International Missionary Council (IMC) to direct a series of extensive studies on the social and economic life of younger churches during the 1930s. Indeed, in Western Christian thinking so naturally concomitant were material abundance and missionary activity that J. Merle Davis, when asked by an Indian Christian whether the gospel had ever been "carried by a people of low economic standards to a group living on a higher economic level," was unable to think of a single instance, "unless it was the witness of the Christian slaves in the Roman Empire to their pagan masters."[3]

An article appearing in a recent issue of the *Los Angeles Times Magazine* referred to modern American missionaries—with their "computers, and air force and millions of dollars in financial support," as a "new breed."[4] The author was right about the affluence of missionaries from North America, but he was wrong in thinking that they are a "new breed." For it is only within the past two hundred years that Christian missions have come to be regarded as the special prerogative of rich Christians. It is true that agencies from the West operate from a conspicuously substantial financial base— sometimes out of headquarters "worthy of multinational corporations," and using expensive technologies to generate the plethora of maps, graphs, statistics, and strategies. But these have been a hallmark of Western missiology ever since William Carey's famous *Enquiry*[5] of two centuries ago.

While missionaries travelling from Western shores in the last century had neither computers nor an air force, they were, by standards of that day, just as well equipped. Even the most modest of missionary expeditions into East Africa, for example, required the employ of hundreds—sometimes even thousands—of native carriers, not infrequently for months on end, to transport missionary goods.[6] And their standard of living, although modest and even tawdry by the standards of contemporary European and American missionaries, was impressive enough to evoke the astonishment, admiration, and envy of Africans.

The adequately equipped missionary to East Africa, for example, found it necessary to take food, cooking utensils, trunks, tents, tools, medicines, sometimes boats, and barter goods sufficient to sustain life for several years in an environment as dangerous to the white man's health as it was uncivilized.[7] Missionaries, of course, were not unlike their fellow countrymen in this regard, and took their cue from the advice of such notables as Sir Francis Galton, President of the Royal Geographical Society, and an expert on survival in "wild countries."[8] The sheer volume of material goods required by Protestant missionaries proceeding to Asia and South America was, when measured against local standards, similarly grand.

As a general rule, Western missionaries no longer take vast supplies with them overseas. But it would be a mistake to think that they are not at least as lavishly supplied as ever. Western "staples"—vehicles, clothing, building supplies, gadgets, food, furniture—all are available in most countries, albeit only to those few who can pay the exorbitantly inflated prices demanded of them. It is no secret, for example, that the price of automobiles in some countries is double, even triple that of an equivalent vehicle in North America. Added to this is the price of fuel—in many poor countries running between ten and thirty dollars per gallon. Missionaries are among those who can, and frequently do, drive automobiles.

Attempts to explain the goals, methods, and accomplishments of Western Christian missionary endeavours during the past two hundred years cannot be adequately grasped without some understanding of the much larger social and economic milieu of which they were simply a pious expression. Throughout the nineteenth and well into the twentieth centuries, a powerful confluence of ideological, economic, and political streams issuing from the West flooded much of the globe. True to the nature of floods, this one, too, affected for good or for ill everything in its path, and there was very little that could be done about it. Some were engulfed and destroyed by the torrent; survivors—among them Western missionaries—were swept inexorably along, like bits of flotsam, wherever the flood took them. In comparison with the mighty vitality of this rushing tide, even the most energetic attempts at resistance were feeble and necessarily largely ineffectual.[9]

Among the ideas which influenced missionary theory and practice from the beginning of the modern era, probably none can match the pervasiveness or the power of Western belief in the inevitability of progress. The law of progress was, in the words of one historian, "the first great lesson that history teaches us."[10]

In the words of a more contemporary analyst:

No single idea has been more important than, perhaps as important as, the idea of progress in Western civilization. . . . From at least the early nineteenth century until a few decades ago, belief in the progress of mankind, with Western civilization in the vanguard, was virtually a universal religion on both sides of he Atlantic.[11]

Not only did missionaries believe in the inevitability of progress, they regarded themselves as its true emissaries. The indolent temperaments or the stubborn conservatism of non-Western peoples might, it is true, *delay* progress, but there could be no doubt about its ultimate triumph. As one veteran missionary explained in the 1897 *Annual Report* of his society, "China . . . would resist [progress] if she could, but she cannot help herself. There are mighty forces at work pressing China forward, to which she must yield whether she will or no."[12]

Missionary apologists never wearied of recounting the dramatic advances made by backward peoples as a direct result of missionary efforts. The most comprehensive of these publications was the massive three-volume study by James Dennis, *Christian Missions and Social Progress*. Written to support the proposition that missions constituted "a supreme force in the social regeneration and elevation of the human race," the evidence marshalled in these volumes promised to be of "striking apologetic import" to readers.[13]

If progress was the destiny of humankind, Western "Christian" civilization was its visible manifestation, a sort of word made flesh, and dwelling among men. There may have been sharp differences of opinion concerning the precise ratio and sequence of those factors which had given rise to Western civilization, but Western missionaries and philosophers, politicians and historians, scientists and dilettantes all regarded the civilizing of the rest of mankind as an almost sacred trust. Even Winwood Reade — a nineteenth-century version of Alvin Toffler — cousin of Charles Darwin, and no friend of missionaries, wrote glowingly of a day when, "by means of European conquest . . . the whole earth [would] be as civilized as Europe."[14]

It seemed obvious, furthermore, that Western ideas, values, technology, social and political institutions, military might, and religion "were not only superior to those found in the rest of the world, but were symbols, pointing to what other nations should and would know in due time."[15]

Missionaries were certain that Western civilization had its roots in the Christian Gospel. For proof, they pointed to Britain — once numbered among the most pagan and uncivilized of nations — now "a glowing and graphic picture of the marvelous change which the Gospel accomplishes."[16] Clergymen back home preached the same message. The pastor of the Broadway Tabernacle Church in New York expanded at length on the theme in an address before the Missionary Societies of Bangor Theological Seminary, Brown and Rochester Universities, and Williams College. He argued that neither commerce nor civilization could by themselves or together elevate man. "Christian Missions," he declared, "are the grand reliance for the elevation of mankind in prosperity, in purity, and in happiness."[17]

As incarnations of that civilization which is the goal of all true progress, missionaries did not view the material advantages which set them above non-Christian peoples as a handicap. To live as civilized Europeans— attractive beacons pointing to that which Christianity could and would eventually accomplish in the backward races—was not merely desirable. It was a duty. There were a few exceptions, but these—some of whom will be touched upon in the final chapter—were accorded by mission societies that special place reserved for eccentrics everywhere: the fringe.

Talk of "progress" and "civilization"—until recently so prominent in Western missiological agendas—now sounds prosaic, quixotic, triumphalist. Yet there can be little doubt that these ideas continue to be at the root of much within the contemporary mission agenda—in altered, though not necessarily muted form. Today mission theory on the "cutting edge" resounds with talk of "development" and "underdevelopment." The West continues to be the standard against which "development" is measured; and Western aid and efforts have, until quite recently, been fueled by the certainty that given enough money, time, and Western expertise, the rest of the world can become what the West now is—"developed." In the popular mind, development is understood to mean movement toward some approximation of Western material and economic standards. Sceptics have been few, and in any case largely disregarded.[18]

It is clear—despite protests to the contrary—that we are not as far removed from our nineteenth century roots as some would like to suppose. Those who, by means of enlightened criticism, would distance themselves from the "misguided" civilizing efforts of nineteenth century missionaries should not be surprised if—as they seek earnestly to forward the West's current development mandate—their most telling and subtle attacks frequently rebound upon themselves.

Western assumptions concerning progress and civilization are only part of the background against which the relative affluence of missionaries must be seen. The overwhelming racial, material, and political ascendancy of the "Christian" nations was not simply a fact, but—in missionary thinking—a providential fact. Missionary racism was of a genre infinitely more benign than that of nineteenth century scientists, it is true. But they were racists, nevertheless.[19] "The missionary," observed the well-known Foreign Secretary of the London Missionary Society, "belongs to a race superior in energy and asserting the right to lead and rule, a race whose wealth is evident to the world."[20]

Racial superiority, of course, carried with it the solemn responsibility known as "the white man's burden." "It is on the Anglo-American race that the hopes of the world for liberty and progress rest," David Livingstone had written in the context of a report that was to provoke Western Christians into indignant action on behalf of Africa.[21]

Likewise politically missionaries were by virtue of their citizenship unavoidably implicated in the subjugation of much of the world by unabashedly imperialist European nations. Western superiority in all things constituted a natural diet for a particularly virulent form of nationalism. Missionaries were not less patriotic than their secular peers. Like other nationalists, they suffered from that myopic condition so aptly described by George Orwell: "The nationalist," he said, "not only does not disapprove of atrocities committed by his own side, but he has a remarkable capacity for not even hearing about them."[22]

This is not to suggest that missionaries were always or even usually blind to many of the injustices inherent in the Western subjugation of much of the world. On the contrary, they were sufficiently critical to earn the reprobation of advocates of imperialism, one of whom accused missionaries of being generally "heedless of [the] great truth. . . . [that] imperialism is a matter of religion."[23] And Harry Johnston, one of the most famous of the British Colonial administrators, described missionaries as "inconvenient champions of native independence."[24]

On the whole, however, missionaries regarded Western imperialism as both natural and, more significantly, providential in making straight the path for the spread of the Gospel. "A European Colonial government," Johannes Warneck observed in 1909, "cannot fail, as the representative of humanity and enlightenment, to . . . prepare the way for the preaching of the Gospel." Western imperialism was, accordingly, best regarded as "one of the powers which God has chosen for bringing the message of salvation to uncivilized peoples."[25]

The extent to which prevailing Western ideas concerning progress, civilization, and power affected missionary theory and practice is obvious. Just how these same ideas may have affected missionary perceptions of their own relative affluence is more difficult to measure, but no less significant. Affluence was a byproduct of Christian influences upon a civilization. Since missionaries were offering Christianity to any who would have it, and since their own relative affluence in a sense constituted "exhibit A" in the case for "Christian" civilization, any radical renunciation of their Western affluence would have been tantamount to a betrayal of their mission. As one missionary delegate explained to his peers attending the 1860 Liverpool conference,

> The Indian looks upon himself as being of an inferior race; and his desire is to rise as much as possible to the level of the white man. . . . Civilised men should [therefore] go amongst them, men who [will] be looked up to by them. . . . [and from those lips they will expect] words of wisdom.[26]

An examination of three crucial areas reveals the extent to which nineteenth century missionary thinking reflected prevailing Eurocentric visions of progress and civilization. In their understanding of the sources and destiny of Western civilization; in their depiction and diagnosis of the maladies of non-Western peoples; and in their flattering perceptions of themselves in relation to non-Europeans; missionaries showed themselves to be true children of their times.

Like their secular compatriots, missionaries were not blind to the obvious superiority of Western civilization, and by means of preaching, education, and medicine they worked hard at sharing its obvious advantages with those less fortunate. They sometimes took heart, furthermore, not only in a Biblical vision of the future, but in the sort of secular ethnocentric one spelled out by an anonymous "French positivist" in the pages of a widely read missionary magazine:

> the colonial expansion of Christian nations will eventually cover the whole world, and India . . . will one day spontaneously embrace the faith of her masters and educators, as she has already adopted their arts, industry and commerce.[27]

If missionary visions of eventual world domination by Western civilization seem to have been unclouded by doubt, their view of the source of that providential superiority was equally clear: European greatness derived ultimately from its close and sustained ties with Christianity. A positive correlation could be observed, furthermore, between the "purity" of a nation's Christianity and the extent of its imperial expansion. "In the providence of God [England] has become the greatest empire of ancient or modern times," explained one missionary-minded clergyman — "Our expansion is directly providential, and links itself with the expansion of another Kingdom, even that Kingdom of Christ. . . . [for] we Britons enshrine the purest form of Christianity current in the world."[28]

Not everyone on "the mission field" saw it this way, of course. In China, especially, missionaries encountered an obstinate unwillingness to understand

> that whatever is best and worthiest in [Western] civilisation is to [Christianity] what the warp is to the woof; that the science, the art, and learning of the West, which the Chinese [coveted], was bound up in a piece with the religion of the West, which they affected to despise.[29]

Chinese refusal to acknowledge the link between Christianity and civilization was lamentable, but understandable, since millions of Europeans likewise closed their eyes to this fact. Nor were missionaries blind to the evils of their beloved civilization so painfully evident in the lives of irreligious compatriots who, in ruthless pursuit of despicable ends, had likewise scattered themselves about the globe. Trafficking in opium, liquor, slaves, and coolies, such Europeans constituted a blotch on the escutcheon of civilization, and drew from missionaries a vast outpouring of indignant and outraged comment. These evil men not only did great injury to weaker peoples; they compromised missionary testimony. For, as missionaries complained, "Every white man is regarded as a Christian . . . [even] the scum of Europe."[30]

But missionary faith in the essential ethical and material superiority of the West itself was not shaken by the activities of unscrupulous Europeans. Such men were aberrations—cultural Judases who for the sake of lucre betrayed their own heritage—whose shameful behavior drove missionaries to redouble their own altruistic efforts. The words of "Britain's Mission," a hymn appearing in the centenary hymnal of the London Missionary Society, tell the story:

> Shall Science distant lands explore
> And trade her wealth convey?
> Shall war be heard from shore to shore,
> And sin extend its sway?
>
> And shall there not be Christians found,
> Who will for Christ appear
> To spread the Gospel's joyful sound,
> And preach redemption there?
>
> Shall Britain's remotest parts
> Transmit her sins alone?
> And not engage with eager hearts
> To make her Saviour known?
>
> O may our dull and languid zeal
> Be kindled to a flame;
> And burn till all the earth shall feel
> The glories of His name.[31]

No less Eurocentric than missionary understanding of the sources, true nature, and destiny of Western civilization were their diagnoses of and prescriptions for the terrible plight of the rest of the world. "In estimating the vile, sunk, and wretched moral condition of the heathen," wrote a Scottish missionary in 1863,

> it matters not whether we look to China, Japan, Burmah, or Hindoostan, lands in which a barbaric civilization has existed longside of the most childish superstition, or to Africa, whose Negro tribes have, since the days of their father Ham, kept on sinking, from age to age, unaided, until a dreary and bloody fetishism has swallowed up all, and made them the lowest of beings that are called men. Look where

we will in heathen lands, we behold the same ghastly scene of death.
... and infidelity ... and piety.[32]

These words, it must be remembered, were written in days before the
absolute value relativism of Western social sciences drove such candid
assessments underground — to be thought rather than spoken — or caused
them to be expressed in more oblique terms. They were the honest observations — seldom contradicted by those so described — of men and women
who were certain not only of their own superiority, but of those obligations
resting upon all those providentially wielding such power and privilege.

At the very root of the wretched state to which non-Western life had
degenerated lay false religion of one sort or another. Heathen religion,
argued the missionary son of the famous Gustav Warneck, was ultimately
responsible for the moral ignorance, deception, bondage to fear and fatalism, selfishness, moral perversion, and gross materialism characterizing
non-Christian peoples.[33]

Since the greatness of the West derived from Christianity; and since the
moral depravity and impotence of the rest of the world was traceable to
faulty religions; it followed that what the world needed was Christianity.
Christianity, aided and abetted by its own progeny — Western civilization —
would perform among the heathen the same miracles it had wrought among
Europeans earlier. By means of Christianity, heathen habits, family life,
commerce, social institutions, and national character would be transformed.
Because the Christian faith was the one "divinely appointed and supremely
efficacious ministry to the higher nature of man, embodying the noblest
rule of righteousness,"[34] any less dramatic result was impossible.

"When the heathen man becomes a Christian," a missionary to Old
Calabar had observed half a century earlier, "he ceases to be the selfish,
brutish, earthly being that he was."[35] "Civilization follows so necessarily in
the wake of Christianity," argued a contemporary, "that the best way to
convey the blessings of the one is to introduce the other, and the more so,
because the worst vices of the heathen arise out of their religion, and are
perpetrated by it."[36]

There can be no doubt that what these men and and others like them
said was true. The human plight in Calabar, for example, was so wretched
as to almost defy description. Not only was West Africa the "White man's
grave"; it was the grave of tens of thousands of Black men as well. There
was nothing idyllic about life in the Africa of early nineteenth century
missionaries. Floggings, mass executions, and torture of the most indiscriminate kind were the order of the day. Twin babies were slaughtered as a
matter of course; chiefs who had died were never buried alone, but took
scores of slaves, wives, subjects, and children with them into the next life;
intertribal war was brutal and endemic; married women were chattels, to
be disposed of at will; filth, reeking stench, and disease were an integral

element of town life. Conversion to the Christian faith brought an amelio-ration of these conditions in due course.[37]

The conviction that progress was inevitable, and that, furthermore, all true progress and high civilization derived from the Christian faith, per-meated the theory and practice of missions. It was a conviction, fur-thermore, substantiated by actual experience in the field. Missionary descriptions of the terrible and oppressive conditions which they observed in India, Africa, and Asia, abound. There can be little doubt as to the essential accuracy of their accounts; and the profound depths of their hor-ror at the cruelty and injustice which they observed should not be trivialized. Today, the Western world continues to register shock at the injustices, torture, and atrocities described in the publications of organizations such as Amnesty International.

Needless to say, such an outlook—combined with their personal and collective experiences abroad—profoundly affected missionary perceptions of their task, their accomplishments, and themselves. This is the context in which missionaries accepted and took advantage of the material and tech-nological superiority which was their special entitlement as Christian West-erners. And while often deliberately or unwittingly implicated in the imperial skullduggery of their "civilized" homelands, they were widely hailed as genuine benefactors of non-Western peoples.

In his introduction to the book *Trade, Politics, and Christianity in Africa and the East*, Harry H. Johnston confessed an "utter lack of faith or interest in most Christian dogmas." His years as a Colonial administrator had, how-ever, caused him to dissent from those who regarded missionary efforts to uplift the weaker races as "a flying in the face of nature." On the contrary, he said, he had been repeatedly impressed with "the splendid work which has been and is being accomplished by all types of Christian missionary amongst the Black, Brown, and Yellow peoples of non-Caucasian race . . ."[38]

Missionaries might have been gratified to hear such praise from a man of Johnston's known integrity and reputation, but probably not unduly sur-prised. They had known it all along, and their admirers had been saying it for years.[39] Obviously, the standard against which missionary accomplish-ments were measured was Western civilization itself. To the extent that the heathen adopted Western ideas and values, desired and actively sought Western material culture, meekly emulated Western political, social, and religious institutions, and submitted without murmuring to Western dom-ination—to that extent were missionary efforts judged successful. Such evi-dence constituted a vindication of their Lord's promise to those who would make the search for His Kingdom and His righteousness a priority (Matt. 6:33).

Such thinking continues to exert a profound influence upon both the ends and the means of contemporary Western missionary efforts. The ring-ing self-confidence is more subdued now; but missionaries from the West necessarily resemble their nineteenth century religious progenitors in numerous ways. Western missionaries, most of whom now come from the United States, are nurtured in the ranks of "an almost chosen people,"[40] citizens of a nation still sufficiently rich, powerful, and self-confident to have its own way in the world; a country, furthermore, imbued with a sense of mission—with what one writer refers to as "the Captain America complex."[41]

Prior to the First World War, pessimism was not yet fashionable, except in a few intellectual circles. The nineteenth century and the earlier part of the twentieth century was a period of scientific and social optimism throughout the European world. But the unseemly and bloody struggle between the "enlightened" nations revealed an incipient evil in Western civilization theretofore unacknowledged, and probably unrecognized, by missionaries from Western lands. This thin edge of British and European self-doubt was driven deeper into the missionary psyche by the shameful pact in 1938 between Hitler and Chamberlain. The subsequent indiscriminate barbarism of the Second World War—with its murder of six million Jews by the world's most "civilized" nation, and its obliteration of an entire city of Japanese civilians by the West's most "Christian" nation—convinced many that the civilization of which they were a part was, after all, a profoundly immoral one. It was with a soul-wrenching shock that the truth began to dawn: it was not Africans, or Asians, or Arabs, or Indians—but their would-be civilizers—who were walking in darkness.

From that time on the fortunes of British and European Protestantism have been marked by an apparently irreversible, accelerating decline. In Britain and Europe of 1900, affiliated Protestants constituted almost 29 percent of the population. By 1985, this remnant had declined to less than 22 percent, with approximately one out of every 4,355 Protestants opting for an overseas missionary vocation.[42]

While the North American pattern is somewhat different, the trend is likewise unmistakable. As one consequence of the World Wars, American perceptions of their providentially dominant role as saviour of the civilized world were reinforced. Americans, carrying their various gospels—of science, technology, modern weapons, democracy, and of course, religion—covered the globe. It is only in very recent times that Americans, especially those living abroad, have begun to recognize the cynical self-serving nature and essential immorality of their nation's dealings with the rest of the world. America is now widely regarded, even by her own citizens, as a national version of Dr. Jekyll and Mr. Hyde—a mild and benevolent character at home, regularly metamorphosing into a sinister and cynically cruel supporter of the most ruthless oppression abroad.

Increasing numbers of North American Protestants, including missionaries—perhaps *especially* missionaries—not only feel betrayed, but are experiencing a deep sense of personal shame and even guilt for their country's collusion with and even open support of tyranny and injustice in Central America, in Asia, and in the uttermost parts of the earth, in a strange perversion of the Great Commission. Contemporary reading of history has, furthermore, raised serious questions about "the good old days," for it is now clear that in her dealings with Indians and African slaves and their offspring, and in her numerous wars — both economic and military — around the globe, "Christian America" neither was nor is as "civilized" as was once fondly believed. Once confidently hailed as a "Christian" nation, America has revealed itself to be neither Christian nor civilized — merely self-righteous and powerful. And so many missionaries have become, in a profoundly literal sense, aliens at home and abroad, an increasingly rare breed of marginal persons ill at ease in a world which is not their home.

The precise nature of the differences between European and North American religious decline vary, but the similarity of the downward trends is unmistakable. Affiliated Protestants as a percentage of the North American population have declined from 54.9 percent in 1900 to 38.7 percent in 1985 — approximately 92 million believers, of whom approximately one out of every 2340 is a missionary.[43]

Still, as rich representatives of a declining yet powerful civilization, Western missionaries continue to enjoy and employ — sometimes with many a guilty pang, but more frequently with only the vaguest twinges of conscience — the affluence which is their birthright. They are not unaware of the burden of credibility this places upon their personal mission to the world's poor — as will be seen in chapter four; nor are they blind to the fact that global resources can support the way of life which they model for only an elite few. But alternatives to relative personal affluence are few, unattractive, and in the thinking of most missionaries, unnecessary. As will be seen in the next chapter, the contemporary missionary rationale for personal affluence echoes that of Western missionaries of a bygone era.

Having thus far dwelt mainly upon nineteenth century influences which had and continue to have a significant influence upon Western practice of Christian mission, it remains to examine briefly certain elements of contemporary North American culture which influence missionary lifestyles and perceptions of "need" in carrying out their work. There is in North America the widespread belief that perpetual economic growth is possible, desirable, and necessary. In the two decades following World War II, "the expectation of plenty ... became the reigning assumption of social thought."[44] The word which perhaps best sums up the plethora of secular values which influence all North Americans — including missionaries — from infancy throughout life is consumerism, the way of life built on the principle that the great goal of human life and activity is more things, better things, newer things; in short, that life *does* consist in the abundance of possessions.

Consumerism is — to use Robert Bellah's expression — a "habit" of the heart that affects everything Americans are and do.[45] When combined with the popular equation of "progress" with technological sophistication, and "civilization" with abundance, Western consumerism makes justification of increasingly high standards of missionary living almost inevitable.

Anthropologist Jules Henry recognized the preoccupation with consumption as long ago as 1963 when he suggested that life in North America could be summed up by two great commandments: "Create more desire" and "Thou shalt consume."[46] American well being, he argued, rested in the faithful obedience of the majority to these two imperatives.

On the one hand, he pointed out, nothing could be more economically catastrophic than a decline in consumer demand. Should buying lag, economic depression, or at least recession, becomes inevitable. Accordingly, consumers are "daily confronted with a barrage of advertising calculated to frighten or flatter them out of reasonable contentment into the nagging itch for goods and services [they] don't really need."[47]

On the other hand, new consumer cravings had to be discovered and created. Nothing could be more economically destructive than an outbreak of contentment. For the majority of North Americans to remain content with last year's shoes, hats, clothes, cars, furniture, electronic gadgets, breakfast cereals, detergents, perfumes, hair styles, and houses would spell the end of the "good life." "To bring into being wants that did not previously exist" became the great mission of advertising and salesmanship—a process compared by economist Galbraith to a humanitarian who, while impressing upon would-be donors the urgent need for more hospital facilities, inadvertently overlooks the fact that the local physician is running down pedestrians to keep the hospital fully occupied! As Galbraith laconically comments: "Among the many models of the good society, no one has urged the squirrel wheel."[48] In North America we have come close.

North American missionaries have not been immune to this fundamental tendency in their society. No sooner is a new product put on the market than Western missionaries will figure out some plausible reason for putting it into missionary service. Specialized suppliers exist whose "mission" is to ensure that Western missionaries do not become "out of date" in either their personal or missiological effects. Missionaries of today can congratulate themselves that the adjective "missionary"—when applied to wardrobe and equipment—no longer denotes the frumpy obsolescence it once did.

The culture in which American missionaries are born and bred has instilled within them the "need" for far more than their nineteenth century counterparts dreamed possible. Nurtured in and supported by churches which, for the most part, have long since succumbed to the "spirit of the age" which surrounds them, Western missionaries have not been very successful in their personal or institutional resistance to the "Laodicean" phenomenon. A prophet is never accepted in the prophet's own country; and while missionary prophets are not likely to be executed by their North American countrymen, too much criticism of the status quo would undoubtedly cost them the financial support of a wealthy and self-satisfied church.

In summary, then, the contemporary Western missionaries find it difficult to deal with the question of personal affluence for a number of reasons.

In the first place, that complex of behaviour and ideas associated with progress and civilization which developed such tremendous momentum in nineteenth century Europe and America continues to exert a powerful though often subliminal influence on the theory and practice of missions, making the rationalization of personal affluence possible. In the second place, missionaries have not been immune to those all embracing processes of enculturation whereby the consumer societies in which they are born and bred and from which they are sent into all the world ensure their own economic survival. And finally, the churches from which missionaries draw their support have virtually ignored Biblical teaching on greed and covetousness, and have sanctified both sins in the patterns of life which they model and support among their members. Positive thinking is the order of the day.

3

The Rationale for Missionary Affluence

It is no disgrace to be poor, but it is mighty inconvenient.

Twain

Over the centuries, those who have been blessed with wealth have developed many ingenious and persuasive justifications of their good fortune.

Galbraith

Missionaries from the West have seldom suffered for want of criticism. From both within and outside mission ranks, there have been those who have been — in their unstinting contributions to the general awareness of missionary defects, mistakes, and misdeeds — generous to a fault. An early notable in this regard was Canon Sydney Smith, who, fearing for the security of British interests in India, used the *Edinburgh Review* to expand on his thesis that missionaries — (in particular the Methodist variety) being "evil," "fanatics," "lunatics," and "conspirators against common sense" — were not to be trusted.[1] Missionary self-defense elicited from Smith an even less flattering appraisal of their ends and means. Railing against the entire "nest of consecrated cobblers" (i.e., missionaries) and their "perilous heap of trash" (i.e., missionary publications), the fuming Canon snorted that "It [was] scarcely possible to reduce the drunken declamations of Methodism to a point, to grasp the wriggling lubricity of these cunning animals, and to fix them on one position."[2]

Another clergyman, writing eighty years later, was equally candid although more restrained in his use of metaphor. In two articles appearing in the *Fortnightly Review*, Canon Isaac Taylor critiqued the strategic and pecuniary shortcomings of mission societies.[3] This unsolicited but helpful genre of missiological literature continues to thrive.[4]

Although censure of Western missionary endeavours is as diverse as the missionary enterprise itself, missionary affluence is a recurring theme throughout. Missionaries have not been unaware of the misunderstanding which their lifestyles abroad engender. "New missionaries going to the field are often surprised at the general comforts which surround the old missionaries on the field," acknowledged one missionary in a chapter addressing the issue of "The Missionary and Luxurious Living."[5]

Taking up his cudgel on behalf of his missionary friends a few years earlier, Meredith Townsend addressed himself directly to a question which, "stated with brutal plainness," was this: "Are not missionaries, especially in India, made too comfortable, too like parsons *in partibus* instead of evangelists?"[6] And in New York, another prominent missionary apologist, smarting from highly censorious accounts of missionary life in the Orient, began his defense by observing that "It would be difficult to say why it is that the idea of self-immolation has always been somehow connected with this particular enterprise, — why," in his words, "one who enters upon it should be supposed to be indifferent to comfort and to all those things which nine-tenths of the activities of mankind are busied with seeking."[7] More recently, a mission executive explaining to some ministers in Southern Manitoba why a young couple en route to Zaire should require more than twice the support from his society than would have been the case had they proceeded under the Africa Inter-Mennonite Board, declared: "I make no apology for the level of support our mission requires of its missionaries."[8] He then went on to outline the admirable support package, which included provision for everything from maternity to eternity. He was rightfully proud, in a paternal sort of way, of the way his mission society took care of its missionaries.

When examining the vigorous defense which Western missionaries have mounted in their own behalf, the image of a sheep before its shearers does not come to mind! For they have not been averse, when accused, to opening their mouths and defending themselves vigorously. This is fortunate. For what is of pertinence in this chapter is missionary response to the perennial charge that Western missionary standards of living are too high.

Within that literature dedicated to the defense of Western missionaries and to the confounding of their critics, responses to charges of high living may, for the sake of convenience, be divided into four broad streams of rationale: economic, domestic, social, and strategic. The defense of the living standards enjoyed by Western missionaries is based upon exceedingly practical and sound considerations which — relating as they apparently do directly to the successful fulfillment of the missionary mandate itself — must be taken very seriously.

ECONOMIC ARGUMENTS FOR MISSIONARY AFFLUENCE

"The cheapest mission is the mission which can keep its missionaries the longest, and get out of them the best service which they are capable of rendering," was the conclusion of Griffith John, a veteran of sixty years of missionary service in Central China. Neither longevity nor effectiveness were conceivable unless missionaries were, in his words, "properly fed and housed, and . . . so provided for that [they are] able to work without distraction."[9] A similar conclusion had been reached by a well-known American medical missionary to Turkey: "Missionary economics," he said, "has to do with the production and conservation of the missionary's vital force."[10] Many missionary fatalities were, according to the Editor-in-Chief of *The Missionary Review of the World*, "needless," and could have been avoided by a more careful attention to the plain teaching of the Scriptures on the subject of the health of the human body.[11]

Before Alphonse Laveran pinpointed the cause of malaria in 1880, and Sir Ronald Ross traced the parasite to infected anopheles mosquitoes, Africa was referred to as the "white man's grave" or the "burial ground of missionaries." Until then, lions, leopards, poisonous snakes, enraged elephants, and crocodiles were all recognized as menaces to health; the mosquito was simply a pest.

Henry Drummond's travels in Central Africa left a deep impression upon him. While there, he saw the graves of Mrs. Livingstone and Bishop Mackenzie. He visited the pathetic cemetery at Livingstonia. He saw missionaries prostrated with fever, suffering in solitude often hundreds of miles from their nearest colleague. He was there to hear the news of Stewart's death, and of the death of a white mother in childbirth. While he was there, the only two British children to have survived thus far died. "In short," comments his biographer, "Drummond saw all the cruel sacrifices, inseparable from the first heroic assaults of Christianity upon the Dark Continent." "I've been in an atmosphere of death all the time," he said when he returned to Scotland.[12]

Just how dangerous was missionary life abroad? By dividing the number of deaths which occurred in each field by the total number of years which missionaries had spent on the field, Dr. William G. Lennox—then of the Harvard Medical School—calculated missionary mortality rates for the major American societies between 1812 and 1928.[13] His figures (Table, page 33) show the number of deaths per thousand in each field.[14] Missionary death rates never approached those of European troops stationed in Africa. Between 1929 and 1936, British soldiers on the Gold Coast were devastated by a rate of 483 deaths annually per 1000![15] Furthermore, figures show that after 1869, mortality rates for Presbyterian ministers in the United States were consistently and dramatically higher than for their missionary counterparts in India.[16] Nevertheless, death on any scale was as unpopular among Protestant missionaries then as it continues to be among people generally.

Of course, missionary mortality was only one—admittedly the most incorrigible—reason why missionary careers were terminated. More frequently, bad health simply invalided a missionary home. Of 3712 missionary withdrawals from service between 1900 and 1928, only 15 percent were because of death, while 31 percent were because of ill health.[17]

TABLE 7
Number of American Missionary Deaths Per Thousand, 1812–1928

Africa	17.1
Near East	13.2
Malaysia and the Pacific Islands	12.4
India	10.4
North China	9.5
Mexico and Central America	9.4
South China	8.9
Europe	7.6
Japan and Korea	6.6
South America	6.2
Central and West China	5.5

A missionary's early departure from the field due to personal discomfort, illness, or death constituted — in addition to the human and strategic costs — a staggering economic loss to the sponsoring agency. The fact that a significant percentage (close to 40 percent) of missionary deaths or withdrawals due to ill health occurred during the first term of service was significant.[18] For as one author explains,

> For a missionary to become generally useful in the missionary field, and to bear his part of the work, requires from three to six years of preparation. The expense, therefore, of getting a missionary upon the field, apart from the original expense of mental equipment in the schools, is not inconsiderable. . . .
>
> If, during this period, the missionary's health breaks down, and he is compelled to give up the work and return home, all of the money, or most of the money that has been spent on his outfit, travelling expenses, and support, while studying the language and learning the work, is practically thrown away.[19]

It was clear that the cheapest and most effective missionary was, beyond doubt, the live one; the live missionary was the healthy one; the healthy one was the comfortable one; the comfortable one was the one whose way of life when abroad most closely approximated that to which the missionary was accustomed back home. For it was only under such conditions that a missionary's "vital force" could be produced and conserved. Wealth and health went together. Philip Southon, an American physician who within two years would himself be buried in Central Africa, explained why a comfortable, European-style residence was an essential part of a missionary's equipment:

> I am now sending my brother an order for things for the home, crockery, glass, cutlery, and lots of little things which really are essential

for a residence in this country. For, as you know, I maintain that we should use all reasonable means to make our lives as comfortable as possible under the circumstances, since our health depends largely upon our degree of comfort or discomfort.[20]

Nor could food be overlooked. No less an authority than Stanley himself is quoted by the Honorary Secretary of the East London Institute in her comments on the cause of missionary fatalities in the Congo: "the cause of death of so many in African exploring parties," Stanley had said, "is poor food. Feed your Europeans on good English provisions, ... pet and care for him, and he will live; give him only native food, and let him rough it, and he will die."[21]

Western missionaries no longer anticipate ill health or an early death as the inevitable price of their calling. They enjoy, along with North American clergy, those preferred life insurance rates which are reserved for those whose life and health expectancy is among the most enviable in the world.[22] This is due, in part, to an eagerness on the part of Western agencies to appropriate the lessons in lifestyle and standard of living of earlier generations of missionaries by steadily improving the conditions and standards of missionary living. During the period between 1960 and 1980, inflation has produced a steady increase in the cost of consumer goods. Nevertheless, disposable personal income for Americans—calculated in constant dollars—has increased by about 60 percent.[23] Economic standards of American missionaries during the same period have, similarly, not only kept pace with inflation, but left it far behind.[24]

The timeless economic argument in favour of missionary affluence is nowhere more clearly summed up than by J. L. Barton, in his 1906 response to the charge that missionaries were living too luxuriously: "Short lives, ordinarily, in the mission field are of little direct value to the work," he wrote, adding:

> In the ordinary course of events, the missionary who can give the longest life of service to the cause is the one who brings the strongest influence to bear upon the people among whom he lives, and who will produce the largest results by his life. It is the missionary's duty to invest his life in the way that will bring forth the largest and most permanent results, and experience has proved that, as a general thing, these results are not obtained by starving the body or misusing it by unnecessary hardships, or causing it to carry unnecessary burdens, and thus wearing it out early in its career.[25]

If his advice sounds strangely out of tune with Christ's words about saving and losing one's life (Luke 9:24), they encapsulate the economic common sense that has characterized the missionary movement from the West since its beginning two hundred years ago. "Avoidance of fanaticism and folly, and the temptation to run to extremes" was, according to A. T. Pierson, the epitome of common sense where missionary health was concerned. He even managed—albeit on questionable hermeneutical grounds—to find scriptural sanction for his point of view in Ecclesiastes 7:16. "Be not righteous over much," quotes Pierson approvingly; "neither make thyself over wise; why shouldst thou destroy thyself?"[26]

DOMESTIC RATIONALE FOR MISSIONARY AFFLUENCE

In order of priority, it is doubtful if any other rationale for maintaining high standards of living can be more compelling than those having to do with a missionary's family life. "One of the most difficult questions to be solved in the work of Christian Missions to the heathen is, what should be done for the children of missionaries?" began the anonymous author of an 1855 pamphlet on this most poignant of all married missionary subjects.[27]

Heartrending indeed are the accounts of earlier missionaries who, because of "the great difficulty of bringing them up in a Christian manner amongst a heathen people,"[28] and for want of appropriately Western schools in the lands of their adoption, felt it their painful duty to send their young children to Europe or America for education. The resulting anguish suffered by both parents and children can scarcely be imagined, although the letters and diaries of grief-stricken mothers do provide a profoundly moving glimpse of their deep distress. A letter expressing the soul-searing agony of a young missionary mother, contemplating the hour of her children's farewell from Burma, could be multiplied thousands of times over, and is worth quoting extensively:

> Our children are but another name for self. You are right in supposing that I have many anxious thoughts about their future lot; how many and how anxious, no human being can ever know . . . From experience and observation, my own as well as others, I am convinced that our children cannot be properly educated and fitted for the greatest usefulness in this country; that I shall wrong my children, seriously wrong them, by suffering them to grow up, inhaling day after day, and year after year, the fatal miasma with which the whole moral atmosphere of this country is so fearfully impregnated. On this point my judgment has long been convinced. Shall we, then, go home with our children, and see them educated under the genial influence of a Christian sky? Or shall we send them away, and commit their best interests, for time and for eternity, to stranger hands, who do not and cannot feel a mother's duties?
>
> As a general rule, I believe a mother's duty to her children is second only to her duty to her Creator. How far missionary mothers may be exempt from this rule, it is difficult to decide. A mother who has spent eight, ten, or twelve of her best years among heathens may

be expected to be well acquainted with their language, manners, customs, and habits of thought and feeling. She has proved herself their friend, and gained their confidence and affection. She is, as it were, just prepared for extensive usefulness. At this point shall she go and leave them, with none to tell them of Him who came to ransom their souls from sin and its penalty? Or, if another is raised up to fill her place, it must be years—years during which many precious immortals must go down to a dark, a fearful eternity, ere she is prepared to labor efficiently among them.

I see no other way than for each individual mother prayerfully to consider the subject, and let her own conscience decide as to her duty. As to my own feelings on this subject, after long, serious, and prayerful consideration, I have come to the conclusion that it is best to send our eldest two back to America in the course of another year, should a good opportunity offer. . . . This surely forms the climax of a missionary's sacrifices. . .

If it were not for the consciousness of doing right, of being in the path of duty, I could not, no, I could not sustain it. . . . Pray for me; pray for those dear children who are so soon to be orphans, an age, too, when they most need the watchful care of parental affection. This thought is at times almost too much for my aching, bursting heart to endure. Had not my Saviour, yes, and a compassionate Saviour, added these two words: "and children" to the list of sacrifices for his sake, I might think it more than was required. . .

Shall we withhold our Isaac? No; may we rather strive to commit ourselves and our precious offspring in faith to his care, who has said, "Leave thy fatherless children to me." They are in one sense orphans. But if rendered so by what we feel to be obedience to our heavenly Father's will, will He not be to them a father and protector? Will He not more than supply the place of the most affectionate earthly parents?[29]

In the course of time, schools offering a Christian or at least a Western educational environment were established. Today, while missionary parents still frequently face the prospect of sending their children to boarding school, modern air travel combined with the availability of numerous special international schools on every continent make the necessary separations of shorter duration and therefore less painful.[30] Nevertheless, as the son of missionaries, it is only as a father that I now begin to fathom the look of muted anguish in my parents' eyes as—year after year—they said their last goodbyes before leaving my sister and me in the care of the dedicated and loving staff of Bingham Academy in Ethiopia.

Missionary children today are, with few exceptions, separated from parents no more than six to eight weeks at a time. Nevertheless, the anguish of separation together with the inevitable twinges of parental self-doubt continue to make the experience painful. Not surprisingly, the care and education of missionary children continues to absorb the attention of Western missionary agencies.[31]

It must be evident that the provision of a Western education abroad is fiscally expensive. Within the various countries in which schools for missionary children or international schools are located, the number of non-missionaries who can afford to send their children to these institutions is negligible. In a country in which most of the inhabitants barely subsist, only the very affluent can contemplate spending three thousand dollars per child per year on their children's education.

In view of the alternatives, this rationale for missionary affluence can be readily appreciated by any parent. "Even if the cheap missionary could induce a fitting wife to share [an ascetic] lot," explained one writer a century ago,

> he will think of the children to come and perceive from examples all around him what on such an income their fate must be. They will be boys and girls with the white energy who have been bred up as natives—that is, they will, unless exceptional persons, belong to the most hopeless class existing in the world. They cannot be sent home or be kept in the hill schools, or be separated in any way from the perpetual contact of an Asian civilization which eats out of white children their distinctive morale.[32]

As Westerners, missionary children are entitled to a Western enculturation which ensures that when they return home, they will not be disadvantaged foreigners. Secure in the knowledge that their children are receiving the education and care appropriate to their social station and nationality, Western missionary parents can get on with fulfilling their part of the Great Commission. Missionary health, especially the psychological and physical well-being of the "weaker vessel,"[33] have been and are being used to justify the modest affluence and privileges enjoyed by Western missionaries, but it is doubtful whether any more powerful or instinctively legitimate rationale for missionary affluence exists.

A SOCIAL RATIONALE FOR MISSIONARY AFFLUENCE

In his instructive pamphlet, "Hints for Missionaries Proceeding to Central Africa," Dr. E. J. Southon's thoughtful instructions on missionary wardrobe—touching upon suits, shirts, collars, undershirts, drawers, socks, scarves, boots, shoes, wading trousers, wading boots, hats and helmets—are prefaced with these words of sage advice:

> In his travels, the missionary should always present the appearance of a gentleman. There is no necessity for discarding civilised habits

because civilisation is left behind; on the contrary, it is for him to carry with him the impress of a society better than that to which he is going; hence, he should always be neat and clean in his appearance, and scrupulously careful that his garb is tidy. An untidy European will surely be criticised by the gentlemanly Arab, if not by natives.[34]

While the substance of Dr. Southon's advice may sound strangely quixotic to the non-Victorian reader, the function which his instructions were calculated to serve is by no means absent from more contemporary missionary concerns. Personal appropriation of those statuses — together with their accompanying roles — which will best facilitate the accomplishment of missionary objectives continues to be at the heart of a missionary's orientation to another culture. Statuses and roles define relationships within any society. Western cross-cultural missionaries are not exempted from this rule.[35]

For good or for ill, the historically close connection between missionaries and the highly visible economic, social and imperial power of the West has made it extremely difficult for them to disassociate themselves from the statuses and roles assigned to the privileged. In the last century, idealistic Church Missionary Society (CMS) missionaries who have tried to do so were regarded by sceptical natives as either hypocrites or failed Europeans.[36]

Contemporary missionaries from the West, no matter how idealistic, inevitably learn that *because* they are *Western* missionaries, they naturally or at least potentially occupy a high status in the social rankings of most economically poor societies. Not only will a missionary attempting to identify materially and economically with the poor not be understood; such a missionary will operate under what Eugene Nida refers to as "a cloud of suspicion . . . since it reverses all the norms of social climbing."[37] Not only the Incarnation of our Lord, but the experience of contemporary missionaries in the field demonstrate that Nida's observation is absolutely correct. An American missionary in Peru wrote to me of his experience in Ecuador. "When we lived in Ecuador," he said, "we did 'go native' and the local people just thought that we were crazy." As he explained,

> They have a conception of "gringo" and in order to gain their respect, we needed to meet their expectations, build a nice house, get a better vehicle, etc. Too close an identification with native culture diminished our standing in the community, and therefore any message we may have [had] for them.[38]

Aversion to the unpleasant side effects associated with diminished standing in a community is indeed a powerful rationale for maintaining and even increasing Western missionary affluence.

STRATEGIC ARGUMENTS FOR MISSIONARY AFFLUENCE

From a strategic point of view, the expansion of Christianity during the past two centuries is impossible to understand apart from the relative affluence of the West. In the words of Latourette, the grand doyen of twentieth century missions historians,

> The expansion both of Europe and of Christianity was facilitated by the new mechanical appliances and the mounting wealth associated with the Industrial Revolution. It was machines which produced the outpouring of goods whose sales sent Europeans to the ends of the earth. Machines speeded up transportation and communication and so reduced the size of the earth that it was possible for Europeans, including Christian missionaries, to cover it. The monopoly of the new machines enabled Westerners to gain the mastery of most of the earth's surface and to impose their will upon other peoples. From the machines was derived the wealth a portion of which, albeit a very small portion, Occidentals devoted to the spread of their faith. It was the exhilaration of the power and the wealth made available and of the doors opened by the machine which accounted in part for that abounding optimism of the 19th century with which the spread of Christianity was so closely associated.[39]

To the economic, domestic, and social benefits accruing to the affluent missionary must be added strategic advantages. The scope, efficiency, and speed of Western missionary strategies bear testimony to both the necessity and the efficacy of money. While the Christian churches in the West are certainly not generous when total annual giving to missions is calculated on a per member basis,[40] the resulting total is nevertheless impressive when considered in the context of economic resources available to the vast majority of Christians in the Third World. North American Protestant mission agencies reported a total income of $1,356.3 million for 1985.[41] Distributed among 764 agencies represented by 67,200 overseas personnel,[42] the money is used to finance a wide range of mission strategies, including education, evangelism, literature, service and/or support, development, aid, relief, childcare and adoption, medicine, media, support of nationals, and other church-related endeavours.[43] It is hardly necessary to point out that these strategies, almost without exception, require considerable financial and technological support in order to be implemented and sustained. Schools, books, hospitals, autoclaves, x-ray machines, vehicles, radio and television sending and receiving equipment, tractors, grain, airplanes, cars, jeeps, trucks, well-drilling machines, computers, scholarships, international conferences and consultations, and the myriad of other vital accoutrements of those mission strategies originating in the West require a scale of affluence unavailable anywhere else in the world.[44]

Without ample supplies of money not only would missionary efforts from the West be severely truncated, but, it is safe to conjecture, would virtually cease. Western strategies, beginning with the support of Western missionaries themselves, are money intensive. To deny itself access to Western affluence would be an act of suicide for the missionary movement. Obedience to the Great Commission would be no longer conceivable for the vast majority of Western Christians. Obedience thus becomes a rationale for affluence. It is scarcely possible to exaggerate the importance of current Western missionary strategies and their concomitant obligations as a rationale for continued missionary affluence. In the words of Rev. C. C. Thayer, for five years a missionary to Turkey under the American Board, "missionary economics require that the missionary be furnished unto every good work."[45]

At a more personal level, likewise, Western missionaries have found personal affluence to be of considerable strategic importance for reasons having to do with their own efficiency and with the compelling attractiveness of their gospel. In the case of the former, no one has better summarized the age old case in favor of missionary affluence than Donald McGavran. Between 1933 and 1935, due to the twin influences of Daniel Johnson Fleming at Union Seminary and the Great Depression which was devastating North America, some missionaries in India formed a "Fellowship for Ventures in Simpler Living,"[46] with McGavran as its founding secretary. He and his family lived for some time on one rupee a day (33 cents) for food, but soon found it necessary to temper idealism with realism. As McGavran explains,

> the association for simpler living soon found out that if we were to carry out any effective work and if we were to maintain fellowship with our fellow missionaries in India, we would simply have to accept the level of expenditure which missionaries in general employed.
>
> If they were to do their work, they had to employ servants. If they did not employ servants, they spent most of their time doing the work which the servants did and very little time doing the Lord's work. Furthermore, the existence of such a plan created considerable friction within the missionary body. Missionaries who did not belong to the association were likely to say, "Oh, you're trying to show us up!"
>
> So after two or three years we simply gave up the idea and settled down to doing good, solid, hopefully fruitful missionary work.[47]

Secondly, Western missionaries have discovered in their relative affluence an exceedingly advantageous apologetic element. This manifests itself in several ways. On the one hand, it is Western missionary affluence which, as part of his general novelty, has often gained for him a degree of attention, influence, and power beyond anything which could not have otherwise been achieved. A rich man commands a hearing not because he necessarily has something important to say, but because he is rich. Missionary novelty has frequently been used to *get* the attention of a people; missionary affluence has just as often been the means of *holding* that attention. There is something about personal pecuniary advantage which inspires great self-confidence in treating with those who are poorer. As a Hindu convert to Christianity recently observed, "It is easy for Western missionaries to equate *richness* with *rightness*, and *poverty* with *wrongness*."[48]

Historically, the display of missionary affluence played a significant role in the initial impression they made upon non-Westerners. In Central Africa, for example, missionaries of the London Missionary Society were immensely wealthy by indigenous standards, and soon functioned not only as religious teachers, but also as employers, chiefs and magistrates. At first, missionaries were somewhat flattered and amused by the effect which their wealth had upon Africans, most of whom had never seen a white man before. "They come in crowds to see the wagons, and they think us a most wonderful people," wrote one young missionary, adding, "they all seem to have a wholesome dread of us."[49] A nearby missionary, relating his construction of a temporary building a month earlier, described the effect which the sight of a European house had upon the Africans: "Many," he said, "look in as they pass, . . . lift their hands in amazement, [and] exclaim 'the white man! the white man!' "[50] For the missionary wishing to be listened to, there is something reassuring about a personal capacity to inspire awe. The material evidences of affluence were not, it is true, miracles; but their effect upon the African was the same. In some mysterious way, their superior way of life constituted, they thought, irrefutable evidence in favor of the truthfulness and vitality of their gospel. As missionaries well knew, it was often the material aspects of Western life that most attracted the unconverted. "They will watch your housebuilding and gardening," two CMS missionaries proceeding to the same part of Africa were told, "and see that you are superior to them in knowledge and energy and are worth listening to therefore on all subjects."[51]

Today, wherever Western missionaries are working among a people whose material circumstances are demonstrably poorer than their own, a similar rationale—if required—is frequently produced to quell any doubts, including self-doubts, about the propriety of missionary affluence. "While committed to a Peruvian church staffed by Peruvians," one missionary wrote to me several years ago,

> we find that Peruvians will listen to a gringo and give him much more credence than one of their own. So, while we have a few Peruvian members [in our mission], they are less persuasive in dealing with their own people than we, the rich, educated foreigners are![52]

The arguments in favor of Western missionary affluence are strong, sensible, and effective. Effective enough to persuade most missionaries that personal affluence, when appropriated and enjoyed with Christian moderation, is — on economic, domestic, social, and strategic grounds — infinitely preferable to the alternative. The next three chapters will examine the case for the alternative.

PART II

CONSEQUENCES OF WESTERN MISSIONARY AFFLUENCE

Missionary rationale for maintaining and even increasing the economic and material disparity between themselves and those whom they would disciple has tended, not unnaturally, to dwell on the positive advantages of personal health, comfort, security, and efficiency. This was the subject of chapter three. The next three chapters will focus on some negative consequences which seem to be an almost inevitable part of the price which missionaries from the West must pay for their privileges.

On the surface, there can be no denying that the advantages of affluence far outweigh the disadvantages. The preference for more rather than less of this world's goods is universal. To my knowledge, there is no human society in which the young are deliberately enculturated to strive for personal destitution! But while the benefits *of affluence relate largely to the comfort, security, and "efficiency"[1] of the individual missionary, the often overlooked* costs *must be calculated in terms of the effects of unbridgeable economic and material disparity upon that complex of social, psychological, didactic, and theological elements which together comprise the gospel communication process itself. What effects — if any — does wealth have upon the missionary as communicator and teacher? And what influence does the material privilege of the missionary have on personal credibility, and on global perceptions of the content and relevance of the good news itself? It is clear that medium and message cannot be separated, each being inextricably, symbiotically linked to and affected by the other. It is the intention of the ensuing chapters to explore some of the negative effects and side effects of Western missionary affluence upon missionaries themselves, upon their message, and upon those who see, hear, and respond to their splendidly packaged gospel.*

Missionaries constitute part of a rich elite whose numbers, relative to the burgeoning populations of poor around the world, constitute a steadily diminishing proportion of the world's total population. Furthermore, the

*economic gulf separating the rich from the poor is widening, despite sincere
but essentially desultory efforts on the part of "developed" nations and
"development" agencies to reverse the trend. Accordingly, the price missionaries must pay for their participation in affluence has never been
higher. For as will be seen, in exchange for the various comforts and
securities of personal affluence, Western missionaries must sacrifice a
measure of apostolic effectiveness and credibility. But this pound of flesh
is a mere scratch beside the cost to personal integrity which a rich missionary — purporting to represent a Lord who became poor for our sakes —
must pay. In the end, all suffer: Christ, who so loved the world that he
became poor; the world of the poor, so loved by Christ that he lived and
died and lives for it; and the rich missionary, who so loves this world that
he cannot give it up for the sake of Christ and for the gospel.*

*Failure to counter wealth's insidious effects upon its missionary endeav-
ors will ensure the continued ebb of the Western churches as a Kingdom
force. Increasingly mesmerized by the deceitfulness of its own riches and
by the cares of its tiny, materially secure, ego-sized world, the richest
church in the world will continue to decline in spiritual fruitfulness despite
its frenetic, high profile, technologically efficient activities (Mark 4:18).
Like her first century counterpart in Laodicea, whose Christlessness and
spiritual destitution seem to have been apparent to everyone but church
members themselves, she will be vomited out of the Body of Christ (Rev.
3:14-21). As will be seen in chapter six, repentance among the secure and
the comfortable is exceedingly rare. But it is possible.*

*The negative dynamics of economic disparity will be examined in the
context of four overlapping spheres of missionary life and work: relational,
communicatory, strategic, and theological. As will be seen, each of these
is affected in profound though not always immediately obvious ways by
the relative affluence of Western missionaries whose professed mandate it
is to lead the poor of this world in the Way of the Cross.*

4

Relational Costs of Missionary Affluence[1]

I have told my missionary friends, "Noble as you are, you have isolated yourselves from the people you want to serve."

M. Gandhi

The whole biblical teaching is rooted in relationship. Money has ultimate meaning only if it enhances human relationship.

K. Koyama

Unlike so many, we do not peddle the word of God for profit.

St. Paul

Those dimensions of missionary life and work most obviously and directly affected by material and economic disparity are those having to do with his social relationships. "No man is an island" means at the very least that one's self-identity is to a large degree determined by the people among whom one lives. A missionary's status—both self-image and identification by others—is significantly influenced by economic standing in one's community. Roles—the behaviour which in missionary or nonmissionary understanding is appropriate to a given status—are similarly affected by the relative affluence of the Western missionary.

Missionary wealth almost inevitably affects interpersonal relationships in at least six ways, each of which is antithetical to all that Christ modelled for his followers.

AFFLUENCE AND MISSIONARY INSULATION

Indeed, it is possible to argue that the primary advantage of wealth is its capacity to provide the wealthy with goods and services which serve to cushion them from the harsh realities of life. The survival instinct which is

45

common to all organisms is, in the case of human beings, supplemented by the desire to proceed from birth to death as comfortably as possible. When compared with the poor, those who are rich are able to achieve astounding comfort on their journey through life, while at the same time being able to postpone — seemingly indefinitely — the unpleasant end of their pleasant journey.[2]

The word *insulate* is thought to have derived from the Late Latin *insulatus*, meaning made into an island. The verb insulate today generally means "to prevent or reduce the transmission of electricity, heat, or sound to or from (a body, device, or region) by surrounding with a nonconducting material."[3] Both the etymology and the definition of this word are instructive in the context of the present discussion, since to a remarkable degree, Western missionaries, because of their affluence, inhabit an island in a sea of poverty. Their affluence constitutes quite literally the "nonconducting material" which protects them from the "heat" and "sound" of the poverty in which the majority of the globe's inhabitants live and move and have their being.

That insularity which the privileged accept as their entitlement manifests itself in virtually every facet of a Western missionary's life. Comfortable, well-furnished residences; closets with several changes of clothing; cupboards stocked with a great variety of nutritious foods; medicine cabinets brimming with efficacious prophylactics and drugs of various kinds; medical plans to deal with a child's crooked teeth or a parent's failing kidney; insurance policies providing for the well-being of loved ones in the event of an untimely emergency; registered retirement savings plans which, by taking careful thought of the morrow, are calculated to assist the aged missionary in the final transition between this life and the next; the costly mobility — by means of personal motor vehicles — to which every Westerner feels entitled; resources sufficient for expensive local and international flights to whisk a family away from danger or to take a family on much needed furlough; educational opportunities unmatched anywhere in the world for children; funfilled, expensive vacations for the family; an abundance of ingenious technological aids of various kinds, each device promising and sometimes delivering efficiency in accomplishing personal and professional ends; such derivatives of personal affluence constitute the "non-conducting material" of which missionary insulation from the "heat" and "sound" of poverty is fashioned.

Such behaviour cannot be hidden from a missionary's neighbours. In a scathing indictment of North American missionaries to Spain, Juan Antonio Monroy observed that "many missionaries arrive in Spain and other countries with the sole intention of taking a vacation in a foreign country." Accordingly, they almost inevitably choose as their ministry bases modern cities with comfortable, sunny climates. Worse, they then proceed to "live in a society limited to themselves, and . . . close themselves off in apartment blocks or . . . chalets surrounded by small gardens . . . in order to be alone.

They don't seek contact with the people, they are not open to friendship."[4] These generalized perceptions are probably not entirely fair, but they are the blunt appraisal of a "native" trying to make sense of North American missionary behaviour.

AFFLUENCE AND MISSIONARY ISOLATION

Independence is the state of being free from the control of another. *Segregation* is the practice of creating separate facilities within the same society for the use of minority groups. *Isolation* is a lack of contact, genuine communication, or interaction between persons or groups within a society.

Perhaps nowhere is personal independence — as distinct from interpersonal dependence — more highly valued than in North America. Alexis de Tocqueville was to comment extensively on this quality when he visited the United States more than one hundred and fifty years ago.[5] While admitting admiration for their "manly independence," he noted an ominous side to American pride in self-reliance: profound isolation from the larger human community.[6]

More recent observers support de Tocqueville. The universally human desire for community and interdependence are, according to one sociologist, frustrated in American society by the almost obsessive love of personal independence which we have been taught from childhood to regard as normal. One common expression of American circumvention of that interdependence upon which all human societies are based is seen, according to Philip Slater, in the high regard for personal privacy:

> We seek a private house, a private means of transportation, a private garden, a private laundry, self-service stores, and do-it-yourself skills of every kind. An enormous technology seems to have set itself the task of making it unnecessary for one human being ever to ask anything of another in the course of going about his daily business. Even within the family Americans are unique in their feeling that each member should have a separate room, and even a separate telephone, television, and car, when economically possible. We seek more and more privacy, and feel more and more alienated and lonely when we get it. What accidental contacts we do have, furthermore, seem more intrusive, not only because they are unsought but because they are unconnected with any familiar pattern of interdependence.[7]

This fierce love of personal independence is not left behind when American missionaries travel abroad. But if independence is expensive in North America, it is much more costly to maintain in other parts of the world.[8] Only the person of considerable means can hope to afford it; conversely, the person wishing to live in an American way must have access to wealth.

Independence is even more costly in nonmonetary terms, however. Not surprisingly, Western missionary communities have from the beginning been marked by a *de facto* racial segregation, since membership is based upon an economic criteria which can generally only be met by Western Christians. This is not to say that all contact with impoverished nonwhites is avoided. On the contrary, it is often the plight of such poor that has figured most prominently in the Western missionary's journeys to the ends of the earth. But such contacts have tended—particularly in places where there are large concentrations of missionaries among even larger numbers of poor—to accentuate the missionaries' absolute independence of and segregation from the poor. This is isolation. There is something both ironic and tragic in the specter of a supremely relational gospel being proclaimed by an isolated community of segregated whites!

Details of a report by two of my students who recently visited one of the largest mission stations in Africa sadly confirm that "the tendency for missionaries to withhold themselves from participation in local community life"[9] is by no means a mere vestige of the past. They could not help but notice that the missionaries on the station were virtually isolated from their closest African neighbours. Any Africans venturing onto the station were menials or merchants, tending gardens, doing wash, delivering loads of wood. It was a world apart—a world of privileged, indulged missionary children enjoying the best education that money can buy in that country; a world of happy, fulfilled, industrious, supremely secure white missionaries, spending their lives in medical, educational, and developmental programmes on behalf of—though not with—Africans; a world of white families, each with its glowing future; a world viewed by its closest neighbours with bitterness, envy, resentment, and sometimes naked hostility.[10] Since Biblical faith is above all a relational faith, it is not only sad, but sinful, when personal possessions and privileges prevent, distort, or destroy missionary relationships with the poor. But this is the almost inevitable price of affluence.

AFFLUENCE AND AN UNBRIDGEABLE SOCIAL GULF

This social gulf makes genuine fraternal friendship so awkward as to be virtually impossible, a phenomenon well documented by Robert Coles in his study of the children of affluent Americans. A wealthy mother's six-word explanation in response to the troubled inquiry of her nine-year-old daughter somehow says everything the rich have ever been able to say concerning their relationships with the poor: "they are they and we are we."[11] Nor have honest observers of Western missionary social behaviour been blind to their apparent inability to establish close friendships with the poor. A friend is an intimate, someone with whom one generally has much in common. In their friendships, people naturally gravitate to those with whom they are not only temperamentally but socially and economically compatible. It is humanly almost impossible for a wealthy family to share a deeply fraternal relationship with a family whose material and economic resources are a pathetic fraction of their own; who cannot afford an education for their beloved children beyond minimal literacy, while the children of the wealthy family anticipates as a matter of course opportunity and money for education up to the very highest levels; whose house is a tiny one-room shack (made of straw or cardboard) with no amenities, while the wealthy family resides in a western-style bungalow, complete with kitchen, bathroom, private bedrooms for each member of the family, carpeted floors, stuffed furniture, closets and bureaus filled with clothes, and personal servants; who must rely solely upon leg power to get anywhere, while the wealthy family has access to car, jeep, power-boat, or airplane; for whom the concept of vacation doesn't even exist, while the wealthy family spends one month of each year travelling and sightseeing, or simply taking it easy in a resort far away from the grind of everyday work.

Between families of widely disparate means and standards of living, friendship is extremely unlikely. With whom does a missionary naturally choose to spend his leisure time? With whom is he comfortable enough to share a vacation? Who is likely to listen comprehendingly, sympathetically, understandingly, to a couple as they pour out the peculiar frustrations, burdens, and perplexities of missionary parenting? With whom is a Western missionary likely to go shopping for family birthday or Christmas gifts? Who is able to commiserate with the missionary about the inadequacy of support level? From whom will a missionary likely seek advice on personal financial matters—investment, banking, saving? In every case, it is very doubtful if the poor would have any part in these aspects of a missionary's life. The social rapport required must obviously be reserved for social and economic peers. The presence of the poor in such situations would be an embarrassment to any missionary of even moderate sensitivity.

It is difficult to deny that economic disparity, and not simply cultural difference, poses a great obstacle to fraternal social reciprocity. Consequently, many Western missionaries—more instinctively than deliberately—associate with the poor only in the context of their missionary work.[12] In other contexts, attempts by the poor to participate in the social life of missionaries can only be a mutually embarrassing intrusion. As long as there is an economic chasm between missionaries and their converts, social fraternity will be hampered. Present economic relationships within the Body of Christ worldwide being more disparate now than they have ever been, former Bishop Azariah's appeal to the delegates of the 1910 Edinburgh Conference still needs to be heard. "Missionaries," he lamented, "except for a few of the very best, seem to me to fail very largely in getting rid of an air of patronage and condescension, and in establishing a genuinely brotherly and happy relation as between equals with their Indian flocks." He concluded his address with his well known challenge: "You have given your goods to feed the poor. You have given your bodies to be burned. We also ask for *love*. GIVE US FRIENDS."[13] Unless Western missionaries are willing to give up their wealth, it is doubtful whether most of them will ever be able to overcome what Robert Coles refers to as "that apartness that goes with wealth."[14] Operating as a part of a small minority having sufficient time and money to live securely and comfortably in a world in which a majority of people are destined to bare subsistence, missionaries must, it is clear, either identify with the privileged or get rid of their wealth.

SOCIAL DISPARITY AND THE ILLUSION OF SUPERIORITY

"Nothing so gives the illusion of intelligence as personal association with large sums of money."[15] Even though the feelings of superiority which inevitably accompany wealth may be dutifully denied with the appropriate protestations of equality required in an egalitarian world, the facade fools nobody. Power, possessions, and esteem are the natural offspring of wealth. Conversely, the state of impoverishment yields only material scarcity, social impotence, and vulnerability.

While awareness of personal superiority is still sometimes expressed overtly, normally the indications are more subtle. One hundred years ago, Westerners expressed their superiority feelings openly without fear of the censure of their peers. Thus Sir Francis Galton — scientific luminary, explorer, and president of the prestigious Royal Geographical Society — could dispense a brand of candid advice to European travellers in Africa that would today result in his censure or incarceration. In Africa there were occasions, he noted, when a traveller had to "take the law into his own hands." At his best, the African ruler could be described as "a savage despot." The typical pattern of civil affairs in that dark continent was expressed by Galton as —

> The simple rule, the good old plan, —
> That they should take who have the power,
> And they should keep, who can.

Accordingly, Galton's proffered advice on how best a Western traveller might handle lawless Africans was harsh, with floggings and penalties based on "the principle of double or treble restitution." Europeans were urged by Galton to look upon mischievous savages "as you would a kicking mule or a wild animal, whose nature it is to be unruly and vicious, and keep your temper quite unruffled."[16]

Unfortunately, instances of missionaries following Galton's scientific advice were not uncommon,[17] and the awareness of superiority was seldom far beneath the surface. Awareness of the social gulf between themselves and Africans was the basis of the unflattering, ironically humorous accounts of African ways which sprinkled the writings of Western travellers. Henry Drummond, not himself a missionary but a staunch advocate of Christian missions, and a popular and influential figure in the Student Christian

Movement between 1884 and 1894, conducted "a scientific examination" of that part of Africa in which a number of British (Anglican and Presbyterian) missionaries were active. The English edition of his published report proved to be immensely popular, selling over 35,000 by 1899. "It is a wonderful thing to look at this weird world of human beings—half animal and half children, wholly savage and wholly heathen," he recorded early on his journey. His opinion of African regal attire—evident in his description of a chief—was bitingly burlesque:

> in books of travel great chiefs are usually called kings, their wives queens, while their mud-huts are always palaces. But after seeing my first African chief at home, I found I must either change my views of kings or of authors. The regal splendour of Chipitula's court—and Chipitula was a very great chief indeed, and owned all the Shire district—may be judged by the fact that when I paid my respects to his highness his court-dress consisted almost exclusively of a pair of suspenders. I made this king happy for life by the gift of a scarlet tennis cap and a few buttons.[18]

Modern missionaries would never be so brash. But they too, surrounded as they are on every hand with evidence of their economic and social ascendancy, must often fight a losing battle against "secret" feelings of superiority over those who can hardly subsist. Thirty years ago it was commonly observed in what may be referred to as the "great man complex"—a condition brought on by the deference which missionaries were frequently accorded by "the natives." The phenomenon was common to other Westerners as well, and is nicely described by Malcolm Muggeridge, in his recollections of teaching in India. "From the moment of landing in Colombo," he recalls,

> I was made conscious of my status as a Sahib. It was like suddenly inheriting a peerage and being addressed as My Lord. Just by virtue of being English and white, if you went to buy a ticket at a railway station, people made way for you. Similarly, in a shop. It was very insidious. At first I found it embarrassing and distasteful; then, though I continued to ridicule it, I came to count upon receiving special treatment. Finally, when for some reason it was not accorded, there was an impulse to become sulky and irritated. From that it is but a small step to shouting and insisting, as in the days of the Raj, I saw happen often enough. Our position in India as a ruling race corrupted all concerned; soldiers . . . missionaries, government officials, planters, businessmen, wives and children; everyone. It also corrupted the Indians.[19]

There are few Western missionaries working among the poor even today who cannot immediately identify with what Muggeridge describes. Nor are modern missionaries any less susceptible to the seeds of corruption which such undeserved deference always carries with it. It is an attitude of entitlement whereby the rich rationalize their own good fortune and blame the victims for their poverty. It is a defensive mechanism which enables the rich to keep more than they need even when in close social contact with destitute people who have less than they need.[20]

Contemporary Westerners compassing land and sea in search of converts may find it difficult to identify with the bullying, the ridicule, the instant intelligence, or the sense of entitlement that accompany social superiority. Nevertheless, must we not at least confess that our obvious affluence and our preference for the company of those, who like us, are affluent, incline us to think of ourselves as teachers rather than servants of the poor? It is hard to behave like a servant when you are rich and powerful, while those whom you serve are poverty stricken and weak. In such situations, it is common to redefine the word "service" to mean whatever we are inclined to do for someone else.

AFFLUENCE AND RELATIONSHIPS OF MISTRUST

Western missionaries are frequently suspected of doing well by doing good. Indeed, it has been observed that when they are no longer doing well—for example, when pressed financially or socially,—they cease from doing missionary good and return home where they can do better!

Of course, human motivation is a complex, sometimes darkly inscrutable phenomenon. That this should be so comes as no surprise to observers of the human predicament, or to those who take the Christian scriptures seriously: "The heart is deceitful above all things, and desperately wicked, who can know it?" The human capacity to assess the motives of one's fellows is remarkably truncated when turned inward. If missionaries have been reticent to speak of material inducements to their calling, others have been more than willing to do so.

In his superb study of the early British missionaries to India, Stuart Piggin demonstrates that among the many noble considerations involved in a candidate's deciding for or against a missionary vocation were at times included personal quests for economic security, respectability, and honour—each of which was to some degree assured those formally associated with a mission society.[21] While missionaries themselves have naturally stressed the self-giving altruism of their service, outsiders have often regarded the relative affluence, security, and social status enjoyed by missionaries to be a sure sign of darker, essentially self-serving motives. As one typically caustic commentator on Protestant missionary life in China in 1885 observed:

The missionary business in China is by no means a bad business to run by that class of clergy who occupy that debatable land which is one grade below gentlemanship, and from which the majority of [them] . . . are recruited. Poverty stricken and without prospects at home, out here they are provided . . . with an assured and liberal income . . . [which] is supplemented by liberal contributions from the resident English merchants. . . . The missionary now lives in a condition of affluence which would be unknown to him elsewhere, a luxurious home with luxurious appliances and table, coolies to carry him about, and an ample margin of dollars. . . . in the course of a few years the missionary becomes tired of his work . . . and hies him back to England. . . . There . . . he can scarcely fail to gain repute — especially among silly women little apt in weighing evidence — as a noble champion of Christianity, whereby he assumes a social status to which his birth and breeding have by no means entitled him.[22]

However overdrawn the Knollys caricature of missionaries might have been, that missionaries often enjoyed considerable material and social advantages, and that these privileges gave rise to suspicion of their motives cannot be denied.

Missionary lore abounds with examples. In South India, Western missionaries for several years answered to the Indian designation "Dora," taking the term to be simply the linguistic equivalent of "missionary." Investigation soon showed, however, that the word actually meant "rich landlord," a status granted to missionaries since, like rich landlords, they were observed to buy land, build walled compounds, houses, schools, temples, roads for their cars, and keep several wives.[23]

In Central Africa, missionaries reported similar confusion in native minds as to their *real* reasons for being there. Missionaries soon discovered that their presence, while creating little hunger and thirst for righteousness, whetted native appetites for the material benefits enjoyed by the white man. One missionary, having spoken daily to the people of the "better way," wearily confessed to being confounded by their utter indifference to what he said, and their rapt preoccupation with what he had. He concluded indignantly: "their only object is evidently just to get what they can out of us."[24] His colleague had earlier been frustrated by the local chief's inability to understand the careful elucidation of his "sole object" in coming to Africa; for his exposition elicited from the chief nothing more than a request for "five or six cloths of different kinds." Concluded the missionary: "It is very difficult to make them understand the nature of our work."[25] The subsequent erosion of goodwill with which their arrival among Central Africans had first been greeted was traced by missionaries themselves to the fact that native expectations of improved material welfare had not been realized, and were apparently unwarranted.[26]

As the foregoing incidents intimate, native misunderstanding and mistrust of missionary motives were, in due course, heartily reciprocated. Missionaries appear to have been unaware of the curious double standard by which they judged themselves and native peoples. Rationalizing the necessity of high material and social standards for themselves, they were deeply suspicious of Africans or Asians who tried to follow their example, labelling them as selfish and worldly minded. Missionaries—earning salaries more than fifty times those of their African colleagues, and enjoying a level of affluence unattainable by most of their converts—expressed disappointment with "worldly minded" native teachers whose "one idea," in the words of one missionary, "seems to be a good education [so] ... they can get more money."[27]

In China, likewise, missionaries whose economic and material resources were immense by local standards, and who commanded salaries from thirty to fifty times greater than those of their Christian Chinese counterparts, nevertheless portrayed the Chinese as "a money-loving people ... [whose] principal divinity is the god of riches, and [whose] one aim is the acquisition of pelf."[28]

Such mutual misunderstanding and mistrust colored social relationships between missionaries and nationals, making genuine friendship at best as difficult as it is unlikely.

One hundred years later, while the economic gulf separating Western missionaries and third world populations is even wider, the social dynamics of suspicion and mistrust remain the same. To argue otherwise is both foolish and futile. Now, as then, few missionaries would admit that membership in the fraternity of missionaries represented a social step up.[29] In a letter to missionary Murray Rogers, Japanese theologian Kosuke Koyama (after eight years as an Asian missionary in Thailand) confided that speculation on the salaries of American missionaries was "a great pass time," but that all such discussions came to a grinding halt the moment an American missionary appeared. There existed an intuitive understanding that such information was highly classified, and might constitute an acute embarrassment to all parties.[30] It is clear that such a discussion could cause a Western missionary confusion only in the context of inordinate disparity between his income and that of his non-Western colleagues. Such secrecy is the culture in which mistrust, misunderstanding, and suspicion have always bred and proliferated.

As in the nineteenth century, so in the twentieth, the instinctive defensiveness which Western missionaries feel about their privileged status continues to be hidden behind the thin camouflage of concern about native selfishness or worldly mindedness. While this is particularly the case between Western missionaries and indigenous evangelists, it is also a problem in relationships between Western missionaries of widely disparate means themselves. One does not need to travel far or long to realize that there exists on many "mission fields" an economic hierarchy. American missionaries—often Southern Baptists—are many times on the top. British missionaries—especially those serving in the more austerely evangelical agencies in the radical tradition of those who, like C.T. Studd—are deeply suspicious of pleasure. Even within those agencies where care has not been taken to ensure strict economic communism, subtly invidious comparisons are frequently made between the dubious dedication of the missionary whose "ministry" account is running over and that of the involuntary ascetic whose "ministry" account is usually dry.

With the "emergence" of "Third World" missionaries, increasing numbers of whom are either finding placement with Western agencies, or who are working in close cooperation with those agencies, the problems attendant upon inequity within the missionary community are even more complicated. Koyama speaks of the economic division of the missionary community in Thailand into "first class" (Western) and "second class" (Asian) missionaries:

> The gap between us was immense in all areas of life. We tried not to compare ourselves with the "first class," and we tried our best, but how could we avoid this comparison? We were living right among them day after day! Once my family was virtually broke ... for one week. I finally went to seek "help" (of "first-aid-kit" kind) at the office of the "first class." I was given a sermon — a good sermon — there. As I came out of that office, feeling like a third class passenger sneaking out of a first class cabin, I met a fellow Western missionary with whom I had studied at the same seminary in the United States, as he drove up in his Volkswagen loaded with items of shopping. He had only been in Thailand a few weeks. Our most "irritating" problem was our most esteemed Western missionaries![31]

Is the suspicion that Western missionaries do good only to do well warranted? Perhaps the answer to that question will not be known until, or unless, the "all these things" package of support and benefits are for some reason no longer available to would-be apostles from the West, and they have to follow their Lord on the same terms as their poorer brothers and sisters around the world. In such circumstances, how many missionaries will go into all the world from North America? No one knows the answer to such questions as this. What is known is that the social distance which comes with economic disparity constitutes an environment in which mistrust and suspicion thrive, and that this is a part of the relational cost which must be paid by missionaries who cling to their material prerogatives as rich Westerners in a poor world. But there is more besides.

AFFLUENCE, ENVY, AND HOSTILE RELATIONSHIPS

With affluence comes social advantage; with social advantage comes personal security and power — power over those with less, power over one's own destiny, the power of choice.

A frequent side effect of economic and social disparity in close proximity is envy—one of that sinister cluster of sins labelled "deadly" by medieval theologians. Although practice has lagged far behind, mission theory has long advocated the establishment of close personal relationships with the people being proselytized. Ironically, therefore, the closer the social ties between missionaries and their third world proteges, the greater the likelihood of envy.

Envy is the feeling that besets us when we observe the prosperity or good fortune of those near us. As Galbraith notes, "Envy almost certainly operates efficiently only as regards near neighbors. It is not directed toward the distant rich."[32] Should gross inequity develop within the context of a family, envy is virtually unavoidable. It is hard to rejoice with those who rejoice, particularly if one is sorrowing. It is painful to see the privileges, advantages, and opportunities which our near neighbours, or brothers and sisters, shower upon their children while ours must experience hunger, privation, and lack of opportunity for betterment. To begrudge the personal and material assets of those who are nearby is a human universal, well documented in personal experience as well as in sociological literature.[33]

The Christian scriptures, in addition to warning against the sin of envy, contain several examples of its operation. The Philistines, envying Isaac because of his great wealth, filled up all of his wells with dirt (Genesis 26:12-16); Saul, envious of David's military successes and popularity with the people, tried to kill him (1 Samuel chapters 18-26); the plan of Darius to reward Daniel's outstanding abilities by making him his chief administrator so maddened his peers that they plotted to destroy him (Daniel 6).

There can be little doubt that the dynamics which produce envy are present wherever Western missionaries work. As psychologist Marjory Foyle pointed out in a recent article on missionary relationships, financial disparity within the mission community itself is a significant factor in the creation and perpetuation of bad interpersonal relationships.[34] The pointedly egalitarian financial policies governing a majority of Western mission agencies suggest that this is well understood by missionaries themselves. This being so, to deny that missionary affluence is a significant contributing factor in the tensions and misunderstanding which seem to bedevil relationships between missionaries and the churches they establish, is to manifest a willful and dangerous myopia. A professor in one of the more prestigious Christian American graduate schools—a man who worked as a missionary in West Africa, and who now instructs future as well as active missionaries—told me that affluence had not been any problem for him, since his African neighbor owned a better color television than he did!

Not all have chosen to deal with the problem by denying that it exists, however. His years as an Asian missionary in Asia made apparent to Koyama what Western missionaries have often been curiously reticent to address openly. "The security which some missionaries enjoy in Asia," he writes, "makes many envious, since it is comparable to the fully chaired university professor in the United States." He continues:

"Threatened life" is the way of life almost universally lived in Thailand and vast areas of South East Asia. I soon began to grapple with the discrepancy between missionary-security and the destiny of the masses without knowing which direction I should take. To my knowledge, this topic has never been taken up at one of those many, many [closed mission business] meetings as either a sociological or theological one.[35]

The subject continues to elude the agendas of missionary conferences and consultations, at least in evangelical circles.

Ironically, nonmissionary Westerners have no difficulty in discerning the envy and hostility which they elicit because of their affluence. Edward Hoagland, a writer who recently travelled — alone and light — throughout the Sudan, relates his embarrassment at parties when, after the normal courtesies were dispelled by drunkenness, the Sudanese would "no longer mask the shock they felt at such a disparity of wealth."[36]

Several years ago, *The Economist* carried a story of a rampage by Chinese soccer fans outside Peking's Workers' Stadium in which a number of foreigners were attacked. The riot was seen as an expression of resentment against Westerners who have been entering China in increasing numbers since 1979, whose presence is "a constant reminder to Chinese . . . of the luxuries not available to them." Only foreigners have access to special shops wherein may be acquired superior local produce as well as imported goods unavailable to ordinary Chinese. Impressive luxury hotels, " . . . where the occasional local Chinese can slip in to gawk but can never hope to be a paying guest," are likewise the forte of only foreigners. "I can't help looking at the foreigners enjoying nice places to eat," complained a Chinese schoolteacher; "I feel angry that it is our country, but the best is reserved for them."[37]

Brewster's Millions, a comic film released in 1985, is built around the truism that wealth brings isolation, not friendship. A recent visitor to Kenya was shocked to discover just how isolated the residents of a large mission station were. He was even more shocked by the hostility of those Kenyans who were the missionaries' closest neighbours. As the missionary jeep in which he was a passenger drove down the road away from the station, he waved to several children along the way. None of the children returned either his smiles or his friendly gestures: two shook their fists, while a third brandished his walking stick menacingly. He noticed that the farther he travelled from the station, the friendlier the people became.[38]

The sociology and psychology of economic disparity being what they are, the Western Church must either grapple seriously with the problem of its affluence, or disappear as a Christian force in the world. Of course, it will continue to send forth committed ambassadors — personal incarnations of the gospel of abundance. But these emissaries will find themselves to be generators of envy and hostility, rather than proclaimers of that freedom which is freedom indeed.

The staggeringly high relational price which Western missionaries must pay for their affluence could perhaps be overlooked, or at least endured, were it not for its insidious effects upon the communication process. For medium and message are both significantly affected by the relationship of the missionary to the convert or would-be convert. If the message of the cross consisted simply in a series of theologically correct propositions about God, human beings, and salvation, then the obligation to preach the gospel could be fulfilled by means of a series of public announcements over the radio. But the Word must always be made flesh, and dwell among men. And the Way has always best been shown by those who can be accompanied by would-be pilgrims. A missionary is above all a Way-shower, whose life must be imitable by his converts. The missionary is not simply a voice box, but a pilgrim who invites others to join him on the narrow way.

5

Communicatory and Strategic Consequences of Missionary Affluence

You yourselves are our letter, written on our hearts, known and read by everybody.

St. Paul

To live is to communicate! Just as we cannot live without blood, we cannot live without communication.

K. Koyama

Zeal does not ensure the propriety of the means which it employs. We need to recognize that zeal for God is not a guarantee that the means used to express the zeal is divinely inspired.

R. Allen

When calculated in the coin of interpersonal relationships, the price which missionaries must pay for maintaining their relative affluence vis-à-vis most Third World Christians is high indeed — especially when considered against Biblical injunctions to brotherly love to which they pay lip service. This was the argument of chapter four.

Missionary rationale for maintaining and even increasing personal living standards usually includes an enthusiastic recital of practical communicatory and strategic benefits deriving solely from the availability of money. As was noted in chapter three, any device which increases the efficiency and the longevity of the missionary or reduces the tedium of missionary tasks not only makes life easier, but is good stewardship. Computers, motor boats, airplanes, cars, jeeps, trucks, durable and comfortable clothing, well equipped residences, schools for missionary children, and countless other amenities which only the rich can afford, not only make missionary work more fun, but more effective, and therefore justifiable. Affluence in this guise is a means to an end. Popular rationalizing — accredited and validated

59

by recourse to military analogy in which the missionary, like the soldier, lives simply but utilizes expensive technical means[1]—seldom takes into account the considerable impact which uncritical use of such means has upon the message itself. For in addition to the relational costs associated with their economic ascendancy, Western missionaries necessarily sacrifice valuable communicatory and strategic effectiveness.

COMMUNICATORY COSTS OF MISSIONARY AFFLUENCE

To communicate is to impart or exchange thoughts, feelings, values, and ideas by means of speech, writing, gestures, and lifestyle. The very essence of mission is communication—verbal and nonverbal. Missionaries are those who, like the apostle Paul, have been committed with the message of reconciliation. Knowing "what it is to fear the Lord," they, above all, "try to persuade men" (2 Cor. 5:11-21). No matter what the shape or the texture of missionary strategy, at the very heart of their *modus vivendi* is "telling," "proclaiming," "preaching," and "convincing," with a view to "baptizing" and "discipling" men and women "from every tribe and language and people and nation" (Revelation 5:9). It is ironic, therefore, that the expensive lifestyles and technological means used by Western missionaries to facilitate the accomplishment of this communicatory mandate frequently ensures that neither the missionary nor the missionary's good news is understood.

Receptor understanding of both messenger and message is powerfully—if indirectly—affected by the relative affluence of the missionary. Medium and message, words and deeds, theory and practice, faith and works, cannot be separated in the life of the one who would remain a credible Christian. The message of the Cross was never intended to consist exclusively or even primarily of a series of theologically correct propositions about the Triune God, man, sin, salvation, the Church, and life after death. Those whose faith is genuine have always been converted. "The demons believe," no doubt correctly, but they make bad missionaries precisely because their lifestyle is at odds with their belief (James 2:14-26). Saying, being, doing—each is an integral part of the Gospel being communicated by the missionary.

Those who would herald the good news must practice a faith which can be both understood and imitated. One of the greatest impediments to credible communication faced by Western missionaries is their relative wealth; for because of it, their personal practice of the faith they proclaim can be imitated only by those whose means make such a lifestyle a realistic possibility.

There are numerous ways in which the relative affluence of missionaries tends to distort or otherwise hamper their effective communication of the gospel. Not surprisingly, missionaries themselves have often been the first to observe—with dismay—the spontaneous generation of misunderstanding which their personal wealth engenders in the minds of the poor both before and after conversion. But they have by no means been the only ones to comment on this phenomenon. Throughout the past two centuries, most missionary endeavour has been undertaken by the "rich" to the "poor." Accordingly, supporters and detractors alike have had ample opportunity to experience or observe, and comment upon, the dynamics of economic disparity upon missionary communication of the Gospel. On the basis of an examination of certain themes which recur throughout missionary related literature, several conclusions concerning the negative effects of missionary wealth upon their communication of the gospel may be drawn.[2]

1. *Wealthy missionaries cannot identify with the life situations of the poor which their message is intended to address.* Inability to relate the good news to the actual circumstances of the people except in theory raises serious questions as to the validity of the good news itself. The reassuring words of a salesman who, for whatever reason, has never tested his own product under adverse conditions, and who is, furthermore, unwilling to do so personally, can and should be treated with scepticism. Applied Christianity — when proclaimed by "needless" missionaries to needy poor — is reduced to a series of personally untested and undemonstrated hypotheses. Such missionaries specialize in how to abound, but do not know how to be in want. Missionary faith — so obviously vibrant and self-assured in the context of their own plenty — may or may not work in the lives of those whose poverty and destitution is endemic. In such situations, missionaries can only model prosperous inversions of the Incarnation depicted in Hebrews 4:15, in effect opting for the comfortable role of high priests who cannot sympathize with the vulnerabilities of the poor, because they have never personally battled the Furies of poverty. The struggle of sincere and idealistic missionaries to imagine themselves in the place of the poor generally leads only to thankfulness for personal and family security, comfort, and material hope, rather than to any attempt to become poor with the poor, to see if the grace of God is in fact as sufficient as they proclaim it to be.

If — as the Bible teaches and communications specialists have recently affirmed — medium and message cannot be separated, then it is not possible to have a "gospel in context" if the missionary medium is himself out of context. Not only *what* is said, but *how* it is said, and *by whom* it is said are equally integral communicatory elements from the perspective of the person *to whom* a message is directed. For example, the statement "Revolution is a good thing" can evoke from a political conservative either hearty agreement or vehement denial — depending upon whether it is attributed to Lenin or to Jefferson.[3] Nothing could be more obvious than the fact that missionaries "communicate to whole men, not simply to souls with ears, [and] . . . whole men communicate — not just souls with mouths."[4] Contrary to the emphases imbedded in most North American mission curriculums, not communication theory, but communicator living, is the key to incarnational communication.[5]

Commenting upon Western missionary ineffectiveness in China one hundred years ago, Isaac Taylor was forced to conclude that unless missionaries were willing "to live among the natives exactly as the natives live," their attempts to communicate the Christian faith would never succeed. "Would a Chinaman," he queried rhetorically, "with his pigtail, feeding on snails, birds' nests, and lizards, have any chance of converting English school boys to Buddhism?" The odds were very slim indeed. It was time, he said, for missionaries to "become brothers of the people . . . give up all European comforts and European society, and cast in their lot with the natives . . . striving to make converts, not by the help of *Paley's Evidences,* but by the great renunciation."[6] In the event, it is safe to assume the discomfit of both critic and criticized. For missionaries, in using the Canon's lack of missionary experience as sufficient grounds for disdaining his advice, inadvertently proved his point. One veteran missionary, having shared his overnight lodgings in a Chinese inn with several squealing pigs, wryly suggested that this might be the ideal place for Canon Taylor to begin his own missionary endeavours![7]

The direct correlation between a missionary's level of identification and effectiveness of his communication is well known. As Eugene Nida has pointed out,[8] at the lowest level of communication, it is not necessary that the source of the message be closely identified with either the message itself or with the receptor of the message. A tourist who is told that he can cash his traveller's check in the bank just around the corner will soon know whether the information source is true or not. Nor does such communication require that the source of the information be closely identified — psychologically, culturally, socially, economically — with the tourist. The identity and nature of the information source is irrelevant.

The second level of communication involves a message which, while not making any permanent demands upon the receptor's world view, potentially affects his immediate behaviour. For example, the person who urges neighbours to get out of town to escape an impending flood is not likely to be taken seriously unless the neighbours also see this person making energetic personal preparations to escape.

Communication at the third level concerns both the immediate behaviour and the value system of the receptor. At this level, the source of the message must identify closely not only with his own message, but with the receptors of it. As Nida explains:

> If . . . someone insists that a man should abandon his carefree way of life, settle down, marry, and raise a family; or if he tries to convince another that he should repent of his sins, become a Christian, and lead an entirely different type of life . . . [then] in addition to identification with his message, he must also demonstrate an identification with the receptors; for the receptor must be convinced that the source

understands his, the receptor's, particular background and has respect for his views.[9]

It is evident that each successive level of communication requires an increasing degree of identification by the source of the message with the receptors, as illustrated by the diagram below:

Identification Required	*Levels of Communication*		
	1. Information	*2. Persuasion*	*3. Conversion*

Minimal
identification
necessary———————> "This is an announcement"

Source must identify   "Let's get out of here!
closely with message————————————> The dam has burst!"

Source must identify
closely with message   "God understands, cares for,
and with receptors———————————————————> loves you. Repent! You must
                                                 be born again!"

The degree to which the source of a credible message must identify with the message itself or with the receptors of that message depends upon the nature of the message being communicated.

Missionaries from the West have succeeded admirably in achieving that degree of identification necessary for effectively communicating at the first level. They have been moderately successful in communicating at the second level, but — due to the nature of the identification required — only rarely have Western missionaries achieved third level communication with the poor. This failure is popularly attributed either to cultural differences or to spiritual blindness, rather than to any counterproductive dynamics deriving from the missionary's personal affluence.

The inadvertent introduction of Islam into Central Africa by the London Missionary Society did cause one missionary to raise the specter of a possible link between his failure and his affluence, however. David Picton Jones, in a letter sparked by two utterly fruitless and frustrating years at his station in Uguha, made some striking observations to the London Missionary Society Secretary in London:

It is a remarkable fact that [our Muslim employees from Zanzibar] have far more influence over the natives than we have ever had — in many little things they imitate them, they follow their customs, adopt their ideas, imitate their dress, sing their songs, and ... speak their ... language. I can only account for this by the fact that [our Muslim employees] live amongst them, in a simple manner like themselves, intermarry with them, and to some extent partake of their notions. Our life, on the other hand ... is far above them, and we are surrounded by things entirely beyond their reach. The consequence is, that they despair of trying to follow us, — indeed they *cannot* follow us, as there is here no trade in European goods, with the exception of cheap cloth, beads, etc. I have found by experience that they are exceedingly ready to imitate anything within their power, especially the young, and I feel sure in my own mind, if we were to bring ourselves nearer their own level — as near to it as our health and character as Christians would allow — we would gradually raise them up to a higher standard, and to a more civilised life. As it is they have nothing to lay hold of, they despair of ever becoming like us, they regard us as being of another (if not a higher) order, and they believe that our religion, however well adapted to us, is to them altogether unsuitable. When I talk to them ... and tell them that [God] is good and merciful, that we always endeavour to do his will, and that we are his children, they will always answer coolly, pointing to the wonderful things in and about our house — *You* are his children *indeed*.[10]

Jones dealt with the problem by firing his Muslim employees, and never again — at least in his correspondence — broached the uncomfortable subject of missionary affluence as an impediment to the Gospel. But his observations are pertinent in a day when the material gulf distinguishing Western missionaries from this world's poor is not merely wider than ever before, but increasing. The inability of wealthy missionaries to identify with the life situations of those for whom their gospel is intended will, it is safe to conclude, render Western missionary communication of the good news increasingly ineffectual.

2. *There does not seem to be a correspondence between what wealthy missionaries preach and what they themselves practice.* This is the second disturbing conclusion which must be drawn from the Western missionary record. Theological and ethical aspects of this problem will be dealt with in a later chapter. Here that apparent dissonance between missionary teaching and practice which is the too frequent outcome of Christian affluence in the context of poverty will be examined as a communications problem.

From the point of view of Christian missions, one of the most obviously detrimental effects of an apostolic lifestyle built around wealth is that such a way of life can be imitated only by others with similar means. Not only *can* human beings imitate, they *must* imitate if they are to survive. Children become recognizable members of a given culture because they learn to imitate the behaviour of status and role models within that culture. Similarly, young believers learn the ways of Christ by imitating mature Christians, such as the missionary.[11] Paul, in the context of his description of the role of an apostle, frankly urged Corinthian believers to "imitate me"

(1 Cor. 4:16). Writing on behalf of Silas and Timothy, Paul congratulated the Thessalonians because — in spite of severe suffering — "You became imitators of us and of the Lord. ... and so you became a model to all the believers in Macedonia and Achaia" (1 Thes. 1:6-7). Quite apart from the questions which poor believers might legitimately raise concerning the Western missionary's disregard for what their own scriptures teach concerning the abundance of possessions, there is the fact that to a large degree, Western missionary communication — contrary to Paul — must consist largely of admonitions to "do as we say, not as we do."

In the words of an open letter written to a high-ranking mission executive, and published in 1971, Western missionaries are

> tied ... spiritually, economically, [and] socially, far more firmly to New York and Paris and London than they are to Delhi or Madras or to the Christian Church in [India]. ... the image of the Church with which people are most familiar is not so much a spiritual movement as a power structure, wealthy and influential, exclusive and sectarian, proudly self-assertive. ... Its offices ... centres of social and political power, symbols of prestige and high-roads to Europe and the U.S.A. or privilege and preference in India.[12]

Despite liberal use — in both writings and speeches — of enlightened phrases such as "self-reliance," "partnership," and "interdependence," the writer goes on,

> this is how it still works out: a Mission board is paying for a foreign missionary couple the rent for an apartment which is as much, or more, monthly than the wages of 20 Indians — and not the poorest at that — who have to support themselves, their wife, their children, from their pay. ... So much for pious statements about living alongside, living as partners, etc.![13]

Although this description of a phenomenon which is borne of economic disparity was written nearly 20 years ago, it is by no means out of date. Indeed, it is more timely than ever. Nor can its application be restricted to missionaries of those churches associated with the World Council of Churches. It is a problem that is always attendant upon wealth and poverty in proximity, and hence is as true of Interdenominational Foreign Missions Association and Evangelical Foreign Missions Association missions as it is of their National Council of Churches and World Council of Churches counterparts. One of the biggest adjustments which Western missionaries to poor nations have to make involves the irony of their metamorphosis — at the very moment when they are most acutely aware of their self-sacrifice — into staggeringly rich tycoons. At the end of his first frenzied year in Zaire, one young medical missionary told of his family's "struggle with the irony of being considered rich. By comparison," he wrote, "we seem like the Rockefellers to many Zairians. . . . we often feel . . . frustrated because we are seen often as rich 'objects' and some come to us regularly just for the 'things' they want to get from us."[14]

The young doctor's exasperation was but a centuries old echo of the experience of thousands of Western missionaries. One hundred years earlier, not too far away on the same continent, a small contingent of young missionaries, having come face to face with the same issue, received this scant reassurance from their venerable Home Secretary:

> Native tribes welcome missionaries amongst them, in the first instance because they hope to be enriched by the presence of these white men. When they find that they have got all that is to be obtained their sentiments change, and as they neither understand nor appreciate the real object of their presence in the country, they too often may turn around and become unreasonable and bitter opponents of their work.[15]

Western missionary claims of personal sacrifice and privation — however genuine in the context of their pecuniary potential in their own society — can only be greeted with incredulity by the great majority of the world's peoples, many of whom would be rich by local standards if they could but trade places with the missionary for a year, a week, or even a day. That missionary motives and intentions should be questioned in such circumstances is hardly surprising; that they should bridle with indignation at those among their poorer brethren who would imitate them is unfair. For not only is imitation the sincerest form of flattery; it is the quintessence of learning. To know what it is that a man is teaching, look not at his notes, but at his students. They are his "letter . . . known and read by everybody" (2 Cor. 3:2).

3. *The gospel of plenty, preached so eloquently and persuasively in the silent language of missionary lifestyle, frequently overrides or distorts poorer people's understanding of the Christian gospel.* This is a phenomenon which is by no means restricted to the sphere of Western religious proselytizing. Since its inception, the United States has felt duty bound to go into all the world and preach the good news of Jeffersonian democracy. This mission, pursued with assiduous sincerity for nearly two hundred years, has been singularly unsuccessful. For the revolutionary message which people around the world have embraced has not been American democracy, but American plenitude, exemplified with compelling if inadvertent persuasiveness by her citizens abroad — servicemen, diplomats, businessmen, educators, tourists, and of course, missionaries.[16]

Curious about his own government's representation of life in the United States, a recent visitor to Moscow attended an exhibit on American culture and technology sponsored by the U.S. Information Agency. He noted that while the high tech portrayal of "The Democratic Process" was virtually ignored, Russian visitors flocked to see "the really good stuff . . . televisions, microwaves, washing machines, computers, stereos," and other symbols of the American gospel of abundance.[17]

Preaching the Gospel of spiritual salvation with their lips, and the gospel of abundance with their lives, Western missionaries have frequently expressed annoyance with the fact that their presence, while creating little hunger and thirst for righteousness, has stimulated within indigenes hearty appetites for the wood, hay, and stubble of Western material culture.

The resulting converts, at one time commonly referred to as "rice Christians," have long been a source of Western missionary exasperation. One early missionary in East Africa, having for several months "spoken to the people . . . almost daily of a better way," confessed himself confounded by their utter indifference to what he said, and their rapt preoccupation with what he had. "Their only object," he concluded indignantly, "is evidently just to get what they can out of us."[18] A year earlier, his Welsh colleague's careful explanation of the "sole object" of his coming to Africa elicited from Chief Kassanga nothing more than a request for five or six bolts of cloth. "It is very hard," concluded the missionary, "to make them understand the nature of our work."[19]

Missionaries then, as now, appear to have been unaware of the curious double standard by which they governed themselves and Africans. Rationalizing their personal need for high material and social standards, their disappointment with "selfish" or "worldly minded" Africans who were eager to follow the missionary example at times bordered on cynicism. African teachers were especially suspect. "Their one idea," one missionary lamented, "seems to be to get a good education and then they can get more money. . . . Our present need is spiritually minded teachers, and not worldly minded."[20]

How African teachers would have answered these accusations we do not know. But it must have seemed to them irritatingly ironic that missionaries—paid fiftyfold that earned by the highest paid African teacher, and occupying positions of prestige and power—nevertheless regarded themselves as possessing that spiritual mindedness and unselfishness which African teachers lacked.

In China likewise, London Missionary Society missionaries—typical of all but the China Inland Mission which had been founded by the radical Hudson Taylor in 1865—not only earned ten times as much as their highest paid Chinese colleagues, but enjoyed many pecuniarily comforting fringe benefits available only to Western missionaries. Like their counterparts in Africa, their vision was such as enabled them to see clearly the materialist mote in Chinese eyes, and not the beam in their own. The Chinese are "a money loving people," concluded a thirty-year veteran, "[whose] principal divinity is the god of riches, and [whose] one aim is the acquisition of pelf."[21]

Today, the same double standard -- on the one hand defending the growing relative affluence of Western missionaries, and on the other hand lamenting expressions of similar, though usually more modest, aspirations on the part of poorer Christian brothers and sisters as evidence of world-liness — is still common. Concerns about the motives and commitment of Africans, Latin Americans, and Asians who use their training to get fiscally secure positions outside their countries continue to sprinkle missionary conversations and prayers. While such concerns may well be justified, those who themselves are assured a physically comfortable and economically secure living by means of "the Lord's provision" — at a North American standard — are not in a very strong position to raise them.

Whether it is acknowledged or not, at the root of these concerns is the affluence of the Western Church and, in turn, her missionaries. While it is true that many whose prospects were limited have bettered themselves economically and socially by taking advantage of opportunities arising out of close association with Western missionaries, it must be no less obvious that missionaries themselves do exceptionally well by most standards, and that missionary motives are not entirely spiritual. What if Western mis-sionary support standards were to be reduced to the level of that enjoyed by their third world colleagues? Is it unduly presumptuous to assume that the missionary force from the West would virtually cease to exist? Given the widespread existence of mission policies which will not allow a mis-sionary to venture forth until his or her support is guaranteed, probably not.

Is it any wonder that Christians from poorer parts of the world — in response to the attractive gospel of plenty which they see so compellingly modelled by emissaries of the Western churches — respond to the implicit invitation by saying "Yes!" to materialism?[22] It is only recently that Western missionaries have discovered, to their chagrin, that the movement of which they are a part has been credited with being one of the greatest secularizing agencies of the past two centuries.[23]

Clearly, the gains associated with affluence (such as those discussed in chapter three) must be weighed against the harder to measure losses which missionaries must be prepared to suffer in their effectiveness as commu-nicators of the Gospel. Clinging to personal affluence makes identification with the poor impossible; it creates an unresolvable tension between mis-sionary teaching and missionary living; and it causes the genuine good news to be adulterated by the pleasant but ultimately death producing gospel of mammon.

The insidiousness of the influence of wealth upon those who have it is aptly illustrated by Jacob Loewen in his account of a seminar on worldview which he conducted for some Indian teachers and their missionary col-leagues several years ago. He explained to the group that each culture has at its center an "axle" from which radiate all of the "spokes" which hold the wheel together and help it to perform its appointed tasks smoothly and without undue difficulty. Wondering whether he was getting through to the teachers, he asked them to name the hub around which their missionaries' way of life revolved. "Money!" was the unhesitating and unanimous response of the group. The missionaries were visibly taken aback.

Asked by the slightly incredulous Loewen how they could be so sure that money was the axle of the missionaries' worldview, the Indian teachers recounted incidents which in their eyes were clear proof that money was at the core of all material and spiritual aspects of Western missionary life and work.

"What about your fathers and grandfathers before the missionary and the white man came," Loewen continued to probe; "what was the axle of their way of life?" "War," came the immediate response. Spokesmen within the group explained that their grandfathers had practiced killing because that was the way to get spirit power. Spirit power had been, in effect, the integrating hub of their grandfathers' way of life. Had their grandfathers been Christians, the teachers explained to Loewen, the Spirit of God would have been the center of their lives, "because He . . . is the most powerful of all spirits."

"And now that all of you are Christians," Loewen persisted, "is the Spirit of God the axle of your Christian way of life, too?"

"No," came the response; "our axle now is . . . money . . . because that is what we have learned from the missionaries."[24]

Loewen's story is reminiscent of an observation made by Alexis de Tocqueville (1805-1895) who, having travelled extensively through the United States, remarked: "I know of no country . . . where the love of money has taken stronger hold on the affections of men."[25] His opinion was shared by Frances Trollope, mother of the famous Anthony Trollope, whose fifty-one month sojourn in America (December 1827-July 1831) inclined her to believe a long time English resident of the country who declared . . .

> that in following, in meeting, or in overtaking, in the street, on the road, or in the field, at the theatre, the coffee-house, or at home, he had never overheard Americans conversing without the word DOL-LAR being pronounced between them.[26]

Missionaries whose lives and values have been shaped in such a milieu are—although often unaware of it themselves—particularly dependent upon and susceptible to the power of mammon. Their mission could not even be contemplated, much less accomplished, without an abundance of money. Both the institutions and the personnel of the Western Christian missionary enterprise bear powerful testimony to the absolute centrality of money. In money, they live and move and have their being. Without money, there would be neither agency nor personnel doing mission from the West. The implications of affluence upon missionary communication are obvious: there is often a great difference between what Western missionaries think they are communicating, and what their poorer listeners actually see, hear, and believe.

STRATEGIC COSTS OF MISSIONARY AFFLUENCE

The efficient and therefore attractive strategic options available to missionaries who have the money to obtain and sustain the expensive technology necessary to implement them were outlined in an earlier chapter. The counterproductive dynamics of affluence-based mission strategies is seldom mentioned, much less considered seriously in all of its far-reaching implications. What follows is an attempt to redress that oversight.

Strategy is the art or science of planning and conducting the Christian mission. Very few Western missionaries do not have something to say on the subject of strategy. Anthropologists, sociologists, development economists, communications experts, theologians, journalists, management specialists, computer programmers, educators, historians, and even marketing consultants — each confident that his or her particular insight provides an indispensable key to more effective strategies — engage in what has come to be known as *missiology*. The myriad books, journals, articles, symposiums, consultations, conferences, seminars, seminary and college curriculums — all devoted to the development, the delineation, and the implementation of mission strategies to reach this or that hidden or neglected or inadequately evangelized or developed people — reflect the earnest and lively interest of Western Christians in the subject.

The highly publicized pecuniary writhings of institutions such as missions and seminaries — and the people who comprise them — is now an established part of the Western Christian landscape. It is understandable, therefore, if questions concerning the adverse effects of their affluence upon the strategies which they devise are seldom raised. Nevertheless, Western missionary strategy increasingly reflects a number of significant inadequacies which are, to a great degree, traceable to the affluence of the Western Church.

1. *Western missionary strategy is characterized by dependence upon expensive technology.* As useful as our expensive machines might be in increasing the speed and the comfort with which missionaries accomplish their professional tasks and attend to their personal needs, ownership, and control of such devices frequently accentuates the distance between missionaries and the people they serve, thus reinforcing the isolation which is a natural part of independent, technological living. Furthermore, becoming accustomed to doing missions with technology, Western missionaries find it difficult to conceive of engaging in mission without it.

An airplane crashes, and donors are assured that the Lord's work will suffer irreparable loss unless the more than half a million dollars needed to replace it comes in quickly. "This need could not have come at a worse time and we must act immediately," read a recent appeal letter from a well known mission agency; "Missionaries are depending on us for flights and the warehouse is full of medical and general supplies waiting to be moved."[27] The keys on a computer keyboard stick, and the anxious and incredibly overworked missionary in Mozambique envisions the closing of Bible school: "If the computer goes out, the seminary closes," he writes, "since most materials are being prepared on a week to week basis on the word processor."[28]

Such appeals and anguished statements by these and other Western missionaries are no exaggeration. They are quite true. The strategies of Western missionaries are increasingly dependent on technology. Without boats, airplanes, four wheel drive vehicles, cars, motorcycles, computers, radios, televisions, refrigerators, electricity, and sometimes air conditioning, missionary work cannot, apparently, be done — at least not by Western missionaries.

There can be no doubt that the speedier life becomes, the lonelier man becomes.[29] Technology has enabled Western missionaries to see the big picture as never before. The Global Mapping Project based at the U.S. Center for World Mission in Pasadena has, for example, identified 17,000 "unreached people groups." Thanks to technology, Western missionaries are able as never before to see the big picture.[30] But also thanks to technology, fewer and fewer are able to identify with the individual persons behind the numbers. Not wealthy Westerners, but often impoverished "national evangelists" end up incarnating Christ and doing the actual mission work. Our strategies become abstract "program" and "people group" oriented. Charts and graphs become a substitute for incarnation and identification. Mobility and speed take precedence over time-consuming personal relationships. As every Western missionary knows, on the field itself — with the exception of modern cities — necessary preoccupation with running and maintaining the technological aids to comfort and efficiency (hence ministry) have sometimes so intruded into the missionary's time as to leave him scarcely any time to engage in missionary work. This is nothing new, although the problem is worse now than it was one hundred years ago. But even then, the complaint by one missionary that he had been "to some extent interfered with ever since [he] arrived, by an extensive storeroom, management of nails, responsibility of meeting caravans, [etc.] . . . "[31] was a common one.

Koyama points out that although race horses run at forty-five miles an hour, cars can travel comfortably at fifty miles an hour, and jets can fly six hundred miles an hour at 35,000 feet above sea level, man walks at only three miles an hour. A person's view of the world becomes increasingly detached and superficial in direct proportion to the speed and the altitude which that person is able to achieve. As Koyama explains,

When we walk (three miles an hour) we see many things, we notice many things, we feel wind, we feel rain, we are warmed by sunshine, we can smell the pleasant aroma as we pass food stalls, we may meet friends or even relatives. We hear children laugh and cry, and see them play. When we walk we see, feel, smell and hear so many interesting things. We are not shut up. We are not rushing at fifty miles an hour. Our pace is three miles an hour on our own feet. That is what makes this seeing, feeling, smelling and hearing possible.[32]

Those who so uncritically utilize technology in the conceiving, designing, and implementation of their missionary strategies need to remember that most persons — "reached" and "unreached" — still walk.

2. *Affluence-dependent strategies cannot and should not be imitated by those whom Western missionaries presume to instruct.* The missionary strategies devised by Western agencies and modelled by Western missionaries is too expensive and too dependent on technology to be emulated by any but the richest churches in the non-Western world. Ironically, so closely associated with affluence and technology are popular Western understandings of mission that we do not recognize the missionary activity of poorer churches for what it is. Referring to the exceedingly numerous underpaid and poorly educated missionaries of African, Asian, and South American churches as "native evangelists," Western missiologists reserve the term "missionary" for those with enough money to do mission in the Western mode. This means, in effect, that unless a person has enough money to buy a return ticket for an international flight, and sufficient financial backing to live overseas as he or she is accustomed to living at home, that person is not a missionary!

Thus, despite the fact that there were an estimated 62,000 Christian foreign missionaries in 1900, a number which by 1987 had increased to 250,400,[33] influential Western missiologists generally speak of foreign mission from the Third World as though it were a recent phenomenon. One frequently quoted source recently put the number of non-Western, cross-cultural missionaries at 15,000, serving under 368 agencies.[34] The criterion used to define "missionary" was, it is clear, one which rendered it impossible to recognize as missionaries any but those associated with societies roughly parallelling Western mission agencies. The thousands of cross-cultural (though not trans-national) evangelists on the cutting edge of church growth around the world are not recognized as missionaries. The publications of Western mission agencies speak glowingly of their evolution into truly international societies, with missionary personnel from Asia or South America joining ranks with Western missionaries. Only the rich need apply. The poor do not and cannot qualify as "real" missionaries.

Forgotten is the fact that the earliest missionaries were natives of an obscure, impoverished, foreign dominated and occupied territory which was little more than a back eddy of the vast imperialist Roman Empire. Imbedded deep within the Western Christian psyche is the notion that missions will naturally and most effectively proceed *from* the political, military, and economically powerful centers to those dominated or impoverished. The institutional structures of Western mission agencies so reflect this model of operation that proposals that this *modus operandi* be reversed are regarded as unrealistic. The financial resources are simply not there. Missions from the poor to the rich are implicitly assumed to be logistically impossible, and in any case, unworkable. Who would listen to a missionary distinguished chiefly by personal want?

Further questions concerning Western affluence-based strategies need to be raised. Can affluent missionaries properly model the way in which the local church can and should relate to the indigenous society? The intuitive negative response to this question is supported by at least one study of missionary work in Colombia, Egypt, and South Korea.[35] Or what about the effects of a Western missionary *modus operandi* which models as its first priority the avoidance of inconvenience, want, or suffering, and which spends prodigious amounts of money and energy to ensure that mission be fulfilled without suffering or inconvenience to the missionary? In such instances, does not the avoidance of personal suffering become a goal to which all other missiological goals are subordinated? That affluence-based strategies should lead to the inability of those converts best able to emulate them to relate the gospel to the poor of their own nations is to be expected, and a miracle when it is otherwise.

3. *Genuinely fraternal strategies in conjunction with poorer churches are usually frustrating and often unworkable from the point of view of both mission agencies and churches.* Money gives power; power results in domination. True partnership between unequals, if not impossible, is extremely unlikely. The slogan of the Whitby Conference of the International Missionary Council in 1947 was *Partnership in Mission.* The reaction of non-Western Christians to the pious goodwill implied in this theme was poignantly expressed by an Indonesian church leader: " 'Partnership in obedience,' yes," he responded to a Dutch delegation, " — the partnership for you; the obedience for us!"[36]

"If you dangle your millions before us, you will make beggars of us and demoralize us," Gandhi warned American missionaries in 1936.[37] His words were both history and prophecy. The relative affluence of Western missionaries has long been and continues to be a key element in seemingly endemic tensions marking the relationship between Western missions and third world churches. Perhaps no single missiological issue has been so hotly debated or so extensively elaborated. Missionary delegates to the Anglo-American conferences — Liverpool, 1860; London, 1888; New York, 1900; Edinburgh, 1910 — repeatedly but apparently futilely grappled with the tensions arising out of the staggering financial inequities between Western missions and their would-be partners in the poorer part of the world. Described by Arthur Judson Brown in 1904 as "a serious problem in missions,"[38] it was still problem enough — following the 1928 meeting of the International Missionary Council in Jerusalem — to warrant the establishment of "The Department of Social and Economic Research and Counsel," under the directorship of J. Merle Davis. Among the several concerns which this department was to investigate and report on was the question of how the rich Western missionary societies and "Younger [i.e., poor] Churches" could best relate in mutually helpful ways. Although the department produced more than a score of volumes in time for the Tambaram meetings of 1938,[39] anything approaching a solution to the complex problems of relationships between rich missionaries and poor churches was not forthcoming. In 1968 it was still described as "the American missionary problem" in the Philippines.[40] Western-based mission agencies continue to search — without success — for equitable formulas whereby fraternity might be practically expressed by means of equal pay for equal work done by Western missionaries and their non-Western colleagues. The problem bedevils virtually every mission agency with Western missionaries in the Third World, Protestant and Catholic alike.

Evangelicals associated with the Interdenominational Foreign Missions Association and the Evangelical Foreign Missions Association — although our deep suspicion of "liberals" has generally made it difficult for us to learn from the similar and much more thoroughly documented experiences of missionaries whose churches are associated with the World Council of Churches — are likewise confounded by the snarled, multifarious complexity of the relationships governing their economically unequal "partnerships" with the third world churches in whose orbit they must now move. In 1971, representatives from the Interdenominational Foreign Missions Association and the Evangelical Foreign Missions Association mission societies convened to explore the issue of church mission tensions.[41] Of the fifteen specific areas of tension identified by the delegates, seven had to do with money.[42] Ironically, non-Western delegates to the conference were conspicuous by their absence, thus providing a mute illustration of the dimensions of the inequity between the sending church/receiving church "partners." The consultation — despite its concern that tensions between two partners be resolved — neglected to invite the weaker partner!

4. *Western affluence results in strategies which cannot effectively reach the poor.* The strategies of Western missions have for the most part bypassed the burgeoning urban poor of the world's great cities — the very people who, if history is in any way instructive, are most likely to prove receptive to the gospel. A New Zealand missionary, well known for his work in Manilla slums, recently spent two years of intensive research in eight of the great Asian cities, seeking, in his own words, "to know how the great mission surge of the last decades had established the church among the urban poor." He was forced to conclude that "the greatest mission surge in history has entirely missed the greatest migration in history, the migration of Third World rural peasants to great megacities."[43]

Neglect of the world's poorest people by the church's richest missionaries is not a case of simple oversight. The fact is, our affluence makes us uncomfortable in the context of insoluble poverty. The very strategies which ensure Western missionary longevity, efficiency, and comfort make residence among the urban poor impossible. Insulation and isolation from the normal crises of everyday living in the slums reduce missionary proclamation of the "better way" meaningless. Western missionaries, intuitively sensing the hypocrisy of ministry without identification, but unwilling or unable to pay the price of identification with the poor, avoid the shantytowns, focusing instead upon upwardly mobile elements of city populations. The tragic result is neglect of peoples who, historically, have always been most responsive to the good news. Despite their antipathy to moratorium, evangelical missionaries from the West are among its chief exemplars with respect to doing mission among the poor.

A second strategically fatal consequence of Western affluence may be observed in our inability or unwillingness to see the West as a desperately needy mission field. Contrary to popular thinking in the West, the scriptures teach that the field is the world. That is, every person ever born is born on the mission field! In the words of a well known Ghanian theologian,

> The idea of one part of the world evangelizing another will not bear scrutiny. Missions are not a movement from the haves to the have-nots, from the educated to the illiterate. They are a movement from the fellowship of faith all over the world to all who stand outside this fellowship, whoever and wherever they may be.[44]

Possibly because of the relative affluence of the West, and because it continues to manifest much of the external paraphernalia that has come to be associated with Christianity, the Western Church tends to see only the non-Western world as a "mission field." Overlooked is the fact that the Western Church is a shrinking church, a church which—it is pointed out by Professor Andrew F. Walls—fails two Latourette tests of Christian expansion: the statistical test and the kingdom test. Statistically, the West is one of the least encouraging areas in the world, manifesting neither the burgeoning numerical growth of sub-Saharan African Christianity, nor the dynamic activity of Latin American Christians.[45] Can it be that our personal affluence is the source of this myopia? After all, there is a precedent. Perhaps the Laodicean Church then, as now, was most comfortable with energetic theorizing, elaborate sociological models, distant global analyses, and with vicarious strategies that relied upon poorer "native evangelists" who could pay the price for actually implementing them at the grass roots level. We do not know. What we are told is that the materially blessed members of the Church in Laodicea were blind to their own spiritual destitution, and were unaware that they themselves constituted a mission field in desperate need of Christ.

There is a third consequence of missionary affluence. By accepting as legitimate the entitlement to affluence which is theirs as Western Christians, missionaries and mission societies forfeit the right to preach a desperately needed prophetic word to a self-satisfied Church which is fat but lean of soul; fulfilled but decadent; awash with talk of God, but spiritually empty. Few are in as good a position to see the spiritual deterioration and advancing decay of the Western Church as are her missionaries on furlough. But by sharing in her affluence, they have forfeited the right to speak the judgment of God. And one of the potentially most compelling voices, calling the Laodicean church in the West to repentance, is muffled—having exchanged the duty to preach for the right to comfort.

It is not biliously pessimistic to suggest that the recent upsurge of interest in missions on the part of young people in the West—as evidenced by student attendance in conferences sponsored by organizations such as InterVarsity Christian Fellowship and Campus Crusade, and in enrollment in the mission studies programs of Christian colleges and seminaries—will not be enough to reverse the creeping impotence of the Western churches. Unless these young men and women are willing to renounce the privilege and security that have come to be a hallmark of the Western way of doing mission, there can be no reversal. Expensive, sophisticated, well documented, highly publicized, high tech strategies, conceived and administered by a privileged coterie of affluent missionaries will not turn the tide against the "powers of this dark world and against the spiritual forces of evil in the heavenly realms" (Eph. 6:12). Indeed, affluence itself is a frequently preferred sector of that spiritual beachhead referred to in scripture as "the world" used by the enemy in his most successful invasion of our Western consumer souls.

It is not a coincidence that the church among the poor is growing both quantitatively and qualitatively around the world—usually in the absence of Western missionaries—while the church in the West continues its comfortable decline. Laodicea was, no doubt, a missionary sending church. But Christ was on the wrong side of the church's door. Philadelphia was, on the other hand, without prospects economically speaking, but Christ was inside, and a great door of opportunity was opened before her. Thus it was (Rev. 3:7-21), and thus it is. God has always preferred human weakness as a vehicle through which to manifest his power.

These, then, are some of the communicatory and strategic costs which Western missionaries have paid and which they must continue to pay for their affluence. When combined with the relational costs outlined in the previous chapter, they may be enough to make affluence a bad bargain from a missiological point of view. But there is a further and integral dimension of missionary life upon which it will be seen wealth takes a terrible toll; a sphere which is really at the very heart of the missionary enterprise— the theological and ethical sphere. The Scriptures constitute the supreme rule for life and faith proclaimed by the Christian missionary. The missionary who submits personal theory and practice to the authority of the Bible deserves a careful hearing. Contrarily, the one whose personal life gives proof of a lack of confidence in the faith being proclaimed should be neither surprised nor disappointed if few converts are forthcoming. This is the subject of the next chapter.

6

Theological, Ethical, and Biblical Considerations on Missionary Affluence

Sell your possessions and give to the poor. Provide purses for yourselves that will not wear out, a treasure in heaven that will not be exhausted, where no thief comes near and no moth destroys. For where your treasure is, there your heart will be also.

But the worries of this life, the deceitfulness of wealth and the desires for other things come in and choke the word, making it unfruitful.

Woe to you, teachers of the law and Pharisees, you hypocrites! You clean the outside of the cup and dish, but inside are full of greed and self-indulgence.

The Pharisees, who loved money, heard all this and were sneering at Jesus. He said to them, "You are the ones who justify yourselves in the eyes of men, but God knows your hearts. What is highly valued among men is detestable in God's sight."

Jesus

"You all know," said the Guide, "that security is mortals' greatest enemy."

C. S. Lewis

Oh the folly of any mind that would explain God before obeying Him! That would map out the character of God instead of crying, Lord, what wouldst thou have me to do?

George MacDonald

Like many other fine things, it lost part of its brilliance when examined too nearly.

Frances Trollope

This chapter is, in many respects, the most important chapter of the book. One might take issue with all that has been said so far concerning the contextual and consequential dimensions of missionary affluence in a world populated by a growing majority of impoverished people. The scriptures, however, cannot be dismissed. No matter how inconvenient the injunction or awkward the admonition, the Bible — because it is God's revelation of himself and of his will for man — must be taken very seriously by all who claim to live by its rule. Missionaries, commissioned as they are to teach others the revealed precepts of God, must be especially careful that there is a harmony between what they say and how they live. As our Savior's brother warned his peers almost two thousand years ago, "we who teach will be judged more strictly" (James 3:1).

This chapter is composed of two major sections, organized along the following lines. In the first part, theological and ethical issues which emerge as a simple result of missionary affluence in the context of poverty will be considered. In the second part, a synthesis of Old Testament and New Testament teaching on the subject of wealth and poverty will be undertaken and applied to the life and work of Western missionaries.

THEOLOGICAL AND ETHICAL CONSIDERATIONS

Each of the relational, communicatory, and strategic consequences discussed in the foregoing chapters has ethical and theological dimensions. It is clear from the Christian revelation that while to be human is to be a social, communicating, and thinking creature, but that at root, we are profoundly theological beings, created in the image of God. As a consequence, there is no facet of life or thought which does not in some way reflect or affect theology.

Thus the social insulation, isolation, independence, and segregation from the poor which are seemingly inevitable *relational consequences* of missionary affluence become profoundly troubling when observed in the lives of those who represent the One who not only emptied himself in order to identify with the plight of fallen man — making himself "nothing, taking the very nature of a servant" — but who instructed all would-be followers to do likewise (Phil. 2:1-11). All too apparent, likewise, are the ethical questions raised by the great gulf between the public preaching and private practice of those whose mandate is to *communicate* the gospel in deed as well as in word. The New Testament calls this disparity hypocrisy. And is not the practice of a *strategy* which can be emulated by only the very rich, and which by its very nature is not capable of relating the gospel to the poor a theological as well as a sociological issue? What follows is no more than a hint of the wide range and complex nature of theological and ethical issues deriving from missionary affluence.

First of all, personal affluence in the context of poverty raises legitimate doubts concerning a missionary's willingness to obey and ability to teach the whole counsel of God regarding mammon. Several merit careful consideration.

1. Is Western missionary preoccupation with material things—with a continual desire for more—really no more than an innocently acquired cultural trait? As I attempted to point out in chapter two, enculturation in a society committed to and structured around the proposition that life consists in the abundance of possessions does have a significant bearing upon a missionary's orientation to life. The Western missionary is the product of a society which devotes more of its collective resources to security than to any other needs.[1] This great preoccupation with financial security is faithfully reflected in the policies of most Western mission agencies—policies for which missionaries are quite rightly deeply grateful. But this security is not gotten cheaply.

In the first place, actual missionary work is often severely curtailed by the necessarily complicated challenge of living like a Westerner in another part of the world. This was the complaint of Charles Hemans, a black Jamaican missionary who worked in East Africa at the turn of the last century. Drawing upon his several decades of experience with missionary life around the world, Hemans' Home Secretary vouchsafed him the scant comfort of his personal conclusion

> that one of the greatest hindrances to the spiritual progress of our missions is in the demands made upon the missionary for purely material things. One is so occupied and constantly worried in the process of attending to house and garden, and directing the labours of ignorant and incompetent people . . . that the mind becomes pre-occupied; attention to spiritual duties is hurried and unsatisfactory, and even the time for personal spiritual improvement is entirely absorbed.[2]

More serious than the problem of wasted time, however, are troubling issues touching upon the theological integrity of the missionary. How can the economically secure and lavishly materially accoutered missionary teach the poor—with any degree of credibility—about simplicity, generosity, contentment, or the costly sacrifice entailed in all genuine discipleship? A missionary must teach these things, for they are in the very warp and woof of his scriptures. And will not the obvious "thought for the morrow" taken by latter day apostles to maintain and even increase personal comfort and security in this life make their teaching on the great joys of the life to come sound rather unconvincing to poverty stricken disciples? Is it possible to maintain both credibility and an affluent lifestyle when teaching the poor what God says about the stewardship of possessions? Biblical answers to questions such as these suggest that emissaries of affluent Western churches dare not excuse their materialist preoccupations by blaming their culture. But there is a second question which must be asked.

2. Is the sin of greed less deadly for Western missionaries than for the poor among whom they live? I believe the answer must be no. If—as I am often reminded by my missionary friends—poverty and wealth are *relative*

concepts, making it possible for the same person to be poor in North America but rich in Africa, then surely it must be conceded that a life of pecuniary propriety in one society may be regarded as profligate in another.

It did not take a theologian to discern as long ago as 1956 that in the West all but one of the "seven deadly 'sins,' sloth, was transformed into a positive virtue. Greed, avarice, envy, gluttony, luxury, and pride were the driving force of the new economy."[3] Of vital concern to Western missionaries must be the question of how and to what degree they unconsciously reflect this inversion of Biblical values. Can it be that even these pious and esteemed representatives of the Western churches have been tainted by that ethical decay which lies at the heart of what is called "consumerism"? The rapidity with which even marginally technological "breakthroughs" are metamorphosed into "necessities" in Western missiology may provide a clue to the answer to this question.

If *greed* be defined as the desire for more than enough in a social context in which some have less than enough, then most who journey from North American shores must accept the fact that most of the world so considers them.

Among the most awkward challenges faced by Western missionaries abroad is the necessity of explaining to the truly needy why Westerners not only "need" to be staggeringly wealthy by the standards of all but a few, but will doubtless "need" more next year. In the eyes of the poor, even the ordinary missionary must seem to incarnate many of those qualities which, by Paul's standards, disqualified a person from office in a church: a lover of money (1 Tim. 3:3), one who has not fled from, but rather embraced great gain (1 Tim. 6:5-11). According to Paul, the children of darkness are characterized by self-indulgence of every kind, and by "a continual lust for more" (Eph. 4:19). "But among you," Paul continues, "there must not be even a *hint* [emphasis mine] . . . of greed. . . . For of this you can be sure: . . . no greedy person . . . has any inheritance in the kingdom of Christ and of God" (Eph. 5:3-5). These are sobering words to those of us who — despite being surrounded by the truly needy — have come to expect as our due steady improvement in our already high standard of living, even if it must be at the expense of those who barely subsist. A third question relates to the affluent missionary's relationship to his Lord.

3. Can the secure, independent, comfortable missionary have any sense of his genuine dependence upon God? In the Old Testament record of relationships between God and His people, security and wealth almost inevitably gave rise to a foolish but spiritually fatal sense of independence. "When you have eaten and are satisfied . . . be careful that you do not forget the Lord your God" was the oft repeated warning as His slave nation prepared to occupy the land flowing with milk and honey (Deut. 6:11-12; 8:10-11; 32:15; Ez. 28:4-5; Hos. 13:6).

Independence from God was not expressed by inattention to prescribed religious services. On the contrary, it was frequently when Israel's relationship with God was at its lowest ebb that worship services evinced an enviable vigor and enthusiasm. No, this independence was a matter of the heart (Ez. 33:31-32; 34:25). God could see it; his prophets preached against it; the poor were made cynical by it; but the rich worshippers themselves were, apparently, oblivious of their hypocrisy.

An obvious manifestation of this independence in the rich Western churches is in the "secret" doubts which our satisfied, secularized minds have concerning the value of prayer. The cliches are there, of course, but can the secure and independent missionary really pray? Does he or she need to?[4] Agnosticism concerning prayer is one result of plenty. Trust in money becomes embarrassingly evident when—as frequently happens—"prayer" letters become thinly veiled appeals for financial support for one project or another.

The secret misgivings which Western missionaries have about prayer is often quite obvious to their poorer brethren in other lands. Jacob Loewen illustrates this in a story from the Choco Church in Panama, where he and another missionary were working with Aureliano, an Indian pastor whose wife was very ill with what was obviously malaria. Pastor Aureliano, having little of the Bible translated into his own language, was overjoyed to read Loewen's translation of James 5:14-15, in which the sick seemed to be promised healing if prayer offered by elders on their behalf were offered in faith. After double checking, just to make sure the Bible really did make such a promise, he asked why prayer should not be offered for his wife.

The missionaries agreed—albeit with secret misgivings about the outcome. What, they wondered, would happen to the touchingly naive faith of these Indian Christians if, as would likely be the case, the woman was not healed? But various Indian leaders were gathered, and the prayer was duly offered. To Loewen's immense relief and surprise, the woman seemed to show some improvement. But she soon suffered a relapse. Later, Loewen observed Pastor Aureliano and the Indian leaders gather once again to pray for the ailing woman. This time, the missionaries were not invited to participate, but the woman was healed.

Later, discreetly inquiring why he and his fellow missionary had not been included in the prayer circle, Loewen was smitten by Pastor Aureliano's reply: "No," he said, "we could not take you along because you two do not believe."[5]

Western Christian agnosticism concerning prayer is by no means deliberate. We try hard to believe. We have our prayer meetings, none more than our missionaries. But the fact is, our affluence and our security make God necessary in only an academic or theological sense. Prayer, as a Biblical study of the subject quickly reveals, is not the activity of people who are in reasonable control of their lives. It is the resort of weak, overwrought, desperate people whose life circumstances call for resources beyond those they possess. A "good" missionary society will take every possible step—by means of elaborate medical, financial, educational, and logistical support systems—to ensure that most of life is well under control most of the time. This is a natural, commendable, and—humanly speaking—desirable course to follow. But it does leave God with, apparently, very little to do in our lives.[6]

Sadly, a strong case can be made in support of the proposition that Western missionaries—true sons and daughters of their churches back home—show no great willingness to lose all things for the sake of Jesus Christ. Far from being, in Paul's words, "rubbish" (Phil. 3:7-8), these material symbols of affluence have become absolutely essential for the continuation of mission from the West. Christ's teaching on the abundance of possessions cannot be taught, because it will not be practiced, by most Western Christians. And this leads to a second category of theologico-ethical issues deriving from missionary affluence which we shall discuss: the money and power-based strategies and statuses generated by the institutional and personal affluence of Western missionaries contradict principles which are at the very heart of Christian mission as prescribed in the New Testament.

The Incarnation and the Cross of our Savior are models for apostolic life and ministry. Although missiological implications of the Incarnation will be dealt with further in the concluding chapter, it is appropriate to touch upon it here in connection with those who cling to their prerogatives as privileged Westerners. One of the conclusions emerging from the 1978 *Willowbank Consultation on the Gospel and Culture* was, not surprisingly, that the Incarnation is a model for Christian witness. Applied to Christian missionary endeavour this meant, the authors of the *Report* went on to explain, a threefold renunciation: of status, of independence, and of immunity.[7] Those Western missions popularly regarded as most progressive typically do their best to demonstrate that they have reversed this pattern: the missionary vocation becomes a distinguished career, longevity of tenure ensuring a pleasant retirement in Florida, and perhaps even the status of "statesman"; a rich variety of home-based support infrastructures reduce local dependence to a minimum; financial, logistical, and medical contingencies are anticipated and dealt with in such a way as to guarantee the missionary immunity from the dire straits of those among whom he works. We save ourselves, we assure ourselves, so that we can save others.

The affluence-based mission of the Western Church—in contrast to the Incarnation-based mission of her Lord—most naturally serves as an ecclesiastical springboard for moving up, not down; her independently secure missionaries find lording both more natural and more immediately effective than serving, although many have convinced themselves that domination *is* service. The great marvel of living in the technological age is that one's mission can be speeded up, rather than—as in the case of Christ—slowing down and finally coming to a complete halt on the cross. We have discovered—to our great relief—that prolonging one's abundant life is not only personally gratifying; it is a demonstrably superior way of marketing the good news than is, say, dying. And thus the gospel is reduced to the proclamation of ideas about the One who was rich but for our sakes became poor, and who personally demonstrated what has proven to be true ever since: that spiritual vitality comes to full potence only through weakness (1 Cor. 12:9-10).

The affluent church—by abandoning the Incarnation as a model for its own life and mission—has demonstrated its fundamental spiritual impotence. For as theologian Trevor Verryn reminds us, "Only the truly strong are able to lay aside their power in an act of self-emptying and assume a position of powerlessness."[8] The strategy of the cross which has ever marked the true servant of God is nowhere more accurately or inadvertently summed up than in the words of the ridicule of the religiously powerful who, satisfied that they had saved themselves no end of trouble by at last disposing of Jesus, chuckled among themselves, "He saved others, but he can't save himself!"[9] Alas for religious teachers of that day and this! In trying to save themselves, they damn both themselves and others.

Added to the self-saving affluence of Western missions, which leaves so little room for that weakness in which God delights, there is a third, deeply theological problem: both the motives and the message of affluent missionaries are suspect, and Biblical teaching on wealth and poverty, the rich and the poor, must necessarily be truncated when conveyed via an affluent channel. The missionary cannot challenge converts to a way of life that he himself is unwilling to live. This is a century old problem which recurs wherever missionaries from the West have gone to do their work among materially poorer societies.

Africans, for example, had great difficulty comprehending the religious motives underlying the missionary presence among them one hundred years ago. A young British missionary, describing Africans as "most friendly . . . to us . . . and [possessing] liberal notions of friendship," went on to explain: "They consider it their duty to supply their friends with food or any such thing as may be acceptable to him."[10] Africans were unimpressed by missionary notions of generosity, however. When missionaries celebrated Christmas a few years later by giving each mission employee and neighboring chief a colored cloth, they found their supply of milk cut off by the disgruntled chiefs, who regarded the size of the gift in proportion to the obvious wealth of the missionaries as parsimonious in the extreme. "The African," concluded one badly ruffled missionary, "has very little idea of gratitude,"[11] a sentiment which, it appears, was heartily reciprocated by the chiefs. Several years later another chief, observing the missionary's great wealth, and in accordance with his own customs, made his request for a small portion of it known to the missionary. His request was denied, but he earned himself a modest place in missionary primary source literature. Even such a "great" chief as Chungu, recorded the indignant missionary, "is not free from the weakness prevalent among African chieftains—a begging propensity. I gave him a good talking to about this, and I hope it will do him good."[12]

Another area of misunderstanding occasioned by the relative affluence of missionaries related to salaries paid to native employees—a problem that continues to bedevil relationships between missionaries and their hosts.[13] Western missionaries—except for a notable few—have studiously overlooked the curious double standard by which they govern themselves and nonmissionaries. Rationalizing the necessity of high material and social standards for themselves, they have frequently evinced a deep suspicion of, and at times a profound disappointment with, converts who try to follow their examples. Such converts, they rightly conclude, are selfish and worldly minded.

The irony of missionary rationale for the low wages paid to their employees in third world countries is captured by Herman Melville in his portrayal of Bildad, the miserly, Quaker shipowner who, having begun as a cabin boy, is now in a position to negotiate wages for crewmembers on his own ship. Young Ishmael stands before him, hoping to be given a berth as cabin boy aboard the soon to sail whaler:

[He] went on mumbling to himself out of his book. "*Lay* not up for yourselves treasures upon earth, where moth—"

"Well, Captain Bildad," interrupted Peleg, "what d'ye say, what lay[14] shall we give this young man?"

"Thou knowest best," was the sepulchral reply, "the seven hundred and seventy-seventh wouldn't be too much, would it?—'where moth and rust do corrupt, but *lay*—'"

Lay, indeed, thought I, and such a lay! The seven hundred and seventy-seventh! Well, old Bildad, you are determined that I, or one, shall not *lay* up many *lays* here below, where moth and rust do corrupt.

"Why, blast your eyes, Bildad," cried Peleg, "thou dost not want to swindle this young man! He must have more than that."

"Seven hundred and seventy-seven," again said Bildad, without lifting his eyes; and then went on mumbling—"for where your treasure is, there will your heart be also."

"Thou, Bildad!" roared Peleg, starting up and clattering about the cabin. "Blast ye, Captain Bildad, if I had followed thy advice in these matters, I would afore now had a conscience to lug about that would be heavy enough to founder the largest ship that ever sailed round Cape Horn."[15]

In summary, missionary affluence is the human culture in which three profoundly theological and ethical problems most naturally thrive: preoccupation with possessions; an exclusive dependence upon power-based statuses and strategies; and ethical double standards. As will become more apparent in the ensuing part of this chapter, a large proportion of the

Christian revelation revolves around the truth that "a man's life does not consist in the abundance of his possessions," and that one of the hardest but most worthwhile spiritual victories to achieve is against the notion that it does. The practical question, as far as the Western missionary is concerned, is whether it is actually possible for a wealthy missionary to maintain credibility when teaching about stewardship of possessions to impoverished people. Can the secure and infinitely better off missionary teach those who barely subsist about sacrifice, about simplicity, about costly discipleship? Can he demonstrate his personal faith in the truth that godliness with contentment is great gain (1 Tim. 6:6-19)? How can the Western missionary teach poor Christians not to become engrossed in the things of this world, because they are all passing away—when his own lifestyle suggests a preoccupation with possessions (1 Cor. 7:30-31)? Is it possible for the affluent missionary to honestly claim, in the midst of his plenty, that he considers everything as rubbish compared to the surpassing greatness of knowing Christ Jesus his Lord, for whose sake he has lost all things (Phil. 3:8)? Is it possible that missionaries from the West so reflect the values of the West that such things can only be "taught," not demonstrated? Honest answers to questions such as these indicate that both the credibility and the integrity of missionary endeavours from the wealthy nations are in jeopardy.

What follows is an attempt to outline the Biblical teaching on wealth and poverty with which every Western missionary should be familiar. This teaching has been virtually neglected in those academic institutions, agencies, and churches most actively involved in the preparation and sending of missionaries. Nevertheless, as Christian teachers, missionaries are not only accountable for this teaching, but will "be judged more strictly" (James 3:1). Accordingly, they must pay close attention both to the way in which they *explain* Biblical teaching on wealth, poverty, and the God-ordained patterns that are to mark the behaviour of the rich to the poor; they must also *apply and model* this teaching in their personal lives.

AN OUTLINE OF BIBLICAL TEACHING ON WEALTH AND POVERTY[16]

Biblical teaching on wealth, poverty, and related issues is abundant and—from the standpoint of the privileged at least—painfully clear. The Bible is a somewhat awkward, sprawling book, written by authors who differed not only in message, style, personality, ability, and era; but who also wrote to and about peoples and situations correspondingly diverse. Accordingly, it must be confessed that any attempt to organize material topically is bound to be a necessarily arbitrary and to some degree unsatisfactory exercise. Nevertheless, it is useful to see the whole counsel of God—spanning some two thousand years—on an issue such as the one under consideration.

In working through the synthesis of Biblical teaching which follows, it is important that the reader keep in mind the several points established earlier in the book: (1) The West is rich. (2) The Church in the West is rich. (3) Missionaries sent by the Western Church are rich. (4) Most of the peoples to whom Western missionaries are sent by their churches are poor. (5) What the Bible says about the rich and the poor has a direct bearing on the Western Church generally, and on Western missionaries specifically.[17]

Old Testament Teaching Which the Rich Find Reassuring

1. Private property is not wrong. Biblical injunctions to generosity against theft indicate that possessions are not wrong, since these injunctions could hardly be applied to generosity with someone else's possessions.
Ex. 20:15 (stealing is forbidden; cf. Deut. 5:19)
Ex. 20:17 (coveting is forbidden; cf. Deut. 5:21)
Ex. 22:1-15 (property may be protected)

2. Wealth can bring happiness.
Eccles. 5:19-20

3. The righteous will prosper.
Ps. 128:1-2
Prov. 3:9-10
Prov. 10:22
Prov. 11:24-28
Prov. 22:9
Prov. 28:22, 27

4. People are sometimes to blame for their own poverty.
Prov. 6:6-11
Prov. 10:4
Prov. 13:4, 11
Prov. 20:4, 13
Prov. 21:5, 6
Prov. 28:19-20

5. Poverty and those who are impoverished must not be romanticized. There are obvious advantages to wealth over poverty. (See the description of famine in 2 Kings 6-7; Jer. 52.)
Prov. 13:23
Prov. 14:20-21
Prov. 22:7
Prov. 19:4, 7
Isa. 32:7

Eccles. 4:1-2
Lam. 4:9-10
Isa. 41:17

It is of no little significance that those parts of Scripture which the rich find most reassuring were, for the most part, written by Solomon, a man who was himself wealthy beyond the imagination of his day (2 Chron. 9:13-28). Not only was his personal fortune vast and ostentatiously displayed, however; it represented a brazen disregard for those God-given regulations which were to have governed the kings of God's people. But he was a man whose obsessive preoccupation with himself manifested itself in tyrannical oppression of his own people, contrary to the Pentateuchal rules for kingship (Deut. 17:14-20). This, predictably, resulted in the tragic division of Israel into two kingdoms (2 Chron. 10:1-19). Solomon ignored Old Testament teaching—including most of his own—concerning wealth. "Better a little with righteousness than much gain with injustice," he noted (Prov. 16:8), even though his name became a byword for oppression. The collapse of his kingdom following his death proved the truth of his inspired declarations that "The Lord tears down the proud man's house. . . . [and] A greedy man brings trouble to his family" (Prov. 15:25, 27). As an example of a pious rich man who didn't practice what he preached, Solomon is one of the most sobering examples in Scripture.

Old Testament Teaching Which the Rich Find Disturbing

1. Material possessions and their concomitant comfort and security are not to be a primary goal of life. A man's life does not consist in the abundance of his possessions. The purpose of life is not to move from birth to death as comfortably as possible.

Deut. 8:3-5
Job 1:21
Ps. 37:16
Ps. 39:5-11
Ps. 49:12-13, 16-20
Ps. 68:5-6, 10
Prov. 11:4
Prov. 15:16-17
Prov. 16:8, 16, 19
Prov. 17:1
Prov. 22:1
Prov. 23:45
Prov. 28:3, 6
Eccles. 2:10-11
Eccles. 4:13
Jer. 9:23-24

2. For the people of God, rights associated with personal property and possessions are not absolute for the following reasons:

a. God is Lord of all creation and all creatures.

Gen. 1-3 (God created everything)

Deut. 10:14-21 (God of gods and Lord of lords, the great God)

1 Sam. 2:7-8 (the foundations of the earth are the Lord's)

1 Chron. 29:14-19 (everything comes from God)

Job 41:11 ("Everything under heaven belongs to me.")

Ps. 24:1-2 ("The earth is the Lord's, and everything in it, the world, and all who live in it.")

Prov. 22:2 ("Rich and poor have this in common: the Lord is maker of them all.")

As Creator and Lord of all things, God has established the rules which most fairly govern the acquiring and use of property and possessions by rich and poor alike.

b. For the people of God, any rights associated with the acquiring, the use, or the disposal of personal wealth are in principle subordinated to an obligation to care for poorer, weaker members of society. That this was a primary concern in the Old Testament is evident in the regulations that were to govern the community life of God's people.

(1) Jubilee

Lev. 25:8-43

The Jubilee year was designed to have a leveling effect. It meant that any economic momentum or advantage which might for any reason — luck, good management or mismanagement, ability or lack of ability — have been gained by one person over another could not be maintained indefinitely. Jubilee was a time of fresh beginnings for the land and for the personal economy of the unfortunate. It made the endless accumulation of properties impossible.

(2) Sabbatical

Ex. 23:10-11

Lev. 25:1-7

Deut. 15:1-6

2 Chron. 36:15-21

The sabbatical was intended for the well being of the poor, the wild animals, and the land itself. Debts were to be cancelled. Failure to practice the sabbatical rests was one reason singled out by the chronicler in 2 Chron. 36.

(3) Tithe

Ex. 22:29-30

Ex. 23:19

Deut. 14:22-29

Deut. 26:1-15

The tithe that was gathered every three years was to be centrally stored for the use of Levites and the poor (aliens, fatherless and widows).

(4) Interest, Loans, Collateral

Ex. 22:25-27

Lev. 25:35-38

Deut. 15:1-11 (What we would call "a sound business principle," God calls a "wicked thought"!)

Deut. 23:19-20

Deut. 24:6, 10-13, 17-18

Interest could not be charged on money loaned to the needy fellow Israelite. Jurisdiction over loan collateral was strictly limited.

(5) Gleaning

Deut. 24:19-20

Harvesting was not to be so efficient as to leave nothing behind for the poor. The story of Ruth and Boaz provides a beautiful example of gleaning laws in practice.

(6) Debt Repayment

Deut. 15:1-11

Debts were to be cancelled at the end of every seven years. "There should be no poor among you," said the Lord (v. 4). These laws were one way of ensuring that there would never be institutional poverty among the people of God.

(7) Treatment of Employees

Deut. 24:14-15

The poor employee was not to be taken advantage of. He or she was to be paid "each day before sunset."

(8) Limitations on the Wealth of Kings

Deut. 17:14-17 (cf. 1 Kings 6-7; 11:1-6)

The wealth which a king could legitimately acquire was to be strictly curtailed. He was not allowed to "accumulate large amounts of silver and gold." Sadly, Solomon's disregard of this command resulted in the oppression of the poor and in the division of his kingdom.

3. Wealth and prosperity are inherently dangerous spiritually. As the King Midas legend tells us, wealth is dangerous because it depersonalizes the wealthy. "Great wealth," argues a tract in a frenzied outburst which nevertheless reflects an outlook which is so universal as to suggest it may be instinctive, "sears the soul, dries up the wellsprings of the heart, thickens the skin, cauterizes the nerve ends, and dulls the sensibilities to the pains and groans of all—save its own."[18]

a. Wealth and security make God redundant, unnecessary, and tempt man to conveniently forget, ignore or even defy God.

Deut. 8:1-20

Deut. 9:4-6

Deut. 31:19-20

Deut. 32:15

1 Kings 6-7; 11:1-13

Ps. 119:36-37
Ez. 28:4-5
Ez. 13:31-32
Hos. 13:6

b. Wealth and security breed a false sense of security.
Ps. 30:6
Ps. 49:5-6
Prov. 10:15
Prov. 11:28
Prov. 18:11,16
Isa. 56:9-12
Jer. 12:1-4
Jer. 17:11
Jer. 49:4-5

c. Wealth and security often spawn pride in one's imagined personal accomplishments or entitlements. Wealth and security are enemies of humility and meekness.
Prov. 18:23
Jer. 9:23-24
Ez. 28:4-5
Hos. 2:8

d. The independence, imagined security, and pride that usually accompany wealth result in profound self-delusion and dangerously distorted judgment.
Prov. 28:11
Eccles. 5:8-15
Isa. 30:9-11
Jer. 6:13-15
Jer. 8:10-11
Hos. 2:8
Hos. 9:7
Hos. 12:6-8

e. Repentance is derailed or distorted by wealth.
Isa. 22:12-13

f. The rich are particularly susceptible to certain sins:
(1) Overindulgence/Gluttony/Insatiable Greed
e.g., Solomon (1 Kings 6-7; 10:14-29; 11:1-6)
Eccles. 5:8-15
(2) Ruthlessness in their dealings with those over whom they have power, that is, the poor and the weak.
e.g., Solomon and Rehoboam (1 Kings 10:14-29, cf. 1 Kings 12:1-24)
(3) Abuse of personal power.
e.g., Ahab and Naboth (1 Kings 21:1-16)
Isa. 30:10-21
Jer. 22:6-12

(4) Contempt for the poor, and callous unconcern for their plight.

Job 12:5

Ez. 16:49

Jer. 22:25-29

(5) Wealth and prejudice against the poor often go together.

Ex. 23:6

Job 12:5

Isa. 5:22-23

(6) Misguided priorities.

Ps. 119:36-37

Isa. 5:22-23

g. Greed, gluttony, and covetousness—sins that have been labeled virtues by our society—are in actuality terrible sins. Recognizing this, earlier Christian theologians included these among the "deadly" or "root" sins.[19]

Ex. 20:17

Deut. 5:21

Prov. 30:12-16

Isa. 57:17

h. On the contrary, godliness with contentment is great gain. Yet discontent with one's lot is at the root of the overindulgence of the rich. God's people are to be content with enough, even if that is only a little.

Exodus 14-17 (Israel's response to what appeared to be survival crises was to indulge in what few will argue was legitimate, vigorous complaint. God's opinion of their complaining is found in Psalm 95:10-11.)

Ps. 73:25-26

We should be content with little, yes, but *our own* little, not someone else's!

i. Wealth and security, and the desire for wealth and security, corrupt those who speak for God.

The one who pays the fiddler calls the tune. Preachers paid to do the job often gear the message to the tastes of the largest donor. The rich have the resources to pay for any message they may wish to hear concerning themselves and their relationship to people and possessions, thus confirming their dangerous but comforting self-delusion. Thus, for example, Balaam was paid by Balak to curse Israel (see Num. 22, esp. v. 15).

Isa. 30:9-11

Jer. 6:13-15

Jer. 8:10-11

Jer. 14:14-16

Jer. 23:14-17, 25-32

Ez. 34:1-5, 17-24

Jer. 44:28

Micah 2:6-11

Micah 3:1-11

Micah 7:1-3

4. Wealth and prosperity are not a sign of righteousness. On the contrary, in the Old Testament they are usually achieved and maintained by means of blatant unrighteousness.

The prosperity of Egypt was built on slavery. The inhabitants of Canaan, a land flowing with milk and honey, were notoriously wicked (compare Num. 13:26-29 with Lev. 18:24-28; 20:23-24). Sodom and Gomorrah, now bywords for sinfulness of the most appalling kind, were affluent (Gen. 13:13; 18:16-29; Ez. 16:49). Many kings of Israel and Judah were not only rich and often apparently successful but notoriously wicked: Baasha (1 Kings 15:33-16:7); Omri (1 Kings 16:21-28); Ahab (1 Kings 16:29; 22:40); Jehoram (2 Kings 8:16-24); Ahaziah (2 Kings 8:25-29); Jehoahaz (2 Kings 13:1-9); Jehoash (2 Kings 13:10-25); Jeroboam II (2 Kings 14:23-29); Menahem (2 Kings 15:17-22); Pekah (2 Kings 5:27-31); Ahaz (2 Kings 16:1-20); Manasseh (2 Kings 21:118); Amon (2 Kings 21:19-26); Jehoahaz (2 Kings 23:31-35). While the scriptures make it clear that the sin of these and other kings resulted in the eventual destruction of both Israel and Judah, yet individually they and their peers enjoyed personal wealth and comfort.

Gen. 6:1-8 (Noah's contemporaries)

Gen. 11:1-9 (Babel builders)

Job 21:7-16 (The immemorial question has been the apparent contradiction between a sovereign God who loves righteousness, on the one hand, and a world in which the wicked are prosperous, successful, and happy while the righteous are poor, unsuccessful, and sorrowful, on the other.)

Ps. 10:2-6

Ps. 37:14-17

Ps. 52:7

Ps. 73:2-17

Ps. 92:7

Ps. 109:1-16

Prov. 11:16

Eccles. 5:8-15

Isa. 1:10-23

Isa. 2:6-9

Isa. 3:15-24

Isa. 5:7-8

Isa. 56:9-12

Jer. 2:34

Jer. 5:26-29

Jer. 12:1-2

Jer. 17:11

Jer. 22:13-19

Jer. 44:15-18

Hos. 10:1-2

Hos. 12:6-8

Amos 5:4-7, 11-15, 21-24

Amos 6:4-7

Amos 8:4-7

Hab. 2:4-12

Zech. 11:4-6

a. Faithfulness to God is no guarantee of personal prosperity or security.

Jer. 44:15-18

b. The rich and the powerful are often to blame for the plight of the poor, either by their actions or by their failure to act.

Prov. 13:23

Eccles. 5:8-15

Isa. 32:7

c. It is not only possible to have too little, it is possible to have too much.

Prov. 30:8-9

d. Preoccupation with personal material advancement and personal security is a sign of spiritual bankruptcy.

(1) It makes our professions of faith a hollow sham to those who are closest to us.

Gen. 13:10-11 and 19:14 (Lot made a fatal decision when he chose the best for himself, displaying his fundamentally hedonistic orientation to life. No wonder his sons thought he was joking when he at last was attentive to God's ways.)

1 Sam. 2:29

(2) It brings moral and physical disaster.

2 Kings 5:15-27

e. Oppression or neglect of the poor leads inevitably to judgment. Solidarity with the poor leads just as inevitably to reward.

Deut. 8:19-20

Deut. 28:15

2 Chron. 36:15-21

Prov. 28:22-27

Prov. 29:14

Isa. 2:6-9

Isa. 3:15-24

Isa. 10:1-4

Jer. 14:11-12

Jer. 18:5-20

Jer. 22:13-19

Micah 2:1-2

Hab. 2:6-12

Zech. 7:11-14

Mal. 3:5

f. Religious orthodoxy without a passion for justice is a hollow sham.

Isa. 1:10-23

Jer. 7:3-7, 21-23

5. God identifies with the poor, the needy, the oppressed.
Ex. 22:21-27
Lev. 25:39-43
Deut. 10:14-20
Deut. 15:7-18
Deut. 27:19
Job 5:8-27
Ps. 9:9, 12, 18
Ps. 10:17-18
Ps. 12:5
Ps. 18:27
Ps. 22
Ps. 35:10
Ps. 37:10-11
Ps. 68:4-6
Ps. 72:2-4, 12-14
Ps. 103:6
Ps. 107:9
Ps. 109:31
Ps. 112:9
Ps. 113:7-8
Ps. 136:17-25
Ps. 138:6
Ps. 140:12
Ps. 146:7-9
Ps. 147:6
Prov. 14:31
Prov. 15:25, 27
Prov. 16:8
Prov. 17:5
Prov. 19:17
Prov. 21:13, 17
Isa. 10:1-4
Isa. 11:1-4
Isa. 26:3-6
Isa. 29:13-21
Isa. 41:17-20
Isa. 53:1-12
Isa. 57:15
Isa. 61:1-8
Jer. 20:13
Jer. 49:11
Hos. 14:3
    a. The Messiah would identify with the poor, the needy, the oppressed, coming not only *for* them but as *one of* them.

Ps. 22

Isa. 53:1-12

b. God's true children always actively identify with the poor, the needy, and the oppressed. Biblical good is never simply passive restraint from doing someone else harm; it is always active, initiative-taking good will toward others.

(1) The person who either oppresses or neglects the poor cannot call himself God's child. Any claim to "Godkinship" by such a person is either an outright lie or an evidence of tragic self-delusion.

Job 30:24-25

Job 31:26-28

Ps. 37:21-28

Ps. 41:1-3

Ps. 94:1, 3, 6

Ps. 112:5

Prov. 25:21 (even the poor enemy!)

Prov. 31:8-9,

Prov. 31:18-20

Jer. 22:3, 16-17

(2) True righteousness always expresses itself in an obedience which concerns itself with the well being of the poor, and is never content with mere conformity to religious rites and the mouthing of pious platitudes.

Ex. 23:6

1 Sam. 15:22-23

Job 30:24-25

Job 31:16-28

Ps. 40:6-8

Prov. 3:27-28

Isa. 1:10-23

Isa. 29:13-21

Isa. 58:1-11

Jer. 7:3-7, 21-23

Jer. 21:11-14

Jer. 22:3

Ez. 16:49

Ez. 33:31-32

Amos 5:4-24

Amos 6:4-7

Amos 8:4-7

Zech. 7:8-10

c. The godly rich relate to the poor and to their possessions according to principles which are detailed and modelled in the scriptures.

Job 30:24-25

Job 31:16-28

Ps. 41:1-3

Ps. 74:21

d. God meets the needs of the poor through the actions and interventions of his obedient people. This was the intent of the laws dealing with the treatment of the poor by the rich.

e.g., Nehemiah 5:1-13

e. True giving to God involves that which we genuinely value — not just our surplus or discards. It is easy to be a cheerful giver when we give away what we neither need nor want. The warm, inner feeling of self-congratulations is very gratifying. But to give what we will really miss — a kind of giving which in the Bible is called sacrifice, and which has always characterized the giving of God's true children — is the giving with which God is pleased. It is an interesting fact that while there is a great volume of criticism in the Scriptures levelled against those whose aid for the poor is either inadequate or nonexistent, there is no instance of prophetic preaching against giving too much.

Lev. 1:3, 10
Lev. 2:1, 4
Lev. 3:1, 6
Lev. 27:1-33
Deut. 17:1
2 Sam. 24:18-25
Mal. 1:6-14

6. True spiritual revival and repentance involves economic reformation and justice. Repentance without the fruit of repentance is meaningless.

Neh. 5:1-12
Isa. 1:10-23
Isa. 58:1-11
Jer. 7:3-7, 21-23
Hos. 4:7
Hos. 8:2
Micah 6:6-16
Zech. 7:8-10

7. Economic repentance is costly, and therefore very rare. But it is possible. The powerful and wealthy usually deal with prophetic preaching by doing away with the preacher, and hiring someone with a more positive approach to their excesses (e.g., Isa. 30:9-11; Ez. 18:5-23). A rare Old Testament account of repentance is found in Nehemiah 5:1-12.

New Testament Teaching Which the Rich Find Reassuring

1. Private property is legitimate.

Matt. 5:42; Luke 6:34-35 (Jesus' followers are to loan to the poor; one legitimately loans only what one owns.)

Matt. 6:2-4; Luke 6:30 (Jesus' followers are commanded to give to the poor; giving away what belongs to someone else is stealing.)

Mark 1:29; Luke 4:38 (Simon owned a house which Jesus frequented; there is no record that Jesus disapproved of private ownership of a house.)

The validity of private property is also implied in numerous parables — for example, the Talents (Matt. 25:14-30), the Unjust Steward (Luke 16:1-8), and the Pounds (Luke 19:12-27) — all of which deal with the use of money without any hint that money is intrinsically evil.

In those cases where Jesus challenges certain people to part with their personal wealth (e.g., the Rich Young Ruler, Matt. 19:21; Luke 12:33; 14:33; 18:22), Jesus is not denying property as a right. On the contrary, he challenges would-be followers to forego this right for his sake. He is not establishing an economic law, but presenting them with a moral choice.

2. Some of Jesus' followers were rich. The Magi were among the first to acknowledge and worship Jesus as the Christ (Matt. 2:1-12); Nicodemus was a member of the Jewish ruling council (John 3:1; 19:39); Joseph of Arimathea is the rich disciple who made arrangements to bury Jesus in his own new tomb (Matt. 27:57-60).

3. Several of Jesus' parables feature astute businessmen who are commended for their profitable investments.

Matt. 7:24-27 (The wise man was rich enough to be able to afford his own house.)

Matt. 25:14-30 (The Master punished the poorest of his three stewards for his failure to invest his money, and rewarded the other two for doubling his money.)

New Testament Teaching Which the Rich Find Disturbing

But as in the Old Testament, so in the New, most of the economic teaching is annoying, meddlesome, unpopular, or distressing to those who are rich. Instruction to Christ's followers concerning the use of their personal resources is both abundant and painfully clear. As members of the best fed, best clothed, best housed society in the world, Western missionaries need desperately to apply this teaching to themselves. New Testament teaching on wealth and poverty may be organized according to the following principles:

1. In the New Testament as in the Old, wealth and possessions, together with the comfort, security, and efficiency which they can provide, are subordinate goods, and neither their pursuit nor their accumulation can ever be regarded as intrinsically worthwhile goals in life.

2 Cor. 4:7-18 ("So we fix our eyes not on what is seen, but on what is unseen. For what is seen is temporary, but what is unseen is eternal.")

Ironically, while the Western church is quick to share that which it claims is most valuable—the good news—its members are sometimes less willing to share that which they claim is unimportant, their material possessions, thus demonstrating the truth of Christ's dictum, "Where your treasure is, there will your heart be also" (Luke 12:34).

Phil 3:8 (Paul could say without fear of contradiction that those things valued by the world were simply refuse to him, since for the sake of Christ he had in fact lost all things.)

2. The personal possessions of Christ's followers are regarded as a trust, to be used for the good of others. Possessions and wealth are of positive value only when they promote his purposes. Otherwise they become a curse.

Matt. 5:42
Mark 8:34-38
Luke 6:27-36
Luke 10:25-37
Luke 14:12-14
Luke 16:19-31
Acts 4:32-35

Heb. 13:5-6 (Freedom from love of money and contentment with one's possessions are absolutely essential for the believer. But can the wealthy believer credibly teach this precept to impoverished brothers and sisters?)

1 Cor. 7:30-31 (We should not be possessive of our possessions.)

3. Wealth and prosperity in the New Testament are not a sign of righteousness, nor are poverty and hardship indications of God's displeasure.

Acts 20:22-24
Acts 21:10-14

As in the Old Testament, in the New Testament personal affluence is generally associated with distance from the Kingdom, mistreatment of the poor, preoccupation with self, and spiritual impotence.

Luke 19:2 (Zacchaeus was wicked and wealthy.)

2 Cor. 8:9 (Christ was poor.)

2 Cor. 11:16-12:10 (Paul was often destitute and suffered much as a direct result of his faithfulness.)

a. Christ (as well as others whose words appear in the New Testament) not only pronounced woes on the rich, but made it clear that it was almost impossible for a rich man to inherit eternal life, and that to be a wealthy disciple is a contradiction in terms.

Matt. 19:16-24
Mark 10:17-31
Luke 6:20-26
Luke 14:25-33

Heb. 13:6 (Freedom from the love of money and contentment with what one has are marks of Christ's true follower.)

James 5:1-6 (There is very little hope for the rich man who continues to thrive at the expense of others.)

b. Sins to which the rich are especially prone—greed (the desire for more than you need even at the expense of those who have less than they need), gluttony, and callous disregard of the poor—are associated by New Testament writers with such sins as idolatry, impurity, and immorality.

Luke 12:13-21 (Christ said to be on our guard against "all kinds of greed." The kind described in this context was of legitimate variety . . . a share in the family inheritance was all the man wanted. Christ saw this as one kind of greed!)

1 Cor. 5:9-11 (The greedy are associated with the sexually immoral, swindlers, idolaters, slanderers, and drunkards. The Corinthians are urged to have nothing to do with such people.)

1 Cor. 11:20-22 (Present economic relationships in the church worldwide are equally scandalous. What would happen if Christian churches in the affluent West covenanted not to partake of the Lord's Supper until all their poor brothers and sisters had enough to eat?)

Gal. 5:16-25

Eph. 4:17-5:7

Eph. 5:3-7 (Greed is a part of the futile way of thinking described by Paul in Eph. 4:17-24.)

Col. 3:1-6 (Greed . . . is idolatry.)

c. Where your treasure is, there your heart will be also.

Luke 12:32-34 (A difficult precept for the rich missionary to teach to the poor. If only Christ had reversed the order—"Where your heart is, there your treasure will be"—He could have made it so much easier for his wealthy followers to save appearances!)

d. Christ's followers are to be in the world but not of it; personal wealth ensures that they are of it, but not in it.

John 17:16-19

e. Preoccupation with self, money and pleasure is an indication of a way of life on the brink of destruction . . . a "last days" way of life.

2 Tim. 3:1-5

4. Wealth and prosperity are inherently dangerous spiritually.

Most wealthy Christians simply do not believe New Testament teaching about the seductive power of wealth in their own lives. And while there are many missionary stories detailing the shipwreck of their converts on the shoals of economic ambition, there are few elaborating the same theme in the personal and institutional manifestations of mission from the West. But the teaching that is so vigorously applied to the lives of poor converts must surely apply to the lives of the relatively wealthy who instruct them!

a. Wealth is the natural culture in which pride and a self-deluding sense of security seem inevitably to flourish. It is fatal to the virtues of humility and meekness.

1 Tim. 6:6-19

b. Wealth deludes both the man himself and those around him concerning his real worth and expertise. It colors and distorts a person's perspective on life itself. As Galbraith put it, "Nothing so gives the illusion of intelligence as personal association with large sums of money."[20] Both experience and New Testament teaching make it clear that Galbraith is right!

Matt. 18:1-9 (The most drastic measures must be taken to ensure that one's activities, attitudes, values, preoccupations, do not cause little ones to stumble.)

Luke 22:24-30 (There is little room in Christ's kingdom for the earthly great.)

Phil. 2:1-4 (Not selfish ambition, but the needs of others, should be the Christian's preoccupation.)

1 Tim. 6:3-16

James 2:1-7 (We tend to favor those who are rich with our company, our friendship, position, a respectful hearing etc.)

c. Wealth deadens a person to his own spiritual need, and tends to produce a preoccupation with this world and, necessarily, alienation from God.

Matt. 13:22

Matt. 22:5

Luke 12:13-21

Luke 14:15-24 (The rich are so busily preoccupied with their own lifestyles they have no time to respond obediently to God's invitation.)

Luke 16:19-31

2 Tim. 6:6-19

James 5:1-6

1 John 2:15-17

Rev. 3:14-21 (The Laodicean church thought it lacked nothing. In fact, it lacked that which is the very essence of the Church—Christ himself!)

d. Wealth makes genuine prayer difficult, since prayer is not the activity of comfortable, secure people, but the desperate outcry of people whose life circumstances are out of their own control.

Synonyms for "prayer" in the New Testament (request, ask, bow down before, fall prostrate before, kneel before, beseech, beg, implore, plead, petition, entreat) can hardly be used to describe the pious cliches mouthed by the rich when their eyes are closed. Self-sufficiency and security are the enemies of prayer, as are materialism and secularism.

e. Wealth comes into conflict with the demands of the Kingdom of God.

Matt. 10:5-10

Matt. 10:37-39

Matt. 13:44-46 (The Kingdom demands everything a man has; the wealthy find it almost impossible to part with their beloved possessions.)

Matt. 16:24-28

Matt. 19:16-24

Mark 10:17-31

Luke 14:15-23

Luke 14:25-35 (Wealthy missionaries appear to be doing well by doing good. The cost of discipleship is another difficult principle for them to teach ... by modelling.)

Luke 16:10-15 (You cannot serve both God and money. The Pharisees — practical businessmen that they were — sneered at the impracticality of this man so obviously out of touch with reality.)

Luke 17:32 (Remember Lot's wife ... she wanted to retain the comfortable life of civilized Sodom.)

Luke 18:18-30 (Rich young ruler must choose between wealth and Christ.)

1 John 2:15-17

f. Wealth tends to produce alienation from one's fellow human beings.

1 Cor. 11:17-34

James 2:1-13

James 5:1-6

g. Wealth tends to become a person's god.

Matt. 6:19-24

Luke 16:13

h. Wealth never satisfies, but breeds covetousness and greed ... a continual desire for more.

Luke 21:34-36 (hearts weighed down with "dissipation" — unrestrained indulgence in the pursuit of pleasure — a picture painted by Jesus himself of our society, dedicated to the pursuit of pleasure, and constitutionally guaranteeing every citizen that "inalienable right.")

Eph. 4:19 (an accurate picture of our consumer society.)

i. Wealth produces spiritual fruitlessness.

Matt. 13:22

Mark 4:18-19 (Money talks ... but it usually doesn't tell the truth!)

Luke 8:14 (Riches and pleasures choke spiritual seed to death.)

j. The love of money can cause us to betray Jesus.

Matt. 26:14-16 (Judas did it for 30 silver coins.)

Acts 5:1-10 (Ananias and Sapphira were more concerned with looking good than with being good.)

5. Christ identified with the poor, coming *for* the poor and as *one of* the poor. Jesus' first recorded public words related to the poor (Luke 4:18-30). He made it clear that God's Kingdom was not intended for the rich, but for the poor. It is true that he came to liberate both rich and poor. Nevertheless, it was as a poor man, rather than as a rich man, that he chose to identify himself with the human race.

Matt. 15:31-46 (It is in the poor that we see and minister to Christ.)

Luke 1:46-56

Luke 2:1-24 (Jesus was born in a stable, and the circumstances of his presentation at the Temple—vv.21-24—indicate that his parents were not rich, but poor. Cf. Lev. 12:8)

Luke 4:16-19 (Jesus' mission was to the poor. Cf. Isa. 58, 61)

Luke 6:20-26 (The poor are blessed, the rich are damned.)

Matt. 8:2, 18-20

Luke 14:12-14

Luke 16:19-31 (Rich man and Lazarus)

John 1:14 (The Word became flesh, and lived for a while among us.)

2 Cor. 8:9 (Jesus became poor for our sakes.)

Phil. 2:1-11 (For our sakes Jesus became nothing, a servant, humbly obedient to the point of death.)

a. Christ's true followers identify with the poor in practical, costly ways.

Those who neglect the poor cannot regard themselves, nor should they be regarded, as Christ's disciples—no matter how orthodox their creeds and confessions, and no matter how enthusiastic their pious rituals. Identification with the needy is a matter of deadly seriousness for Christ, and therefore for all of his true followers. Lack of concern in this area is a sure indication that Christ is not within.

Matt. 25:31-46

Luke 11:37-42 (The Pharisees neglected justice and the love of God.)

Luke 14:12-14 (Invite the poor to banquets.)

Acts 2:42-47

Acts 4:32-37

Acts 11:27-30 (Practical response to impending famine.)

Acts 20:35 (Paul worked hard to help the weak.)

It is no wonder that early believers were not called Christians, but followers of "the Way" (Acts 9:2; 19:9, 23; 22:4; 24:14, 22)!

2 Cor. 8:1-15 (The poor churches of Macedonia pleaded for the privilege of sharing with the needy.)

2 Cor. 9:1-15 (We reap not only *what* we sow; we reap *more* than we sow. God loves a cheerful giver.)

Gal. 2:10/Acts 21:17ff.

Gal. 6:7-10

Phil 4:14-19 (Philippian church contributed to needs of Paul.)

Heb. 6:4-12 (It is possible for Christians to begin well in this matter of helping the poor, and to then become lazy.)

Heb. 13:16 (Sharing our resources with others is a sacrifice with which God is pleased.)

James 1:27

1 John 3:7-20 (Significantly, assurance of salvation for John rests—not upon the recollection of some altar call experience in the past, but upon one's relationship with his possessions and with the needy. In the words of James 2:19, "the demons believe," i.e., insofar as orthodoxy is a matter of mental assent to a series of propositions about God, Jesus, the Holy Spirit,

etc., the demons are believers! But their "belief" does not produce conversion. Only the converted are God's children.)

Rev. 3:14-21

b. God has chosen to work through the poor and the weak rather than through the rich and the strong.

Matt. 1:18-21

Luke 1:26-38 (Mary, the humble fiancé of Joseph, a carpenter, was chosen to bear the incarnate Son of God. This cost her her reputation, and saddled her with not only the life-long stigma of conceiving a child out of wedlock, but with a life of sorrow and misunderstanding as the earthly mother of a man who so irritated the respectable guardians of Jewish orthodoxy that he drove them to murder. This is a part of the human cost of obedience and divine favor.)

1 Cor. 1:16-31

2 Cor. 12:7-10

James 2:5

Rev. 2:8-11 (Smyrna—poor but rich.)

Rev. 3:7-13 (Philadelphia—weak, yet strong.)

Rev. 3:14-21 (Laodicea—rich, yet impoverished.)

c. Not our religious orthodoxy, but our relationship with the needy, is the true indicator of our standing with God.

Matt. 25:31-46 (Sheep and goats)

Luke 10:25-37 (The Good Samaritan)

d. Identification with the poor in the New Testament involves relating to *specific persons*, rather than to an abstract sociological class. To identify with "the poor" as a class necessitates little more than wringing one's hands on their behalf, giving some money to charitable causes, and indulging in the very satisfying exercise of haranguing those who benefit most from the maintenance of the status quo. It costs almost nothing, and the rewards in terms of self-satisfaction are immense. But to identify with actually poor persons requires a different kind of identification—one costly in terms of personal resources, time, and agenda. And it is identification of this kind that marks the true follower of Christ. To have the former without the latter is nothing but hypocrisy. To have the latter is a basic requirement of every disciple, and gives that disciple the moral right to speak boldly against that structural evil which is often a significant factor underlying the poverty of large proportions of the world's poor.

Luke 10:25-37

6. Genuine repentance involves genuine giving, which is always sacrificial. The giving which God honors involves parting with that which we genuinely value and need—not just a ritual dumping of our surplus or discards. True worship involves sacrificing that which is most dear to us . . . our own bodies.

Rom. 12:1-22 (To "sacrifice" one's body means, among other things, to

think humbly about ourselves; to spend our lives on behalf of others . . .
sharing with God's people who are in need, practicing hospitality and asso-
ciating with people of low position. Whatever else the "sacrifice" might
mean, there is never much in it for the sacrifice itself, as Levitical regulations make clear.)

Mark 12:41-44 (The poor widow's two copper coins—worth only a fraction of a penny—were of much greater significance than the large donations
of the rich. Note also that Jesus does not appear to have been unduly
concerned with whether the recipient of the gift was worthy or not. In this
case, the widow gave all that she had to a corrupt Temple regime. Jesus
did not regard this as waste, since he was more concerned with the widow's
motives than with the relative merits of the recipient. Cf. Mark 14:1-9 . . .
woman who wasted the expensive perfume on Jesus' feet.)

John 12:1-8

a. Christ's followers are not called to self-fulfillment, but to self-denial.

Mark 8:31-38 (Peter, rebuking Jesus for his morbid negativism, is dis-
concerted to hear that the more positive agenda he had in mind for Jesus
is inspired by Satan. "Out of my sight, Satan!" Jesus said. "You do not
have in mind the things of God, but the things of men.")

Acts 14:22

b. Christ's followers are not called to be first, but last; not masters, but
servants. For the wealthy person living among the poor, this goes absolutely
contrary to natural practice, necessitating a redefinition of "service" so that
the ruler sees himself as the servant of the ruled.

Mark 9:33-37

Luke 13:22-29

c. Love is the distinguishing mark of Christ's disciple. Love without costly
sharing with the needy is not Christlike love.

John 13:34-35

John 14:23-25

Heb. 13:15-16

d. The generosity of Christ's follower is to be uncalculating, and should
extend even to undeserving enemies.

Matt. 5:38-48

Luke 6:27-36

Luke 14:12-14 (The poor who cannot repay should be invited to missionary celebrations.)

Romans 12:17-21

e. Genuine repentance always contains a practical, economic dimension.

Luke 3:7-14 (It is interesting that all of the "fruit in keeping with repentance" spelled out by John the Baptist involved economic relationships.)

Luke 19:1-9 (Zacchaeus not only paid back four times as much as he
had extorted, he gave half of his possessions to the poor. "Today," said
Christ, "salvation has come to this house.")

Acts 2:42-47

Acts 4:32-5:11 (There were no needy persons in the earliest church. Ananias and Sapphira were more concerned with looking good than with being good, as are many today.)

Acts 10:2 (Cornelius "gave generously to those in need.")

Acts 19:23-41 (Wide-scale repentance in North America would undoubtedly have severe economic repercussions. Nothing could more quickly undermine our way of life than an outbreak of widespread contentment, or conversion to Christ's view of the importance of possessions.)

7. Repentance for the rich is rare, but possible. There can be no doubt that Jesus had many dealings with the rich. What, then, was he trying to say to them? Their situation did not have to remain as it was. They could be converted. Conversion would result in the fruit of repentance. Repentance would involve them in radically new relationships to their wealth and to the poor.

Luke 19:1-9 (Although the rich young ruler did not repent, and very few of the Pharisees repented, Zacchaeus did.)

a. Those within the church who are rich are to be commanded "not to be arrogant nor to put their hope in wealth ... to do good, to be rich in good deeds, and to be generous and willing to share."

1 Tim. 6:17-19 (This is difficult to do if you are rich yourself.)

8. Many religious leaders and missionaries of New Testament times loved money. Insofar as the Western Church still regards itself as the leader of the world wide community of believers (witness the call for "teachers" on the personnel requirement lists of mission agencies!), we are to all appearances in a position analogous to that of the Pharisees of Christ's day.

Matt. 23:23-26

Luke 11:39-42 (Christ describes the Pharisees as "full of greed.")

Luke 16:9-15

Teachers will be judged by a standard more rigorous than that applied to others (James 3:1). To be a wealthy Christian teacher is to be in a dangerous predicament indeed, since the teacher must practice what one preaches. To do anything less is to forfeit not only one's credibility, but one's claim to be Christ's disciple as well! "My mother and my brothers are those who hear God's word and put it into practice," Jesus said (Luke 8:21. Cf. Matt. 7:21-27; Luke 6:46; 11:28; Jas. 1:22-27). The just shall *live* by faith, not just talk about faith (Heb. 10:38; 11, 12).

2 Cor. 2:17 (There is money to be made in peddling the word of God!)

Phil. 3:17-21 (Those whose lives, priorities, preoccupations revolve around personal security are living as "enemies of the cross.")

1 Thes. 2:5 (Pious masks often are a cover for greed.)

1 Tim. 3:3 (The one who loves money is disqualified from leadership in the local church.)

1 Tim. 6:3-5 ("Godliness" can be lucrative.)

2 Peter 2:1-3 ("Christian" teachers whose greed motivates them to "minister" are nothing new.)

Jude 3:16

a. Some who claim to follow Christ do well by doing good. They are not genuinely interested in the poor, only in using the poor as a way for personal advancement of one sort or another.

John 12:1-8 (Judas was not really interested in the poor. He supplemented his living handsomely by personal use of what was given to him for the poor.[21]

9. Obedience, not theological orthodoxy, distinguishes the true follower of Jesus from the fraud.

Acts 6:7

Acts 7:53

Heb. 10:30 (The righteous one will *live* by faith.)

CONCLUSION

Let no one think that possession of wealth is the only sin, or that only the wealthy sin. *All* — rich and poor — have sinned and fallen short of the glory of God. The poor have sins to which they are particularly susceptible. But wealth is the context in which the faith of the rich is tested. The gospel is for the rich, as well as for the poor — although the rich might at times not recognize the "good news" as *good* when it is focused so painfully on their pleasantly desperate plight.

It is clear that Christianity was never designed to make people comfortable and at ease with wealth and power. Nor, predictably, has genuine discipleship ever been widely popular among the rich. Wealth on any wide-scale has never been the norm in human experience. Subsistence, rather than abundance, has been the distinguishing mark of most societies. The modern missionary movement from the West, coinciding as it has with the relatively widely distributed affluence of the traditionally missionary sending nations, is now confronted with theological and ethical dilemmas engendered by its own affluence.

In view of the fact that Western missionaries must often number themselves among the rich of this world, the teaching of the Old and New Testaments on the subject of the wealthy and the poor makes very uncomfortable reading, and impossible teaching for those who live privileged lives among the poor. This is perhaps one reason why missionaries from the West are focusing on the upwardly mobile classes of the world's great cities, and why Protestant missionaries at least have *little to say to* and even *less to do with* the inhabitants of the slums.[22] This may be one reason why the door of opportunity in Christian mission today is not open before the wealthy Laodicean church, but before the impoverished Philadelphian church. Affluent missions are becoming increasingly marginalized in the great spiritual mission of the church.

Even the least self-examined person cannot but feel uncomfortable when confronted with the plain teaching of the scriptures in these matters. In the face of the discomfort induced by the probings of God's revelation, a person has recourse to one of three possible options: (1) one may ignore the teaching altogether; (2) one may engage in the transparently dubious exercise of self-justification by explaining why an uncomfortable teaching doesn't apply to one's personal situation; or (3) one may repent and be converted.

PART III

THE CHALLENGE OF WESTERN MISSIONARY AFFLUENCE

"But how can God bring this about in me?"—Let Him do it and perhaps you will know.

George MacDonald

There is a profound sense in which this concluding section can never be finished, at least not in the pages of a book. Most of what needs to be said remains to be written in the flesh and blood of everyday life. Some readers will, no doubt, be frustrated by the discovery that I have not spelled out the precise details of that repentance which leads to conversion, and to which the scriptures clearly call us. A little reflection, however, will show that no one can write a discipleship agenda for someone else. Each disciple is called from a particular place, at a particular time, to a particular obedience, by a personal Savior and Lord.

As Western Christians we rightly regard the poverty of our fellow human beings as a gigantic problem about which we seem able to do very little; we have proven less willing to view our personal affluence as an even greater problem. Global poverty is an acute material problem, no doubt; but Western affluence is a profoundly spiritual one. Is it not at least as difficult for us members of the Western Church to overcome our affluence as it is for our poverty stricken brothers and sisters in the rest of the world to survive their poverty? Unless we come to see our Western world through the eyes of Jesus and the writers of our scriptures, we will continue to excuse the personal and collective covetousness and greed that have made us "great," and above the locked door to the heart of the richest church the world has ever seen will be written—in splendid gilt lettering—the word "ICHABOD." And her Savior will remain on the outside (Rev. 3:17-20).

7

Grappling with Affluence

If anyone would come after me, he must deny himself and take up his cross and follow me. For whoever wants to save his life will lose it, but whoever loses his life for me and for the gospel will save it.

Jesus

Heroes, being men of marked character, are deemed by the vulgar herd to be eccentric: their very superiority prevents their being estimated. The circumstances of their death shakes weak Faith, but the true Christian through Death to Life sees clearly, how God of seeming evil works lasting good. To die for one's country is a great gain: to die for one's Saviour, to fill up what remains of His sufferings, is sweeter.

Cust

There are two kinds of Christianity — success-Christianity and failure-Christianity. Jesus said, "Unless I fail, my work will be useless."

Kagawa

She had not learned that the look of things as you go, is not their look when you turn to go back ... nature is like a lobster pot: she lets you easily go on, but not easily return.

George MacDonald

We come now to the most difficult part of the book. The broad outlines of the argument so far have proceeded along the following lines: In chapter one, the fact and scale of Western missionary affluence was outlined. In chapter two, the cultural and social milieu which make it possible for Western missionaries to accept uncritically their rising material expectations and standards of living in a world populated by a growing majority of impoverished inhabitants was examined. Chapter three focused on Western missionary rationale for maintaining and even increasing the disparity between themselves and the poor. These three chapters together served as introduction to salient features of the context in which the theory and practice of Western Christian mission are conceived and implemented.

In chapters four through six, attention was focused on overlooked, ignored, or denied — but always troublesome — consequences of missionary affluence in a world increasingly polarized between the rich few and the impoverished many. The quality of their relationships with the poor, the clarity of their communication of the Good News to the poor, and the credibility of their theologies, it was argued, have been and continue to be deeply and negatively affected by the growing affluence of Christian missionaries from the West.

AN ATTEMPT AT GAINING PERSPECTIVE

If knowledge were synonymous with virtue, the book could end here. But since it is not, it remains to suggest an answer to that embarrassingly practical question which is the inevitable corollary of all that has been said so far: What can be done? Is it really true, as Ivan Illich insisted almost twenty years ago, that "There is no exit from a way of life built on $5000 plus per year."?[1] The last decade of Western missionary experience seems to support his pessimism; but are change, repentance, conversion — the stock in trade of missionary preaching — possible only for nonmissionaries?

One point may without hesitation be conceded: the narrow path of discipleship has never been popular among those whose numerous and bulky possessions make passage through the narrow gate and negotiation of the narrow way impossible. It has always been easier for a poor man than for a rich man to enter the Kingdom of Heaven — in spite of the fact that the rich man with his M.Div. and his Kittel's is well prepared and splendidly equipped to speculate and articulate on eternal verities. But did not some of Christ's first followers come from the ranks of the then wealthy? The rich young ruler found it impractical to give up all that he had to be Christ's disciple, it is true (Luke 18:18-25); but Levi must have been a man of considerable economic means, and he repented (Luke 5:27-30). His testimony argues against Illich, therefore. He — along with Zacchaeus, Barnabas, Paul, Luke and numerous others — is proof that there *is* an exit from our blatantly materialistic way of life!

It must also be admitted that missionaries from the West are not unaffected by the press and pull of a social ethos which, if examined closely, is shaped, inspired, and directed by the deep conviction that life consists in the abundance of possessions, especially more, better, up-to-date possessions. In a more innocent age, it was possible for missionaries to believe that their comfortable way of life was the inevitable outcome of national life organized in a Christian way, and that, given enough time and sufficient conversions, the poorer peoples of the world would enjoy the good life. Not only were Christianity and civilization inseparable, but, in the sober judgment of some of the best of the West's nineteenth century Christian minds, no one could "become a Christian in the true sense of the term, however savage [they] may have been before, without becoming . . . civilized."[2] Well after the dawn of the twentieth century, with the "civilized" nations in the throes of one of the most bloody and pointless struggles in the pathetically war-strewn record of humankind, it was still bravely asserted that

The civilisation which is called Western is the slowly developed product of religion . . . [and has] surged forward to its present high water by means of the internal pressure of its inner Christian elan, . . . an impulse which is but the expression of a Christian principle of life moving within.[3]

We no longer believe this to be so. The West has been demystified. We now know with terrifying certainty that for 999 out of 1000 of our fellow human beings, there is no possible road to our way of life in the foreseeable future. The stark and brutal truth is that the natural resources of our planet are sufficient to support "civilized" life for only a tiny fraction of its human population. Accordingly, Western missionaries must be prepared as never before to test the truthfulness of their assertion that "Christ is the answer" in the context of personal material want.

There is a third point which must be remembered. It is not necessary to be wealthy in order to do the Lord's work. The North American experience of wealth on a wide scale is, in terms of historical precedence, an anomaly. As Galbraith points out,

the experience of nations with well-being is exceedingly brief. Nearly all, throughout all history, have been very poor. The exception, almost insignificant in the whole span of human existence, has been the last few generations in the comparatively small corner of the world populated by Europeans.[4]

At the turn of the nineteenth century—when what is thought of as the "modern missionary movement" was in its infancy—the per capita gross national products of the developed and nondeveloped worlds were separated by a factor of less than two; by 1913, the ratio stood at three to one, widening to seven to one by 1970.[5] As indicated in the first chapter of this book, the gap continues to grow at an accelerating rate. The possibility of the Christian mission being carried out without vast financial resources or an elite corps of highly paid professional Western missionaries is not merely a theoretical possibility. For the major part of the Church's existence it has been a necessity, and as the twentieth century draws to a close, it is increasingly clear that most missionary endeavour has been, is being, and must continue to be undertaken by missionaries from the poorer churches.[6] One of the most difficult but unavoidable lessons the Western Church will be compelled to learn is, according to theologian David Bosch, "how to become again what it originally was and was always supposed to be: the church without privileges, the church of the catacombs rather than of the halls of fame and power and wealth."[7]

It has become popular in our day to speak of sinful social structures. While it is true that evil manifests itself at every level of human expression, it is vain to imagine that by changing the context, we will re-create the human being. A cathedral constructed of flawed bricks will be structurally unsound, no matter what its structural design. Accordingly, the emphasis in the ensuing pages will be on personal change, that is, on the "bricks" of Western mission. The culture that shapes us, the law that governs us, the education that conditions us, and the institution that employs us, are all significantly influential, but they are not absolutely determinitive. On the other hand, it would be foolish to imagine that the Western missionary, no matter how disagreeable he may find the selfish excesses of his own society, can escape entirely from its influences. To borrow Trevor Verryn's apt metaphor, "[the Western missionary] cannot help but carry something of [the West's] atmosphere with him, like the smell of stale cigarettes clinging to the clothes of a nonsmoker who has been in a room full of people smoking."[8]

When it comes to transforming international or national political, social, economic, or religious institutions, it is true that the efforts of one person must seem comically inadequate. We yearn for "structural change" which will make personal change easier. In the colorful words of the once editor of the *Edinburgh Review*, we feel "like flies on the chariot wheel; perched upon a question of which we can neither see the diameter, nor control the motion, nor influence the moving force."[9] But fatalism has never been a strong forte of Western missionaries. Like the Apostle Paul (Rom. 7:14-25), they well know that the line between good and evil cannot, according to their Bible, be drawn between opposing political or economic ideologies, or along racial, social, national, or even religious lines: for both good and evil dwell within the heart of every person born. They know, furthermore, that the goal of the Christian life is not the creation and maintenance of a personal utopia in this life. To manifest the fruit of the Spirit in a less than perfect environment is not only a more worthy, but a more realistic, goal in a creation groaning under the tyranny of the forces of darkness.

And so the missionary is urged to begin his lifelong wrestling with afflu-ence — not with his nation; neither with his church or his mission society; nor even with his family; — but with himself. If there is to be any repentance, it must begin here. Jesus never called his disciples to a life of conformity to each other, but to himself.

The chapter will be structured along the following lines. It is recognized, first of all, that in grappling with questions arising from personal affluence, the Christian missionary must begin with a clear understanding of the pro-foundly theological dimensions of the issue. Ideas have consequences. The One who searches and knows the secrets of the human heart reminds us of what we already instinctively know: as one thinketh in the heart, so that person is. However dimly understood or inadequately applied, God's revelation to humankind by means of his words and through his Living Word must be the basis of all Christian missionary belief and action. The Bible is our map. Jesus is our best example of how to follow that map.

It follows that only with such a theological orientation can practical problems and objections be dealt with *Christianly*, rather than just pragmatically, and, where need be, changes can be made, new directions can be taken, and relationships between rich Christians and mammon can be transformed. The conscience, someone once noted, is like a sun dial. The person who comes to it in the night with only a flashlight will discover that it will obligingly tell any time one might wish; but during the day, with the sun shining upon it, it must tell the truth. The parallel between the Christian conscience and the word of God is clear.

Fourthly, we who struggle frequently need to be reminded that we are not alone. Not only is God with us, but there is a great cloud of witnesses, past and present, who—personally, creatively, but above all faithfully, having grappled and continuing to grapple with this great issue—encourage us to increased personal and corporate effort and endurance.

Finally, those of us committed to carrying out with fidelity and integrity the mission entrusted to the Church can and must help each other, encouraging, spurring one another on to love and to good deeds (Heb. 10:24-25).

THEOLOGICAL MOORINGS

Among the richly varied theological motifs running through the pages of the New Testament, three are of such broad significance as to touch upon every other facet of Christian faith and practice: the Incarnation, the Cross, and weakness as power.

The Incarnation

The Incarnation is the very heart of the Christian faith. "In the beginning was the Word," John wrote; and "The Word became flesh and lived for a while among us" (John 1:1, 14). Paul, echoing this most elementary of Christian teachings, reminded the churches in Galatia that "When the time had fully come, God sent his Son, born of a woman, born under law, to redeem those under law" (Gal. 4:4-5). Western missionaries have been among those most committed to the proclamation of this good news. Growing personal affluence and temporal security have made it increasingly difficult to regard the Incarnation as a model for personal action. For much of Western evangelicalism, *Incarnation* is merely a *theologically descriptive*, rather than a *strategically prescriptive*, term (Phil. 2:1-11). It is from the Incarnation, rather than from Marshall McLuhan, that missionary communicators learn that the *medium is the message*. The Living Word must always be made vulnerable flesh.

The Incarnation teaches us that power, speed, mobility, comprehensiveness, efficiency, and success are not the measure of missionary strategy. God so loved the world that he gave his only Son; that Son came into the world—not with an impressive show of force, but as the powerless, vulnerable, "illegitimate," child of a peasant mother. All the creative and sustaining power in heaven and on earth was his (Col. 1:15-17), yet he willingly entered his own creation as a helpless, dependent, suckling infant, occupying only one or two square feet in the bottom of a manger, needing to learn obedience and grow in wisdom. The Word made flesh grew up poor, lived his life surrounded by and in sympathy with the poor, and died poor. In carrying out his mission to save the world, he walked about Palestine for three years, often delayed by crowds and hampered by the religious establishment. Coming in the "fullness of time," he was to all practical purposes unaware of unreached people groups in the world next door. Had his Father miscalculated?

Could not his credibility have been enhanced had he come as the privileged, gifted, wellbred, highly educated, cultured, heir apparent to the throne of some powerful, affluent kingdom? Would it not have been better for him to postpone his debut until the age of the global village—with its jets, computers, telecommunications networks, mass media, public health programs, and human rights organizations at his disposal, to make the accomplishing of his mission more realistic? Was the life of Christ really the preposterously naive, ill conceived, amateurish fiasco that it appears to have been by modern missiological standards of strategic planning and performance?

The answer, of course, is clear. There *were* more appropriate ways for him to authenticate his claims to being the Son of God. There *were* more effective ways of inaugurating the Kingdom of God. Even then, in the absence of motor vehicles, airplanes, computers, and highly technical communications media, there *were* more efficient ways of proclaiming the good news. Despite the absence of marketing consultants and advertising specialists, surely there *were* practical means available for the packaging and selling of the Word made flesh to the general public.

The fact is, the Messianic *modus operandi* was not accidental, but deliberate. The temptation to prove his sonship and fulfill his mission by means of demonstrations of and association with power was deliberately and utterly rejected (Matt. 4:1-11; Luke 4:1-13). His mission would—because it should—unfold in poverty, weakness, and obscurity. The inspiration behind Peter's subsequent suggestion that Christ's mission should be carried out by a more attractive means was traced to Satan himself, when Jesus' scathing rebuke could scarcely have been harsher: "Out of my sight, Satan!" Jesus said to Peter (Mark 8:31-33).

The missiological lessons of the Incarnation are clear. "As you have sent me into the world, I have sent [those whom you gave me] into the world," Christ prayed as he pled with his father for those who, like him, were "not of the world" (John 17:16,17). "Your attitude should be the same as that **of Christ Jesus," Paul reminded believers at Philippi, whose methods for achieving personal objectives appear to have been only too natural (Phil. 2:5).** At the very least, the Incarnation means giving up the power, privilege, and social position which are our natural due. Christ's mission in Christ's way must always begin, proceed, and end with the great renunciation. And this sacrifice is made not merely with reference to "what could have been" back home, but by the standards of the people among whom the missionary is called to incarnate the gospel. This does not leave much room for the power-generating, status-inflating, career-building, self-protecting affluence to which emissaries of the Western churches have become accustomed.

There are those who have suggested that a Western missionary should not try to identify too literally with a lower group if, in the eyes of this lower group, he has an ascribed right to a higher status. Such a course of action, it is argued, will not only be misunderstood by people, "since it reverses all norms of social climbing"; it will surround the missionary with "a cloud of suspicion."[10]

That misunderstanding and suspicion are among the penalties paid by all who go against the social norms of a society cannot be denied. But that this should be regarded as sufficient reason to continue to enjoy the privileges of affluence is more than doubtful; it is wrong. Jesus, in lowering himself and becoming of no reputation *did* suffer lifelong misunderstanding, suspicion, and eventual death—because he did not operate according to the social expectations associated in the Jewish mind with the role of Messiah. Much that is distinctive in his good news runs dangerously contrary to human conventions, and sounds suspiciously like bad news! Those who love their enemies, bless their persecutors, refuse to store up treasure on earth, give way before others, and surrender their lives in selfless service, are frequently, quite rightly, regarded as a threat to the status quo. This is not the behavior of natural man, but of those whose King is not of this world. God's wisdom has always seemed, to fallen man, foolishness.

Western mission agencies—if they wish to be truly Christian—must return to this "foolishness" of their Lord. No matter how enlightened the technique, how massive the budget, how sophisticated the technology, or how numerous the well-qualified personnel, nothing but God's strategy revealed in the Incarnation will prevail against either "the powers of this dark world" or "the spiritual forces of evil in heavenly realms." However strange or inappropriate our spiritual weapons may seem to the natural man, they are the only ones that work in the spiritual battle.

The Cross

The cross, likewise, is not merely a symbol of the atonement, but a prescription for the only way of life promised to all who would follow Jesus.

The New Testament attaches tremendous importance to the crucifixion of Christ. It is the very heart of Apostolic teaching. Our Savior's death on this diabolical instrument of suffering was the central act in the drama which brings salvation to humankind. In his death, Christ made himself one with sinners, absorbing our richly deserved punishment. "He is the atoning sacrifice for our sins," John assured his readers (1 John 2:2; 4:10); and Paul, addressing the self-righteous Galatians, reminded them of the central fact of the Gospel: "Christ redeemed us from the curse of the law by becoming a curse for us" (Gal. 3:13). This is good news indeed!

But there is a disturbing, and therefore often ignored, thread of truth in New Testament teaching about the cross. Those who would follow Christ look forward not only to the comforting prospect of "pie in the sky in the sweet by and by," but to suffering and death in the here and now. For Jesus deliberately chose to make the fellowship of the cross an integral part of what he offers each would-be disciple. "Anyone," he said, "who does not take up his cross and follow me is not worthy of me" (Matt. 10:38). These words were spoken in the context of the natural tendency of his followers, then as now, to put family concerns before obedience to God.

As Jesus approached his own terrible, mortal suffering, Mark records that he called the crowds to him along with his disciples, and said: "If anyone would come after me, he must deny himself and take up his cross and follow me" (Mark 8:34). In this instance, his unvarnished account of the rejection and suffering that lay just ahead for him earned him Peter's love-inspired remonstrance. "You do not have in mind the things of God, but the things of men," was Jesus' response to a suggestion which, if followed, would have put him in collusion with the forces of darkness (Mark 8:31-33).

Do not these words constitute a serious challenge to the Western way of doing mission? The cross, that instrument of dreadful suffering and shame, not only results in our salvation, but prescribes the way of life for all who follow Christ! The cross not only gives life, it takes it. The cross achieves reconciliation between God and humankind, it is true; but it also divides, separating those whose kingdom is not of this world from those at home with the spirit of their age. For Christ's followers, the cross is not only the power of God unto salvation; it is the guarantee of misunderstanding, persecution, and suffering at the hands of those to whom it is a foolish and obnoxious stumbling block (1 Cor. 1:17-18; Gal. 6:12-14). There is nothing attractive, easy, secure, comfortable, convenient, strategically efficient, economical, or self-fulfilling about taking up a cross.

Many, regarding themselves as Christ's disciples because they have accepted, at a superficial level, what Christ offers through the cross, are in actual fact nothing of the sort. Encountering such "believers" in Philippi, Paul tearfully acknowledged that "many live as enemies of the cross of Christ . . . [for] their mind is on earthly things." The fellowship of the cross was foreign to these church members. They were not conformed to Christ's death. "Their destiny is destruction," was Paul's sorrowful conclusion (Phil. 3:17-20).

For such people, the cross means judgment. Their lives, shaped, directed, and consumed by self-gratification, are a mute but effective denial of the Christ whom they profess to follow. Horrified at the prospect of a personal cross, they choose the security of surrender to the enemy of their souls rather than the foolishly painful cross of the lover of their souls. Living out their lives in pleasant, self-fulfilling ways, according to the wisdom of their particular world, like corns of wheat that refuse to fall into the ground and die, the potential for multiplying life is never realized.

In the highly competitive drive to meet increasingly expensive institutional commitments and expand (or at least maintain) membership ranks, personnel recruitment by Western churches and mission agencies does not often dwell upon the call to the fellowship of the cross. Great care is taken to show the extent to which the agency or denomination is prepared to attend to the needs and wants of its missionaries; comprehensive support packages ensure that no needless suffering will be incurred on the part of either the missionary or the missionary's family. The enlightened strategies of the mission are duly elaborated, replete with success testimonials calculated to convince the potential still-wavering recruit that this is the mission society for him or her. New Testament teaching on self-denial is reinterpreted to mean little more than a comfortable life abroad. There are exceptions, of course. But, like the affluent churches it represents, much that the West calls "mission" is no longer an example of participation in the sufferings of Christ. "He saved others; he cannot save himself" has been conspicuously rewritten in missionary flesh to read, "Western Christians save themselves and their children; perhaps if we are fortunate they will save a few of us too."

The Western Church is invited to join the fellowship of the cross. Western mission structures, policies, strategies and personnel need to reflect the Way of the Cross. Of the many responses to the controversial "Laymen's Foreign Mission Inquiry" of 1932,[11] the most theologically apposite criticism was that of Japanese reformer Toyohiko Kagawa: "Can Christianity exist without the Cross?" he asked. " 'Re-Thinking Missions' tries to interpret to us Christ without the Cross as Christianity. . . . nothing is said about the inevitability of paying the price of the Cross in order to bring in the Kingdom of God."[12] His words apply equally to more contemporary, evangelical missions from the West. Mission that does not operate according to the principles of the cross—the heavy, awkward, impeding, unappealing, death dealing cross—may be mission, but it is not *Christian* mission.[13] For the mission or the missionary that is *Christian* in the profoundest sense of that term, self-denial is not merely a periodically inconvenient necessity, but a radical strategy marking all of those who are in step with Christ. Since we battle not against flesh and blood, the weapons of our warfare are not carnal, but spiritual (2 Cor. 10:3-4).

Weakness

The third paradoxical element characterizing mission done in the New Testament way is *weakness*. Humankind has always been awed and cowed by power. Power of various kinds—military, political, social, economic, ecclesiastical—is avidly sought and clung to in the natural course of human affairs. We Westerners are a privileged people; privileges require protecting; protection requires power, in the case of missions, the power of money, excellent organization, well educated missionaries, and skillful strategies.

According to the New Testament, on the other hand, obedient followers are not to either strive for or maintain personal power and privilege; all that they do is marked by personal vulnerability and self-giving. The mission which truly serves its Head never looks for ways of gaining and wielding power, but for ways of subjecting itself on behalf of others. No other pattern is consistent with incarnational or cross bearing mission.

The Power of God unto salvation began with the powerlessness of a poor infant, in the presence of an assortment of peasants, shepherds, and common barnyard animals. The mortal struggle against the terrible forces of evil in our universe (Eph. 6:12) pitted all the violent power of which Satan was capable against the pathetic weakness of a newborn infant.

The infant survived, and grew, but came to a tragic and early end. Unable to answer charges of political insurrection brought against him by the people he had come to save, he died. Unable to defend either himself or his followers, he hung—helpless, painracked in body and spirit, a victim of trumped-up charges—on a cross between two thieves. His mother, tearful witness to her first born's death agonies, must have recalled with bitter irony the joyful outpouring of hopes and expectations with which she had greeted the news that this child would liberate Israel (Luke 1:46-55). How naive she had been then! How differently her son's life had unfolded before her: he had not brought down rulers from their thrones—they had brought him down instead; he had tried to lift the humble, but had been trampled by them in return; he had on occasion filled the hungry with good things, and sent the rich empty away, but the rich now had their revenge. Her son's weakness was no match for their power. Of course, we now know that not the crucifiers, but the Crucified, manifested the mighty power of God which transformed persons, nations, and the course of history.

The Apostle Paul's Damascus Road conversion—from power to weakness—made him the most effective of the earliest missionaries. Having understood the futile incongruity of utilizing worldly power in carrying out Christ's mission, in his letters to the Corinthian Church Paul repeatedly returns to the theme.[14] "God chose the weak things of the world to shame the strong," he reminded the quarreling church (1 Cor. 1:27). He made it clear that to be a missionary (an apostle) meant, in God's mysterious strategy, to be "on display at the end of the procession" (1 Cor. 4:9), least among the prisoners of war, condemned to a public death. He was a spectacle, yes, but not the spectacle of affluence, efficiency, and comfort modelled by many of his Western apostolic counterparts.

"It seems to me," said Paul, "that God has put us apostles on display." What was it that people watching the procession would notice about these missionaries? Not their strength, but their weakness; not their honor, but their dishonor; not their healthy bodies, fine wardrobes, and comfortable homes, but their poverty, rags, and homelessness; not the flattering accolades of the powerful, but curses, slander, and persecution at the hands of everyone. In short, to be a missionary meant to become "the scum of the earth, the refuse of the world" (1 Cor. 4:8-13)! Like his Savior's before him, Paul's life did not have a happy ending, a "missionary statesman" surrounded by devoted supporters and fellow veterans in a Christian retirement village somewhere on the Mediterranean. He spent his last days almost alone, in a Roman dungeon, a frail old man whose life was finally snuffed out by executioners at the behest of a powerful state. It is hard to imagine a weaker, more vulnerable person than this. Yet, as Japanese theologian Kosuke Koyama observes,

> Through Paul who was imprisoned, beaten, stoned, shipwrecked, threatened by all kinds of people, hungry, thirsty, cold and exposed, God touched the foundation of history, and he let Paul touch it too.[15]

What is the significance of these three themes for the Western mission today? Any mission strategy worthy to be called "Christian" must be consistent with Biblical teaching on the Incarnation, the cross, and weakness. A strategy conceived and generated from afar—within the protected confines of an American church or educational institution—is not an incarnational strategy; a strategy which guarantees security, comfort, and privilege for its practitioners knows nothing of the cross; a powerful, all-encompassing, grandiose plan calling for the mobilization of tens of thousands of North Americans and the expenditure of millions of dollars to support them cannot possibly express itself in that weakness which is, according to the Bible and supported by the facts, the only vehicle whereby God's power may be made perfect.

For the affluent Western Christian mission, grappling with its economic power at the theological level will mean subjecting all personal, family, ecclesiastical, and strategic plans, policies, practices, or considerations, to these three questions: (1) Does it reflect the Incarnation, or is it essentially self-serving? (2) Is the cross both the message and the method, or is self-preservation the bottom line? (3) Are people more impressed by its stability and strength or by its weakness? The answer to each of these questions will determine the "Christian-ness" of both the missions and the missionaries of the Western churches.

SETTING THE DIRECTION

Having outlined those elemental features—with their timeless, implicit call to repentance—which have ever distinguished *Christian* mission from *mere* mission, it remains to explore the nature of that tangible fruit which true repentance produces (Matt. 3:8). Repentance is always proven by deeds (Acts 26:20).

The Scriptures do not speak of revolution, but of repentance. This is significant. Revolving wheels and social revolutions frequently have much in common: In the case of the former, one full revolution leaves the tire slightly further down the road, a little worn, perhaps, but otherwise the same. The parts of the tire relative to each other remain unchanged. Thousands of such revolutions simply wear the tire out. Human revolutions have proven similarly ineffective in transforming the human predicament. Repentance, on the other hand, means a deliberate change in direction, leading to genuine conversion. A much more radical concept than is revolution, it is profoundly Christian.

Repentance is a hopeful term, because—unlike revolution—it does not suggest that turning and transformation occur simultaneously. A change in one's direction is not synonymous with arrival at one's ultimate destination. Change in direction is simply an essential beginning, making the prospect of reaching a specific goal realizable. When issued to Western mission, the call to repentance is simply a call to begin moving in a new direction—the direction pointed to by the Incarnation, by the cross, and by the paradox of weakness.

Of course, to the unrepentant, talk of repentance has never been popular. Indeed, it is safe to say that had early Christians refrained from insisting upon this aspect of the "good news," not only would their message have been more palatable to unbelievers, their lives would have been spared.

Obstacles to Repentance

Since it is within specific social milieus that one must repent, those who contemplate embarking upon a new direction in mission do well to remind themselves of the sort of obstacles which they will invariably encounter. Humankind has ever evinced a remarkable capacity to make ridiculous that which threatens personal privilege. The missionary choosing to part direction with more pragmatic peers will find that practical problems, thoughtful objections, and complex relational considerations will most certainly abound at all levels—institutional, family, and individual.

At the *institutional* level, that stabilizing inertia which is built into policies can hardly be avoided. Nonconformists within any organization are rightly perceived to be dangerously centrifugal. Christian obedience has never been successfully legislated. The institution, as the abstract yet tangible expression of the collective identity of its members is more than the sum of its parts, for its life will extend well beyond the years alloted to any of its particular members. In addition to providing its members with an accredited religious and social identity, it also serves to both define and legitimate their personal ends and means. It is exceedingly difficult for an institution to engage in the sort of self-criticism which can lead to repentance. Nor can an institution repent on behalf of its members. Troublesome questions concerning policies and practices are, therefore, frequently dealt with by ostracizing or dismissing the one who raises them. Reformers—whether they be politicians, theologians, or missionaries—are to their institutions what prophets are to their home countries: embarrassing blots on the institutional escutcheon, they are not welcome (Luke 4:24). The self-justification mechanism which is an attribute of all institutions will be one of the most difficult challenges faced by the person or the family wishing to grapple with the challenge of Western missionary affluence.

Why should this be so? John Woolman's comments on the complacency with which high-placed Christians of his day regarded personal complicity in the economically complex question of slavery seem to apply equally to the unwillingness of many Western missionaries to deal with the problem of affluence: "Customs generally approved and opinions received by youth from their superiors become like the natural produce of a soil, especially when they are suited to favourite inclinations," he observed.[16]

When Christian leaders of high reputation themselves engage in culturally acceptable but dubious practices, similar behaviour at the individual level is easily rationalized. However natural this tendency might be, personal accountability to God is by no means thereby abrogated. "For as justice remains justice," Woolman warns,

> so many people of reputation in the world joining with wrong things do not excuse others in joining with them nor make the consequences of their proceedings less dreadful in the final issue than it would be otherwise.
>
> Where unrighteousness is justified from one age to another, it is like dark matter gathering into clouds over us. We may know that this gloom will remain till the cause be removed by a reformation or change of times and may feel a desire ... to speak on the occasion; yet where error is so strong that it may not be spoken against without some prospect of inconvenience to the speaker, this difficulty is likely to operate on our weakness and quench the good desires in us, except we dwell so steadily under the weight of it as to be made willing to endure hardness on that account.[17]

The power of the institution over the individual can hardly be overemphasized. Missionaries can and must be critical about their institutions where these come into conflict with personal obedience. Testimony against

Western missionary affluence will be a lonely and costly task. Nonconformity arouses fierce resistance against it, even in pious missionary circles. James Gilmour's ascetic adaptation to Chinese life one hundred years ago was regarded by his colleagues with hostility because of its implicit criticism of their way of life.[18] The little band of Western missionaries to India who, under Donald McGavran's leadership, formed the "Fellowship of Venturers in Simpler Living" in the 1930s, soon lost heart due in large part to "the considerable friction in the missionary body" which "the existence of such a plan created."[19] To have invidious comparisons drawn between one's own comfortable way of life and that of an apparently more dedicated colleague is always distressing, and stirs the self-justification instinct to vigorous action. Sydney Smith's explanation of the collective ire of English clergy against social reformer Elizabeth Fry rings true: "She is very unpopular with the clergy," Smith explained, "[because] examples of living, active virtue disturb our repose, and give rise to distressing comparisons: we long to burn her alive."[20]

A number of Western mission agencies, while not addressing the problem of their affluence by renouncing it, have recognized the morally questionable pattern of relationships which have long characterized and bedeviled Western missions and non-Western churches. They have begun to move away from the traditional Western stresses on *independence, autonomy*, and *self-sufficiency*, restructuring along lines more consistent with Biblical teaching on the Church as the Body of Christ. In these societies, the emphasis is on the *interdependence* of Western and non-Western churches and institutions. At the institutional level, this has resulted in structures which—in terms of power, policies, and personnel—are becoming more genuinely international. This is a hopeful sign, and if pursued, will be the salvation of Western missions abroad.[21]

Little needs to be said here concerning *family* and *personal* obstacles to simpler missionary living. As was pointed out in chapter 3, humanly speaking there is much to be lost, and little to be gained from pursuit of a deliberate policy of economic austerity. At the family level, children, spouses, parents, and in-laws complicate obedience to some of Christ's more extreme commands (e.g., Luke 9:57-62; Matt. 10:34-39). Despite all that Christ said about the danger of riches, we believe—at least where our families are concerned—that poverty is even more dangerous. To risk the misunderstanding of our next of kin is a heavy price to pay for what they will doubtless regard as foolhardy economic eccentricity. The necessity of preparing our children to "fit" into the materialistic culture of the West makes privilege abroad absolutely essential. Excusing personal participation in the Western love affair with mammon on the grounds that our materialist excess is simply "cultural" is too strong a temptation for most of us to resist. The powerlessness and loss of personal influence which must inevitably accompany renunciation of affluence-based status is too great a price to pay.

A Place To Begin

Formidable as these barriers to repentance might seem, a beginning must be made in attempting to surmount them. The suggestions following are merely that—suggestions. To prescribe any uniform pattern of discipleship is to ensure Pharisaism. The disciple is not called to *look* good, but to *be* good. This is the essence of Christian integrity. Obedience is a matter of the heart, and its external patterns cannot be legislated or institutionalized.

1. *Individual.* We instinctively long for the security of conformity. We do not mind paying the price of discipleship—provided the sacrifice can be made in the company of similarly sacrificing and approving peers. Peter, upon hearing of the fate awaiting him, was curious about what lay ahead for John. Jesus' words to Peter are his words to all of us whose personal obedience is contingent upon the obedience of the group: "If I want him to remain alive until I return, what is it to you? You must follow me" (John 21:18-22).

While the call to follow Jesus in self-denial is a profoundly personal matter, the fact that self-denial can never be lived in isolation from others means that it can easily degenerate into a display of self-righteousness, or into an insistence that others conform to the same external standards. The individual who senses the urging of the Spirit to personal repentance must guard diligently against the sin of pride, and must be prepared to be misunderstood by his or her peers. As Koyama notes,

> If we go we must be prepared to go the way of self-denial. We want to go, but we do not want to be mocked. Bishops, theologians, and church leaders are prepared to go as long as their spiritual, intellectual and ecclesiastical prestige is safely protected.[22]

Each missionary must, furthermore, come to grips with the fact that many of the underlying values which have shaped and which continue to power Western societies are not godly, but godless. Thinking it no longer "worthwhile to retain the knowledge of God," Western societies display increasing evidence that "God [has given] them over to a depraved mind, to do what ought not to be done" (Romans 1:28). Sadly, at all levels, even in its expression of mission, the Western Church appears to be more comfortable with "the mind of the West" than with "the mind of Christ."

Simpler personal lifestyles are necessary. The missionary is not, after all, a saint living in the Millenium, but a soldier engaged in a cosmic conflict in which no treaty is possible—only defeat or victory. Travelling lightly is absolutely essential. The disciple is not the owner, but the steward of those material possessions and personal talents entrusted to him or her. These talents are not to be wasted by burying them in the ground of self-indulgence.

"Needs" must not be defined by Western standards, but by local conditions. Real renunciation – not just the appearance of renunciation – must be practiced (Acts 5:1-11). It is sometimes necessary to sell our personal possessions so that those who have real needs may be helped (Acts 2:45). Our human tendancy has ever been to accumulate possessions – even at the cost of indebtedness – and then excuse ourselves from giving on the grounds that we have no money to give. There is nothing very notable about a willingness to part with spare cash for the sake of the needy. It is only when a Christian, for the sake of others, willingly parts with dearest possessions that the mind of Christ is manifest.

2. *Family.* The family has perhaps been the most frequent resort of those who explain their unwillingness to obey Christ's economic instructions. "I will follow you," Christ is often told by conscripts and volunteers, "but first . . . [my family]" (Luke 9:57-62). But is obedience in this crucial area possible only for those without a family? The children of Western missionaries are, like their parents, privileged beyond the wildest prospects of the majority of children who have ever lived. I write as the son of missionaries – as a beneficiary of the costly privileges and special environment so lovingly provided for all such children abroad.

In an age of growing want, the services and privileges accorded to the children of Western missionaries are by no means being curtailed. On the contrary, every effort is being made to enhance current programs and to provide new ones. Naturally, we want "the best" for *our* children. Books, articles and consultations on "missionary family" and "missionary kids" take relative affluence as a given. The possibility of voluntary poverty at the family level is never raised. This reinforces the idea that Western missionary families need not question the status quo. Nor are the issues facing the children of the tens of thousands of poor non-Western missionaries ever broached. Although numerically a majority, and strategically at the cutting edge, it is as though they didn't exist.[23] Even the curriculums of those schools catering to the children of Western missionaries pointedly exclude incorporation of the language, perspectives, or content of indigenous educational systems. Third world missionary parents and their children must do the best they can with their negligible resources, while the children of affluent Western missionaries look forward as a matter of course to special facilities, special care, special education, and a special place among the world's elite.

There is a singular lack of critical sensitivity to the impact of schools for missionaries' children – often conspicuously exclusive enclaves of Western culture and values, bastions of privilege which the poor can only see from outside – upon missionary children themselves and upon the people from whom they are so carefully insulated and isolated. Many children of Western missionaries take up the vocation of their parents. There can be little doubt that enculturation to the entitlements of privilege make it difficult for them to operate along lines of genuine sharing, fraternity, and mutuality with non-Western Christians. That missionary children, when they become missionaries themselves, should perpetuate within the Western missionary enterprise a *modus operandi* which is increasingly suspect, and which has for decades been relatively impotent, is not surprising. But it is sad.

As to those non-Western peoples in a position to observe most closely the privilege accorded to Western missionaries and their children, does not such institutionalized privilege serve to confirm in their minds that the *real* good news is the good news of *plenty*?

As parents, we need to heed the lesson of Old Testament parents who put their children first. Lot and Eli come to mind as examples of parents who made their children's well being a priority. *Lot,* choosing to put his own economic security before that of his uncle, did exceedingly well materially (Gen. 13). This may have been the beginning of a steady erosion of his spiritual integrity, for when he later warned his sons-in-law about Sodom's impending doom, "his sons-in-law thought he was joking" (Gen. 19:14). *Eli* is another example of one who put his sons before his obedience to the Lord (1 Sam. 2:1-36, especially v. 29), with similarly dire consequences. By his indulgence, he unwittingly doomed his beloved sons. *Elkinah* and *Hannah*, on the other hand, are examples of parents for whom the well being of a first born son was of less importance than obedience. Samuel was their son of promise. In accordance with her vow, Hannah took her small, just weaned son to the temple, where he was to be raised by Eli—a man who had already demonstrated his paternal incompetence by ruining his own sons (1 Sam. 1-3).

Is it more harmful for children to share the experiences of the rich or the experiences of the poor? If the teaching of the Bible is taken seriously, the answer to this question must be obvious. To quote John Woolman once again,

> In our present condition, to love our children is needful; but except this love proceeds from the true heavenly principle which sees beyond earthly treasures, it will rather be injurious than of any real advantage to them. Where the fountain is corrupt, the streams must necessarily be impure.[24]

3. *Mission Agencies.* Mission boards and agencies cannot insist that member missionaries lower their standard of living. But they can try to provide a milieu in which those who choose to do so are given understanding, acceptance, and encouragement. Change, apart from radical conversion or catastrophe, comes slowly to an institution. But why should not the problems associated with missionary affluence be grappled with frankly and regularly at mission conferences and consultations? Although the subject does not appear on the agendas of many missiologists or administrators, it frequently troubles individual missionaries, especially those in their first term of service. The candor with which agencies and denominations share their needs for more money is well known. Could not the other side of the

equation be dealt with as well—not in "missionary only" gatherings, but in meetings in which the poor themselves are invited to share their perceptions of Western missionary economics?

Several years ago, in answering the question "How does a missionary function and relate in today's Asia?" Renuka Somesakhar offered some practical suggestions to Western missionaries serious about overcoming the handicap of their affluence. "In the past," he pointed out,

> those missionaries endeared themselves most to the people, who lived within the economic framework of those with and among whom they worked. To persons coming from affluent countries acceptance of "lower wages" seems like a big sacrifice. But it is lower in comparison with which standard. . . . Mission boards and missionaries themselves have done considerable amount of discussion on this point. Unfortunately, seldom, if ever, the host country is consulted on this extremely important matter which, in the last analysis, does influence greatly the function and relationship of a missionary to Asians.[25]

It may be that societies of a new kind will need to be generated.[26] Protestants can learn much from Catholic orders of missionaries who—like our Savior—choose poverty or parity rather than wealth as a basis for missionary service. Is there no room in Western evangelical missionary circles for a "great renunciation"? The Moravians, the Salvation Army, the Oxford Brethren at Calcutta, the Universities' Mission to Eastern Africa, and the China Inland Mission—like the Jesuit fathers—operated on principles of apostolic simplicity, austerity and self-denial. They provide proof that Evangelical societies need not be organized around the principles of plenty. Catholic missionary orders have long, often effectively, practiced it; missionaries sent by the Confessional churches continue to spend time and money discussing and writing about it; Evangelicals—alas—have in recent years virtually ignored it, at least in practice.[27]

Must we conclude that this kind of obedience is impossible for evangelical missionaries? Is it heresy to suggest that the One whose grace is sufficient for the weakness and poverty of Catholic or non-Western missionaries is inadequate in the case of evangelical Western missionaries? Only those who will answer "NO" to these questions with their lives need consider missionary service. For all others, mission must remain simply a career.

4. *Training Institutions and Sending Churches.* Can secure, rich clergy in their pinstriped suits, or tenured seminary professors, operating out of their comfortable and well equipped environments—credibly challenge Western missionaries to consider the "crucified mind" strategy in matters of personal and family privilege? Can congregations of churches that have deliberately moved into the comfortable suburbs in order to avoid the inconvenience, frustration, and hopelessness of being surrounded by the poor of our inner

cities insist that their missionaries follow a more radically Biblical pattern? I think not. Kipling's verse captures the incongruity of those who might be insensitive enough to try:

> The toad beneath the harrows knows,
>   Exactly where each tooth point goes;
> The butterfly upon the road,
>   Preaches contentment to that toad.

As long as we North American Christians and leaders demonstrate that we have learned only to abound, it will be hypocritical to insist that missionaries from among us should learn how to be in want. The Laodicean Church cannot inspire its members to great sacrifice for the sake of Christ. Only a community of believers who themselves have chosen to reject the materialist spirit of the age can stir its members to pursue genuine self-sacrifice abroad. A wealthy church is bound by the rules of propriety to support its missionaries according to its own ever-inflating notions of adequacy. On the other hand, missionaries so supported are not morally obligated to conform to Western standards of consumption and privilege. They are free — indeed morally obligated as Christ's followers — to practice stewardship of these resources according to the dictates of their consciences.

Nor are those North American training institutions busily engaged in the preparation of missionaries in a morally strong position to admonish missionary graduates to choose the narrow way of self-denial. The embarrassingly brazen trumpeting of their own imagined superiority over other institutions, together with an unblushing willingness to make the convenience and comfort of their facilities and services a selling point, smack of the competitive spirit of the age, and not of Christ. That such practices are the rule rather than the exception in North America make it clear that the humility which is a prerequisite of self-denial is simply not there. Such self-promoting ecclesiastical and academic environments will — except by the accident of a "genetic throwback" to the Church's Ancient Root — produce their own kind of offspring. Soldiers of Jesus Christ emerging from such a milieu will be prepared to expect comfort, rather than to endure hardness (2 Tim. 2:3).

But a beginning can be made. A number of seminaries and colleges are offering courses designed to grapple with the complexities of being rich Christians in an age of hunger. Some are becoming more critically aware of the evil which the Bible calls greed, but which is sanctified and legitimized by the term "consumerism" in Western society. A number of them have incorporated this element into their mission curriculums. At Fuller Theological Seminary School of World Mission, for example, Elizabeth Brewster teaches a course entitled "Incarnation & Mission Among the World's Urban Poor," in which an effort is made "to gain a Scriptural and experiential perspective for mission outreach among Third World Poor . . .

[on the] assumption . . . that the incarnation of Christ provides a Biblical model for ministry."[28]

In my own institution, two courses required of all students in the department of mission studies deal directly with the challenge of the affluence of missionaries. One of these, "Rich and Poor: The Problem of Affluence in Mission," surveys and applies scriptural teaching regarding ethical and practical aspects of issues growing out of wealth and poverty in proximity. A second course, "Missionary Identification," explores the significance and implications of the Incarnation as a normative model for Christian ministry. Where mission courses touch upon strategy, cognizance is taken of the implications of the Western missionary's relative affluence upon the effectual implementation of a given strategy.

More can be done. All students, but especially those contemplating foreign missionary service, should be given every encouragement to familiarize themselves with the great cloud of witnesses for whom the Incarnation and the Cross of our Lord have been not only the means of salvation, but models for mission. We need models—heroes, if you will—who can inspire us to move beyond the expectations of convention. Not forgetting Jesus and Paul, the lives and the writings of men and women such as Roberto de Nobili, Henry Martyn, Allen Gardiner, Coleridge Patteson, John Williams, Mary Slessor, Hudson Taylor, James Gilmour, Dan Crawford, Malla Moe, Toyohiko Kagawa, Daniel Johnson Fleming, Bruce Olson, Mother Teresa, Ron Sider, Stephan Kovalski, Viv Grigg, Niall O'Brien, and others too numerous to mention—people much admired but seldom emulated—must be studied and imitated. Those who have struggled notably with the lethal materialism which Western Christians have so heartily embraced must be introduced to the next generation of Western missionaries. Students preparing for missionary service must be inspired to make Kagawa's conversion prayer *their* lifelong prayer: "Oh God," he prayed, "make me like Christ."[29] His prayer was answered.

We need also to hear the stories of godly missionaries and evangelists who, because they are poor, and in many cases scarcely literate, are largely unknown to us. Too often, these men and women, responsible for most of the growth of the church around the world, are known—if at all—only as characters in a story told by a Western missionary. Cannot they tell their own stories? Listening to them, one is both inspired and humbled: *inspired* because God's Spirit is not restricted to working through affluent Western missionaries; *humbled* because the role of Western missionaries in these stories is often so incidental.[30]

Needless to say, teachers and leaders of missionaries should themselves model simplicity in lifestyle and contentment in personal ambition if they are to help their students to do the same. Physical facilities likewise should—in the midst of a society which makes fun and comfort supreme values to which all other considerations are subjected—model plainness, not ostentation. Better far to err on the side of austerity than luxury!

THE FELLOWSHIP OF VENTURERS IN SIMPLER LIVING

For any individual to attempt to address adequately the complicated multifarious issues raised by this book would not only be presumptuous but futile. I am acutely aware of my personal inadequacies in writing a book such as this. Perhaps I have written some things that either should not have been said, or which should have been said in a different way; and I have doubtless overlooked aspects of the problem that should have been addressed. My only plea is also an invitation: as members of the Body of Christ, we need each other.

I am proposing the resurrection — in slightly modified form — of the "Fellowship for Venturers in Simpler Living" founded by Donald McGavran in India nearly sixty years ago. I conceive of it as an international forum in which problems, examples, ideas, and proposals relating to the topic of missionary affluence can be discussed and grappled with. The Fellowship will revolve round a modest publication — to be issued at least once a year to members — a kind of ongoing, open discussion in which members may freely share their problems, questions, observations, visions, and insights with one another.

Initially, at least, membership will be restricted to those who write to me concerning some aspect of the challenge of doing mission out of affluence. Professors, missionary supporters, missionaries, administrators, church leaders, students, observers, and others with a personal interest in the subject — Westerners and non-Westerners alike — are invited to use this as a means of encouraging, guiding, inspiring, and admonishing each other "toward love and good deeds" (Heb. 10:24). The challenges of modelling economic Christlikeness at the individual, family, and institutional levels will be frankly acknowledged and vigorously grappled with.

CONCLUSION

In the final analysis, Christian stewardship is not something we do, but something we become. Not a technique but a way of living. Two ways in which a missionary may resist the mesmerizing pull of Western materialism are well illustrated in the encounters of two Greek heroes, Odysseus and Jason. Odysseus, having heard of the deadly but irresistibly appealing call of the Sirens, was determined to experience the pull without succumbing to its effects. Accordingly, he had himself bound to the mast of his ship, and the ears of his oarsmen plugged with beeswax, after issuing firm instructions that he was not under any circumstances to be released until the ship had sailed well past the island inhabited by the Sirens. As the boat approached the island, Odysseus began to hear the song of the Sirens, gradually, inexorably, succumbing to its spell until at last he writhed and struggled in his bonds, begging his crew to let him heed the deadly song, and cursing them for ignoring his frenzied appeals. As the boat drew past the island, and the voices of the Sirens faded into silence, Odysseus was able to assert self-control once again, and reflected on his desire to rush to what must have been certain death. His method of resistance illustrates the way of bonds and restrictions. It is not pleasant, but it can be effective in saving us from our own desires.

Jason and his Argonauts faced a similar peril, as — approaching the island whose shores were lined with the bleaching bones of thousands of sailors who had been unable to resist the appeal of the Sirens — they began to lose the will to resist the Sirens' deadly pull. Fortunately, as the story goes, Princess Medea had the presence of mind to urge Orpheus (Greek god of music) to counter the Sirens' song with the music of the gods. This he did so effectively, accompanying himself on his lyre, that the music of heaven drowned out the sound of the Sirens, thus neutralizing its mesmerizing effects, and saving the lives of all on board.

As evangelical missionaries, we can choose to respond to the appeals of mammon in three ways: (1) we can give in to its deadly appeal; (2) we can bind ourselves by rules and regulations which make it impossible for us to respond as we would like; (3) or we can drown out the Sirens' invitation to death by listening instead to the music of the Spirit, and by learning to sing His song.

". . . And the things of earth will grow strangely dim in the light of his glory and grace."

Notes

FOREWORD

1. R. Pierce Beaver, ed., *The Gospel and Frontier Peoples* (South Pasadena: William Carey Library, 1973), p. 81.

2. Jean-Marc Ela, *African Cry*, translated by Robert R. Barr (Maryknoll, N.Y.: Orbis Books, 1980), pp. 71-80.

3. Adrian Hastings, *A History of African Christianity 1950-1975* (London: Cambridge University Press, 1979), p. 228.

INTRODUCTION

1. See Jon Bonk, "Affluence: The Achilles' Heel of Missions," in *Evangelical Missions Quarterly*, Vol. 21, No. 4 (October, 1985), pp. 382-390; and "The Role of Affluence in the Christian Missionary Enterprise from the West," in *Missiology: An International Review*, Vol. XIV, No. 4 (October, 1986), pp. 437-461.

2. Letter of Johnstone to Bonk, Feb. 26, 1985.

3. Letter of Waddell to Bonk, November 7, 1986.

4. Letter of Strickland to Bonk, December 17, 1986.

5. Letter of McAllister to Loge, April 16, 1987, Irian Jaya.

6. See Jill Neimark, "The Power of Positive Thinkers: How One Company Created a Work Force Full of Optimists," in *Success* (September, 1987).

1. THE FACT AND THE EXTENT OF WESTERN MISSIONARY AFFLUENCE

1. Robert Moffat, *A Missionary Prize Essay on the Duty, the Privilege, and Encouragement of Christians to Send the Gospel to the Unenlightened Nations of the Earth* (Newcastle: Pattison and Ross, 1842), p. 50. The author of this essay should not be confused with the more famous London Missionary Society missionary of the same name.

2. William P. Walsh, *Christian Missions. Six Discourses Delivered Before the University of Dublin, being the Donnellan Lectures for 1861* (Dublin: George Herbert, 1862), p. 51.

3. It is important to remember that late 19th century racism exemplified by Josiah Strong was not peculiar to Christians; indeed, as I have attempted to show elsewhere, the racism of Christians — being based, as it was, upon the doctrine of monogenesis — was far less sinister than the scientific racism of the times, with its "survival of the fittest" assumptions and its varied theories of polygenesis. See Jon Bonk, " 'All Things to All Persons' — The Missionary as a Racist-Imperialist, 1860-1910," in *Missiology: An International Review*, Vol. 8, No. 3 (July, 1980), pp. 285-306.

4. Josiah Strong, *The New Era; or, The Coming Kingdom* (New York: Baker & Taylor Co., 1893), pp. 79-80; and *Our Country: Its Possible Future and Its Present Crisis* (New York: Baker & Taylor Co., 1885), as cited in Sydney E. Ahlstrom, *A Religious History of the American People* (New Haven: Yale University Press, 1972), p. 849. See also Sydney Ahlstrom's chapter, "Annuit Coeptis: America as the Elect Nation," in *Continuity and Discontinuity in Church History: Essays Presented to George Huntston Williams on the Occasion of his 65th Birthday*, edited by F. Forrester Church and Timothy George (Leiden: E. J. Brill, 1979), pp. 315-337.

5. Bernard E. Quick, "He Who Pays the Piper . . . : A Study of Economic Power and Mission in a Revolutionary World" (Unpublished Manuscript, Princeton Theological Seminary, n.d.), p. 52.

6. Harvie Conn, "Missions and our Present Moment in History," an address to the Joint October 29-November 1, 1985 Meeting of the American Association of Bible Colleges (AABC) and the Association of Evangelical Professors of Mission (AEPM) held in Chicago.

7. For a summary of the difficulties and pitfalls inherent in the use of GNP as an instrument to measure the relative economic well being of nations, see *World Resources 1987*. A Report by The International Institute for Environment and Development and The World Resources Institute (New York: Basic Books, 1987), p. 239.

8. This table, appearing in The World Commission on Environment and Development, *Our Common Future* (New York: Oxford University Press, 1987), p. 30, utilizes data in the World Bank's World Development Report 1986 (New York: Oxford University Press, 1986).

9. All GNP figures in this chapter are taken from Table 15.1 in *World Resources 1987*, pp. 240-241, cited above. I have deliberately chosen to list those poorer nations with the highest concentration of North American Protestant missionary personnel, as indicated in *Mission Handbook: North American Protestant Ministries Overseas*, 13th Edition (Monrovia: Missions Advanced Research and Communication Center, 1986), p. 585. These are neither the poorest nor the most well to do of the 181 different countries in which North American missionaries work.

10. See the tables detailing the "Comparative Distributions of Mission Personnel" in *Mission Handbook*, p. 584.

11. See Irving B. Kravis, et al., *World Product and Income: International Comparisons of Real Gross Product*. Produced by The Statistical Office of The United Nations and The World Bank. (Published for the World Bank by The Johns Hopkins University Press, Baltimore, 1982). This volume is the fifth of six reports in the series so far.

12. These figures are taken from Box A.2 on p. 270 of *World Development Report 1987*.

13. The Report of the Commission on Environment and Development provides as a fair representation "a nation in which half of the population lives below the poverty line, and where the distribution of household incomes is as follows: The top one-fifth of households have 50 per cent of total income, the next fifth have 20 per cent, the next fifth have 14 percent, the next fifth have 9 per cent, and the bottom fifth have just 7 per cent." See Box 2-1, *Our Common Future*, p. 50.

14. Western consciences have frequently derived solace from the conviction that "non-Western people don't need as much, because money goes farther in their countries." One also hears, on the other hand, that missionary salaries must be

increased to keep pace with higher and constantly inflating costs of living in these same countries. Although these statements are clearly contradictory, both are frequently asserted by Western missionaries.

15. See *Mission Handbook*, pp. 545-560.

16. Ibid., scattered.

17. A useful conspectus on the personnel and reported incomes of the twenty-five largest agencies is found in *Mission Handbook*, pp. 601-604. The agencies listed in this comparison include a mix of big, middle-sized, and small agencies. Figures for Canadian agencies are similar.

18. See *Mission Handbook*, pp. 331-54, 511-16.

19. These figures were provided by the mission agencies themselves over a period of approximately one year. It is important to understand that the dollar amounts generally include provision for transportation, medical insurance, housing, and pension. Salary or support for a married couple may be calculated by simply doubling the figures. Additional allowance for the support and education of missionary children is the usual practice. It is also important to note that the actual salary received by a missionary with a given agency will depend upon the cost of living in the country or the city to which he or she is assigned. Furthermore, many of those working with independent or Interdenominational Foreign Mission Association (IFMA) associated agencies are chronically undersupported. On the other hand, many missionaries with these agencies have access to special "ministry" accounts upon which they may draw for ministry-related expenses such as a motor vehicle, a refrigerator, a power generator, etc.

The figure for the Southern Baptists represents the guaranteed basic cash provision. In addition, Southern Baptist missionaries receive numerous supplementary benefits, including U.S.A. housing allowances, longevity allowances, comprehensive medical insurance, life insurance, outfit and refit allowances, furlough transportation allowances, local leave allowances, allowances for the education of children, and retirement grants. The overall support package is reviewed regularly on the basis of the U.S. Department of State Indexes of Living Costs Abroad, Quarters Allowances, and Hardship Differentials. All in all, Southern Baptist missionaries are among the best provided for in the world.

20. This is the title of a book by David M. Potter, *People of Plenty: Economic Abundance and the American Character* (Chicago: University of Chicago Press, 1954).

21. A letter from David Picton Jones (Uguha) to Ralph Wardlaw Thompson (London), December 2, 1884, located in the Council for World Mission Archives (Central Africa-Incoming-5/5/C) at the University of London.

22. See Richard Lovett, *James Gilmour of Mongolia: His Diaries, Letters and Reports* (London: Religious Tract Society, 1893), pp. 211-213.

23. From the Foreword of *The Economic Basis of the Church*. Preparatory Studies and Findings, Meeting of the International Missionary Council, at Tambaram, Madras, India, December 12-29, 1938. See "The Madras Series," Vol. V, Edited by J. Merle Davis (New York: International Missionary Council, 1938).

24. See J. Merle Davis, *The Economic and Social Environment of The Younger Churches*, The Report of the Department of Social and Economic Research of the International Missionary Council to the Tambaram Meeting—December 1938 (London: The Edinburgh House Press, 1939); a partial list of the specific studies may be found on pp. 225-27.

25. "Economic Disparities on the Mission Field" is the title of chapter 3 of *The Economic Basis of the Church*, pp. 25-35.

26. Ibid., p. 31.

27. Daniel Johnson Fleming, *Ventures in Simpler Living*. The book, written in 1933, appears to have been published by Fleming himself, being printed by The Polygraphic Company of America, New York, and made available through The International Missionary Council, New York.

28. This is the title of a chapter in his book, *Ethical Issues Confronting World Christians* (Concord: Rumford Press, 1935, to be obtained from The International Missionary Council, New York), pp. 109-122.

29. Daniel Johnson Fleming, *Living As Comrades: A Study of Factors Making for "Community"* (New York: Published for the Foreign Missions Conference of North America by Agricultural Missions, Inc., 1950).

30. *Mission Handbook*, pp. 39-40.

31. Harry F. Wolcott, "Too True to be Good: The Subculture of American Missionaries in Urban Africa," *Practical Anthropology*, Vol. 19, No. 6 (Nov.-Dec. 1972), p. 252.

32. Wolcott, "Too True to be Good," p. 253. William Reyburn and Jacob Loewen discussed social dynamics disparity frequently and creatively in the pages of *Practical Anthropolgy*, but mission agency policy has seldom, if ever, attempted to address the issue.

33. The report is No. 22 of a series of Lausanne Occasional Papers emerging from the Consultation on World Evangelization held in Pattaya, Thailand, June 16-27, 1980. The full title of the report is: *The Thailand Report on The Urban Poor: Report of the Consultation of World Evangelization Mini-Consultation on Reaching the Urban Poor* (Wheaton: Lausanne Committee for World Evangelization, 1980).

34. Dana Jones, "The Road to Celia's," *Evangelical Beacon*, Vol. 60, No. 16 (August 31, 1987), pp. 12-13.

2. THE HISTORICAL AND CULTURAL CONTEXT OF MISSIONARY AFFLUENCE

1. David M. Potter, *People of Plenty: Economic Abundance and the American Character* (Chicago: University of Chicago Press, 1954), p. 76.

2. Ibid., p. 67.

3. J. Merle Davis, *The Economic and Social Environment of the Younger Churches*, p. 1.

4. David DeVoss, "The New Breed of Missionary," *Los Angeles Times Magazine* (January 25, 1987), pp. 14-18; 20-23; 34-35.

5. William Carey, *An Enquiry into the Obligations of Christians to use Means for the Conversion of the Heathen* (London: Hodder & Stoughton, 1891 [reprint of 1792 edition]). Carey's book, while modest by the scale of the studies generated by contemporary missiologists, nevertheless constitutes the "source" of a continuing genre of Western missionary literature that reached its apogee with the publication in 1983 of the *Encyclopedia of World Christianity*, edited by David Barrett (London: Oxford University Press).

6. Thomas O. Beidelman, "Contradictions between the Sacred and the Secular Life: The Church Missionary Society in Ukaguru, Tanzania, East Africa, 1876-1914," in *Comparative Studies in History: An International Quarterly*, Vol. 23, pp. 73-

95. Beidelman's comments on these caravans (pp. 79-82) are most helpful.

7. See E. J. Southon, "Hints for Missionaries Proceeding to Central Africa," a 49-page pamphlet prepared for the London Missionary Society. Southon, an American medical doctor and missionary with that society, gives some indication of the material supplies required to support Western life in Africa (London: Printed for the Directors [of the LMS] by Yates & Alexander, 1880).

8. See Francis Galton, *The Art of Travel; or, Shifts and Contrivances Available in Wild Countries* (London: John Murray, 1855).

9. In Volume IV of his *History of the Expansion of Christianity: The Great Century, A.D. 1800-1914: Europe and the United States of America* (London: Eyre and Spottiswoode, 1941), pp. 9-21, Kenneth Scott Latourette lists thirteen distinguishing characteristics of the nineteenth century, each influencing to some degree missionary perceptions of the world, of themselves, and of the Christian gospel.

10. William Samuel Lilly, *Christianity and Modern Civilization. Being Some Chapters in European History with an Introductory Dialogue on the Philosophy of History* (London: Chapman & Hill, 1903), p. 25. See also Neil Arnott, *A Survey of Human Progress, from the Savage State to the Highest Civilization yet Attained. A Progress as Little Perceived by the Multitude in any Age, as is the Slow Growing of a Tree by the Children who Play under its Shade—but which is Leading to a New Condition of Mankind on Earth* (London: Longman, Green, Longman, and Roberts, 1861).

11. This quotation is taken from one of the most thorough and masterful studies of its kind, Robert Nisbet's *History of the Idea of Progress* (New York: Basic Books, 1980), pp. 4, 7.

12. Griffith John, *London Missionary Society Annual Report*, 1897, p. 47. The writer was by then a veteran of more than thirty years as a missionary in China.

13. James S. Dennis, *Christian Missions and Social Progress: A Sociological Study of Foreign Missions*. 3 Volumes. (Edinburgh: Oliphant, Anderson and Ferrier, 1898), p. ix. Similar studies include W. Douglas Mackenzie's *Christianity and the Progress of Man as Illustrated by Modern Missions* (Edinburgh: Oliphant, Anderson and Ferrier, 1898); James Johnston's *A Century of Christian Progress and its Lessons* (London: James Nisbet & Co., 1888); and the book by James L. Barton, *Human Progress through Missions* (New York: Fleming H. Revell Co., 1912).

14. W. Winwood Reade, *The Martyrdom of Man* (London: Kegan Paul, Trench, 1909 [1872]), pp. 504, 502.

15. Robert Nisbet, *History of the Idea of Progress*, p. 308. See also the chapter "The Doctrine of Civilization," pp. 154-200 in *Doctrines of Imperialism*, by A. P. Thornton (New York: John Wiley & Sons, 1965).

16. J. Logan Aikman, *Cyclopaedia of Christian Missions: Their Rise, Progress, and Present Position* (London: Richard Griffin and Co., 1860), p. iv. See also Richard Whately, "On the Origin of Civilization. A Lecture by His Grace the Archbishop of Dublin. To the Young Men's Christian Association" (London: December, 1854).

17. Joseph P. Thompson, "Christian Missions Necessary to a True Civilization," *Bibliotheca Sacra*, Vol. 14, No. 56 (October, 1857), p. 847.

18. Among those who have bravely raised questions about the legitimacy of Western notions of "development," Bob Goudzwaard, author of *Aid for the Overdeveloped West* (Toronto: Wedge Publishing Foundation, 1975), and Ivan Illich, author of *The Church, Change and Development* (Chicago: Urban Training Center Press, 1970), need to be heard. See also the writings of Andrew Greeley, E. F. Schumacher, and Pascal Bruckner.

19. See my article, " 'All Things to All Persons'—The Missionary as a Racist-Imperialist, 1860-1910," *Missiology: An International Review*, Vol. 8, No. 3 (July, 1980), pp. 285-306.

20. R. Wardlaw Thompson, "Self Support and Self Government in the Native Church as Affected by Considerations of Race, Previous Religion, and Present Social Conditions," in *Centenary of the London Missionary Society. Proceedings of the Founders' Week Convention, at the City Temple, Holborn Viaduct, London, E.C., September 21st to 27th, 1895. Papers and Speeches in Full* (London: LMS, 1895), pp. 349-350.

21. David Livingstone, *Missionary Travels and Researches in South Africa; Including a Sketch of Sixteen Years Residence in the Interior of Africa, and a Journey from the Cape of Good Hope to Loands on the West Coast; thence across the Continent, down the River Zambesi, to the Eastern Ocean* (London: J. Murray, 1857), p. 679. See also Andrew F. Walls, "The Legacy of David Livingstone," *International Bulletin of Missionary Research*, Vol. 11, No. 3 (July 1987), pp. 125-129.

22. George Orwell, "Notes on Nationalism," in *England Your England and Other Essays* (London: Secker & Warburg, 1953), p. 52.

23. Allan MacDonald, *Trade, Politics and Christianity in Africa and the East* (London: Longmans, Green and Co., 1916), pp. 55-56.

24. Harry H. Johnston, *A History of the Colonization of Africa by Alien Races* (Cambridge: Cambridge University Press, 1899), p. 151.

25. Johannes Warneck, *The Living Forces of the Gospel: Experiences of a Missionary in Animistic Heathendom*. Authorized translation from the German by Neil Buchanan (London: Oliphant, Anderson and Ferrier, 1909), pp. 171, 174. See also "the opinion of an educated African youth" under the title, "Are African Native Races Profited by Foreign Rule?" in *The Illustrated Missionary News*, Vol. 22 (July, 1888), p. 111.

26. These words were spoken by Fred A. O'Meara, Chaplain to the Red Indians on Lake Huron, and Superintendent of Indian Missions for the Church of England there. See *Conference on Missions Held in 1860 in Liverpool: The Papers Read, the Conclusions Reached, and a Comprehensive Index, Showing the Various Matters Brought under Review* (London: James Nisbet & Co., 1860), pp. 212-213.

27. W. Garett Horder, "Prophecy of a Positivist," *Chronicle of the London Missionary Society*, Vol. 59 (November, 1886), pp. 455-456.

28. J. F. T. Hallowes, "Our World-Wide Empire," *Chronicle of the London Missionary Society*, Vol. 59 (October, 1894), p. 225. See also his earlier article, "The Expansion of England in Relation to the Propagation of the Gospel," in Vol. 51 of the *Chronicle of the London Missionary Society* (May, 1886), pp. 197-200.

29. T. W. Pearce, "Western Civilisation in Relation to Protestant Mission Work," *Chronicle of the London Missionary Society*, Vol. 55 (August, 1890), p. 239. The point of view expressed by Pearce was a common one. See, for example, Benjamin R. Cowen, *The Miracle of the Nineteenth Century. Do Missions Pay?* (Cincinnati: Cranston and Sons, 1891); Ray Palmer, *The Highest Civilization a Result of Christianity and Christian Learning*. A Discourse Delivered at Norwich, Conn., Nov. 14, 1865, on behalf of The Society for Promoting Collegiate and Theological Education at the West, in Connection with the Annual Meeting of the Board of Directors (Albany: J. Munsell, 1866); or John Cumming, "God in History," in *Lectures Delivered Before the Young Men's Christian Association 1848-1849*, Vol. IV (London: James Nisbet and Co., 1876), pp. 35-78.

30. Horder, "Imperialism and Missions," op. cit., p. 81.

31. "Britain's Mission," *Centenary Missionary Hymnal*, compiled and edited by Stanley Rogers (London: London Missionary Society, 1895), p. 75.

32. Alexander Robb, *The Heathen World and the Duty of the Church* (Edinburgh: Andrew Elliott, 1863), p. 1.

33. Johannes Warneck, *Living Forces of the Gospel . . .*, op. cit., pp. 81-134, passim.

34. James S. Dennis, "The Social Influence of Christianity as Illustrated by Foreign Missions," in *Christ and Civilization: A Survey of the Influence of the Christian Religion upon the Course of Civilization*, edited by John Brown Paton, Percy William Bunting, and Alfred Ernest Garvie (London: National Council of Evangelical Free Churches, 1910), pp. 487-488.

35. Alexander Robb, *The Heathen World and the Duty of the Church*, p. 74.

36. William Pakenham Walsh, *Christian Missions: Six Discourses Delivered before the University of Dublin; being the Donnellan Lectures for 1861* (Dublin: George Herbert, 1862).

37. For a glimpse of life in Calabar during this time, see the excellent biography by James Buchan, *The Expendable Mary Slessor* (Edinburgh: The Saint Andrew Press, 1980).

38. Allan J. M. MacDonald, *Trade, Politics and Christianity in Africa and the East* (London: Longmans, Green & Co., 1916), pp. vii-xix. See also Harry H. Johnston, *A History of the Colonization of Africa by Alien Races* (Cambridge: Cambridge University Press, 1899), p. 146.

39. See, for example, Thomas Laurie, *The Ely Volume; or, The Contributions of our Foreign Missions to Science and Human Well Being* (Boston: ABCFM, 1881); William Warren, *These for Those: Our Indebtedness to Foreign Missions; or, What We Get for What We Give* (Portland: Hoyt, Fogg and Breed, 1870); John Liggins, *The Great Value and Success of Foreign Missions. Proved by Distinguished Witnesses; Being the Testimony of Diplomatic Ministers, Consuls, Naval Officers, and Scientific and other Travellers in Heathen and Mohammedan Countries; Together With that of English Viceroys, Governors, and Military Officers in India and in the British Colonies; also Leading Facts and Late Statistics of the Missions* (London: James Nisbet & Co., 1889); Robert Young, *The Success of Christian Missions: Testimonies to their Beneficent Results* (London: Hodder & Stoughton, 1890); etc.

40. See the book by Walter Nicgorski and Ronald Weber, editors, *An Almost Chosen People: The Moral Aspirations of Americans* (Notre Dame: The University of Notre Dame Press, 1976).

41. Robert Jewett, *The Captain America Complex: The Dilemma of Zealous Nationalism* (Philadelphia: The Westminster Press, 1973).

42. See Robert T. Coote's interpretive essay, "Taking Aim on 2000 AD," pp. 35-80 of *Mission Handbook: North American Protestant Ministries Overseas*, 13th Edition (Monrovia: Missions Advanced Research and Communication Center, 1986), pp. 57, 79-80. My calculations here and below are based on his figures.

43. See Coote, ibid.

44. See David E. Shi, *The Simple Life: Plain Living and High Thinking in American Culture* (New York: Oxford University Press, 1985), p. 248. Chapter ten, "Affluence and Anxiety" is worth reading in this context.

45. Robert N. Bellah, Richard Madsen, William M. Sullivan, Ann Swidler, and

Steven M. Tipton, *Habits of the Heart: Individualism and Commitment in American Life* (Berkeley: University of California Press, 1985).

46. Jules Henry, *Culture Against Man* (New York: Random House, 1963), p. 19. For a lucid description of the mechanics of this process, see John Kenneth Galbraith, *The Affluent Society*. Third Edition, Revised (New York: New American Library, 1976), Chapter 11.

47. Dorothy Sayers, *Letters to a Post-Christian World; a Selection of Essays*. Selected and introduced by Roderick Jellema (Grand Rapids: Wm. B. Eerdmans Publishing Co., 1969), p. 145.

48. Galbraith, *The Affluent Society*, p. 124-128.

3. THE RATIONALE FOR MISSIONARY AFFLUENCE

1. See Sydney Smith, "Critique," *Edinburgh Review* (January 1808).

2. "Critique," *Edinburgh Review* (April 1809), pp. 40, 42.

3. Isaac Taylor, "The Great Missionary Failure," and "Missionary Finance," in *The Fortnightly Review*, Vol. XLIV, New Series (July-December 1888), pp. 488-500 & 581-592, respectively.

4. See, for example, Ado K. Tiberondwa, *Missionary Teachers as Agents of Colonialism: A Study of their Activities in Uganda* (Lusaka: National Educational Company of Zambia, 1978); Soren Hvalkof and Peter Aaby, eds., *Is God An American? An Anthropological Perspective on the Missionary Work of the Summer Institute of Linguistics* (Published jointly by International Work Group for Indigenous Affairs in Copenhagen, Denmark, and Survival International in London, 1981); David Stoll, *Fishers of Men or Founders of Empire? The Wycliffe Bible Translators in Latin America* (London: Zed Press, 1982); or K. P. Yohannan's *The Coming Revolution in World Missions* (Altamonte Springs, Florida: Creation House, 1986).

5. J. L. Barton, *The Missionary and His Critics* (New York: Fleming H. Revell Co., 1906), p. 164.

6. Meredith Townsend, "Cheap Missionaries," *The Contemporary Review*, Vol. LVI (July, 1889), p. 1.

7. F. F. Ellinwood, "Asceticism in Missions," *The Chinese Recorder and Missionary Journal*, Vol. XXII, No. 1 (January, 1891), p. 1.

8. The meeting took place near Steinbach, Manitoba. Other details shall remain anonymous.

9. Griffith John, *A Voice from China* (London: Religious Tract Society, 1907), pp. 214-215.

10. C. C. Thayer, "Missionary Health Economics," *Missionary Review of the World*, Vol. 26 (February, 1903), p. 128.

11. A. T. Pierson, "The Needless Sacrifice of Human Life in Mission Work," *The Missionary Review of the World*, Vol. XXVII, No. 2 (Old Series), (February, 1904), p. 81.

12. George Adam Smith, *The Life of Henry Drummond* (New York: Doubleday & McClure, 1898), pp. 209-211. See Henry Drummond, *Tropical Africa*, 3rd ed. (London: Hodder & Stoughton, 1889), especially pp. 15-16, 22-23, 41-45.

13. See William G. Lennox, *The Health and Turnover of Missionaries* (New York: The Foreign Missions Conference, Advisory Committee, 1933). The denominations studied included the Presbyterian Church in the United States of America, the Congregational, Methodist, and Episcopal Churches, the Northern Baptist Con-

vention, and the Young Women's Christian Association. This valuable study followed his earlier studies, *The Health of Missionary Families in China: A Statistical Study* (Denver: University of Denver, 1921), and *A Comparative Study of the Health of Missionary Families in Japan and China and a Selected Group in America* (Denver: University of Denver, 1922).

14. Lennox, *The Health and Turnover of Missionaries*, p. 120. See also the Frontispiece (Figure 40) of the book, and his entire chapter, "Death Rates," pp. 113-127.

15. Lennox, p. 120.

16. Lennox, p. 118.

17. Lennox, pp. 78-79. In his chapter, "Reasons for Withdrawal" (pp. 77-112), Lennox demonstrates that most of the deaths and illnesses could have been prevented.

18. See Lennox's chapter, "The Years of Service," pp. 54-76.

19. J. L. Barton, *The Missionary and His Critics*, pp. 162-163. See also the chapter in Lennox, "Opportunities for Saving," pp. 181-199.

20. A letter from Southon to Thompson, Urambo, July 12, 1881, see my dissertation, " 'All Things to All Men'? Protestant Missionary Identification in Theory and Practice, 1860-1910, with Special Reference to the London Missionary Society in Central Africa and Central China" (University of Aberdeen, Scotland, 1984), (hereafter referred to as "All Things to All Men"), p. 67. See also Daniel Johnson Fleming, *Living as Comrades: A Study of Factors Making for "Community"* (New York: Published for the Foreign Missions Conference of North America by Agricultural Missions, Inc., 1950), pp. 23-24.

21. Mrs. Gratan Guinness, *The New World of Central Africa, With A History of the First Christian Mission on the Congo* (London: Hodder & Stoughton, 1890), p. 518. Mrs. Guinness was quoting one of Stanley's "Fourteen Rules for Life in Africa."

22. See, for example, the actuarial tables used by the Presbyterian Ministers' Fund Insurance Company.

23. *Statistical Abstract of the United States, 1981*, (U.S. Census Bureau, Washington, D.C.: Government Printing Office, 1981), p. 423.

24. A comparison of mission finances during the same period of time indicates that mission finances have more than kept pace with inflation. Compare the figures appearing in the *Occasional Bulletin of Missionary Research*, Vol. IX (Dec. 8, 1958), with those in the *Mission Handbook: North American Protestant Ministries Overseas.* 12th Edition. Edited by Samuel Wilson. (Monrovia: Missions Advanced Research and Communication Center, 1979), passim.

25. J. L. Barton, *The Missionary and His Critics*, pp. 163-164.

26. A. T. Pierson, "The Needless Sacrifice of Human Life in Missionary Work," p. 84. There have always been Western missionaries who have not heeded this advice, and these have suffered—if not ill health—the censure of their missionary peers. See Andrew Porter, "Evangelical Enthusiasm, Missionary Motivation and West Africa in the Late Nineteenth Century: The Career of G. W. Brooke," in *The Journal of Imperial and Commonwealth History*, Vol. VI, No. 1 (October, 1977), pp. 23-46. From Hudson Taylor and James Gilmour in the nineteenth century, to Bruce Olson and Viv Grigg in the twentieth, missionaries who eschew Solomon's advice have been regarded with suspicion by their Western peers.

27. "Remarks on the Provision that Should be Made for the Children of Mis-

sionaries" (New York: Anson D. F. Randolph, 1855), p. 5.

28. "Remarks," p. 15.

29. Mrs. A. M. Edmond, *Memoir of Mrs. Sarah D. Comstock, Missionary to Arracan* (Philadelphia: American Baptist Publication Society, [1854], pp. 184-186, quoted in "Remarks on the Provision that should be made for the Children of Missionaries," pp. 13-14. Groves S. Comstock and his wife began service in British held Arracan [Arakan] in 1835. Both soon died of cholera: she in 1843, and he in 1845. See Maung She Wa, G. Edwards and E. Edwards, *Burma Baptist Chronicle* (Rangoon, 1963), pp. 106-110.

30. The number and range of educational institutions at the service of missionary children around the world may be seen in *The ISS Directory of Overseas Schools* (Princeton: International Schools Services, 1988). The *Overseas Schools Profile* (Whittier, CA: Association of Christian Schools International, 1986) provides vital information—including history, curriculum, organization, faculty, enrollment, facilities, and finances—on more than 125 schools for the children of missionaries in 56 countries.

31. The books, service agencies, and conferences devoted to the subject of missionary children make this evident. See C. John Buffam, *The Life and Times of an MK* (South Pasadena: William Carey Library, 1986); Betty Jo Kenney, *The Missionary Family* (South Pasadena: William Carey Library, 1983); Edward E. Danielson, *Missionary Kid—MK* (South Pasadena: William Carey Library, 1984). Among the several associations devoted primarily to the concerns of missionary children and parents, Association of Christian Schools International (ACSI, 28-L Northwood Lake, Northport, AL 35476) is well known, as is INTERFACES (International Family and Children's Educational Services, Box 11233, Richmond, VA 23230). Less well known is the recently established MU KAPPA International (7500 West Camp Wisdom Road, Dallas, TX 75236), described in their brochure as "a fraternal association for MKs." The International Conference on Missionary Kids has convened in Manila (November, 1984) and in Quito (January, 1987). A third ICMK conference is being planned for Nairobi in 1990. The compendiums are available from Missionary Internship, Box 457, Farmington, MI 48024.

32. Meredith Townsend, "Cheap Missionaries," *The Contemporary Review*, Vol. LVI (July 1889), p. 5.

33. See Daniel Johnson Fleming, *Living as Comrades* p. 24; F. F. Ellinwood, "Asceticism in Missions," p. 5; J. L. Barton, *The Missionary and His Critics*, pp. 164 & 169; Betty Jo Kenney, *The Missionary Family*. See also Marjorie A. Collins, *Manual for Today's Missionary: From Recruitment to Retirement* (South Pasadena: William Carey Library, 1986), chapters 22 & 30.

34. E. J. Southon, "Hints for Missionaries Proceeding to Central Africa" (London: Printed for the Directors of the London Missionary Society by Yates & Alexander, 1880), p. 2.

35. For a creative explication of missionary roles, see the articles by husband and wife team Jacob A. and Anne Loewen, "Role, Self-Image and Missionary Communication," and "The 'Missionary' Role," in *Culture and Human Values: Christian Intervention in Anthropological Perspective: Selections from the Writings of Jacob A. Loewen* (South Pasadena: William Carey Library, 1975), pp. 412-427, and 428-443, respectively. Also stimulating and insightful in this regard are William D. Reyburn's articles on "missionary identification," helpfully reprinted on pp. 746-791 of *Readings in Missionary Anthropology II*, enlarged 1978 edition, edited by

William A. Smalley (South Pasadena: William Carey Library, 1978).

36. Thomas O. Beidelman, "Contradictions between the Sacred and the Secular Life: The Church Missionary Society in Ukaguru, Tanzania, East Africa, 1876-1914," in *Comparative Studies in Society and History: An International Quarterly*, Vol. 23 (1981), pp. 73-95, but especially p. 89.

37. Eugene Nida, *Message and Mission: The Communication of the Christian Faith* (New York: Harper & Row, 1960), pp. 164-165.

38. Letter of Moore to Bonk, December 11, 1985, Peru.

39. Kenneth Scott Latourette, *The Unquenchable Light* (London: Eyre and Spottiswoode, 1940), p. 83.

40. See *Yearbook of American & Canadian Churches, 1987*. Annual. Fifty-fifth Issue. Edited by Constant H. Jacquet, Jr. (Nashville: Abingdon Press, 1987), especially the section entitled "Church Financial Statistics and Related Data, United States and Canada." Jacquet's figures indicate that per member per annum giving to benevolences—of which foreign missions is a small part—was $56.74 for U.S. churches, and $45.62 for Canadian churches. See also David B. Barrett's article, "Silver and Gold Have I None: Church of the Poor or Church of the Rich?" in *International Bulletin of Missionary Research*, Vol. 7, No. 4 (October 1983), pp. 146-151.

41. See the 13th edition, *Mission Handbook: North American Ministries Overseas* (Monrovia: Missions Advanced Research and Communication Center, 1986), p. 611.

42. Ibid., p. 11.

43. Ibid., p. 618. These are the general ministry categories reported by the 764 agencies represented in the 13th edition.

44. While it is popular to believe that the Western missionary enterprise has been sustained largely by the "widow's mites" of numerous ordinary donors, the financial support of most agencies relies heavily upon the generosity of rich individuals who, by means of purpose established foundations, trusts, and endowments, have often singlehandedly made possible many of the capital intensive strategies and programs of Western missions. Outstanding among these largely anonymous donors in the nineteenth century were men such as jam manufacturer William Hartley, treasurer of the Primitive Methodist Missionary Society; chemical manufacturers James and John Campbell White, who provided most of the finance necessary for the Free Church of Scotland's Livingstonia Mission; or Robert Arthington, the millionaire largely responsible for both the timing and the strategy used by the several societies instrumental in the missionary occupation of Central Africa. See Brian Stanley, " 'The Miser of Headingly': Robert Arthington and the Baptist Missionary Society, 1877-1900," in *The Church and Wealth: Papers Read at the 1986 Summer Meeting and the 1987 Winter Meeting of the Ecclesiastical History Society*, edited by W. J. Sheils and Diana Wood (Oxford: Published for The Ecclesiastical History Society by Basil Blackwell, 1987), pp. 371-382. See also A. M. Chirgwin, *Arthington's Million: The Romance of the Arthington Trust* (London: The Livingstone Press, 1935). The pattern continues, although now as then donors remain largely anonymous as far as the general public is concerned. R. G. Letournou in the U.S., and the Reimer family of Reimer Express in Canada, are well known for the literally millions of dollars given to further the establishing of Christian missions around the world. Few indeed are the mission societies without similar, if more modest, benefactors.

45. C. C. Thayer, "Missionary Economics: Personal Efficiency," *Missionary Review of the World*, Vol. 26 (July, 1903), p. 517.

46. Fleming was, at the time, Professor of Missions at Union Theological Seminary in New York, himself a former missionary to India. See his *Ventures in Simpler Living* (New York: The International Missionary Council, 1933). McGavran did his Ph.D. at Union Seminary and Columbia University under Fleming.

47. Letter of McGavran to Bonk, January 26, 1988, Pasadena.

48. Tony Malik, converted in 1975, now a missionary with Venture Teams International. These remarks were made in the context of his lecture on "Hinduism," delivered before the students of Winnipeg Bible College and Theological Seminary on October 17, 1985.

49. Letter of Thompson to Mullens, October 1, 1887, Mabisi, as cited in Bonk, "All Things to All Men," p. 66.

50. Letter of Jones to Thompson, November 14, 1887, Fwambo, as cited in Bonk, "All Things to All Men," p. 66.

51. Instructions to Dr. E. and Mrs. Baxter, July 31, 1888, cited by Thomas Beidelman in his article, "Contradictions between the Sacred and the Secular Life: The Church Missionary Society in Ukaguru, Tanzania, East Africa, 1876-1914," *Comparative Studies in Society and History*, Vol. 23, No. 1 (January 1981), p. 85.

52. Letter of Moore to Bonk, December 11, 1985, Peru.

II. CONSEQUENCES OF WESTERN MISSIONARY AFFLUENCE

1. "Efficiency" in the Western mind is most frequently associated with speed and comfort. Slow is frustrating; fast is good; faster is better. Discomfort is to be avoided at any cost; comfort is good; more comfort is better. Missionary use of technology increases the speed and the ease with which Western missionaries carry out their tasks. Technology is expensive, and inaccessible to all but the rich. But speed and ease are thought to justify all. This is well understood by North American church members, whose generosity in funding projects or machines that contribute to "efficiency" is well known.

4. RELATIONAL COSTS OF MISSIONARY AFFLUENCE

1. "Relational" is used in a strictly non-technical, inclusive sense to refer to both social and psychological aspects of missionary cross-cultural relationships.

2. See "Table 16.3 Health Indicators, 1964-90," World Resources 1987: A Report by The International Institute for Environment and Development and The World Resource Institute (New York: Basic Books, 1987), pp. 252-253. Missionary longevity makes them a good risk for insurance companies, a number of which offer life insurance policies to missionaries at preferred rates.

3. *Collins English Dictionary of the English Language* (London & Glasgow: William Collins Sons, 1979).

4. Juan Antonio Monroy, "Why do Protestant Missionaries Fail in Spain?" *Milligan Missiogram* Vol. VI, No. 3 (Spring, 1979), pp. 5, 18. See also the pamphlet by Mavumilusa Makanzu, "The Twentieth Century Missionaries and the Murmurs of the Africans," *Apophoreta of African Church History* - 3 (Aberdeen: Department of Religious Studies, University of Aberdeen, Scotland, in association with the Scottish Institute of Missionary Studies, 1974).

5. de Tocqueville was a French nobleman who is today best known for his book *Democracy in America*, containing descriptions and observations made in the course of less than one year of travel in the United States in 1831-1832. The book has remained in print ever since, and continues to be cited as an accurate and still useful commentary on the American way of life. Alexis de Tocqueville, *Democracy in America*, 2 vols (New York: D. Appleton and Company, 1901). Since that time, countless others have commented on the American love of independence. See, for example, Jules Henry, *Culture Against Man* (New York: Random House, 1963), and Philip Slater, *The Pursuit of Loneliness: American Culture at the Breaking Point* (Boston: Beacon Press, 1970).

6. Alexis de Tocqueville, *Democracy in America*, Vol. 2 (New York: D. Appleton and Company, 1901), p. 786.

7. Philip Slater, *The Pursuit of Loneliness: American Culture at the Breaking Point* (Boston: Beacon Press, 1970), p. 7.

8. This is why the U.S. Department of Labor publishes the quarterly bulletin *U.S. Department of State Indexes of Living Costs Abroad, Quarters Allowances, and Hardship Differentials*. As the July 1987 edition of this publication explains, "the indexes should not be used to compare living costs of Americans in the United States with the living costs of foreign nationals living in their own country, since the indexes reflect only the expenditure pattern and living costs of Americans" (p. 1). A number of U.S. based mission agencies use the data in this publication as a helpful point of reference when undertaking similar calculations on behalf of their own missionaries.

9. This was the assessment of veteran missionary and author Arden Almquist in his book, *Missionary Come Back!* (New York: The World Publishing Co., 1970), p. 26.

10. Letter of Peters and Nelson to Bonk, November 1, 1987, Nairobi. The observations of youthful visitors are often superficial, it is true. But sadly, this was not the case in this instance. The view that this large enclave of Western missionaries is profoundly isolated was subsequently corroborated by several whose judgment cannot be so lightly dismissed. Two of these are Kenyans — the one an active churchman and chairman of the Religious Studies Department of a large university in Nairobi; the other a missionary-educated official within the Kenyan Department of Education. The third is a well known American professor of missions, who is a regular visiting lecturer at a nearby African Bible School.

11. Robert Coles, *Privileged Ones: The Well-Off and the Rich in America*. Volume V of *Children in Crisis* (Boston: Atlantic Little, Brown Books, 1977), p. 77.

12. J. Herbert Kane, in reflecting on a lifetime of work as a missionary and instructor of missionaries, wrote recently that he regretted his failure as a missionary in China "to cultivate more social contacts. Most of my contacts were related to work." See his article "My Pilgrimage in Mission" in *International Bulletin of Missionary Research*, Vol. 11, No. 3 (July 1987), p. 132.

13. *World Missionary Conference, 1910. To Consider Missionary Problems in Relation to the Non-Christian World* (Edinburgh: Oliphant, Anderson & Ferrier, 1910), Vol. IX, p. 309.

14. Robert Coles, *Privileged Ones*, p. 14.

15. John Kenneth Galbraith, predicting the crash of the stock market. See "The 1929 Parallel," in *The Atlantic Monthly,* Vol. 259, No. 1 (January, 1987), p. 62.

16. Francis Galton, *The Art of Travel; or, Shifts and Contrivances Available in Wild Countries* (London: John Murray, 1855), pp. 60-61.

17. Stuart Watt, a Church Missionary Society (CMS) missionary to East Africa in the late nineteenth century, tied up and flogged several porters caught stealing. One of the porters subsequently died. A. M. Mackay, another much admired Church Missionary Society missionary, shot and wounded several mutinous porters. See Beidelman, "Contradictions between the Sacred and the Secular Life: The Church Missionary Society in Ukaguru, Tanzania, East Africa, 1876-1914," in *Comparative Studies in Society and History: An International Quarterly*, Vol. 23 (1981), pp. 80-82. London Missionary Society missionaries in Central Africa during the same period engaged in similar corporal punishment of their African charges, as I relate in my study, *The Theory and Practice of Missionary Identification*, Volume 2 in the Studies in the History of Missions Series (Lewiston/Lampeter/Queenston: The Edwin Mellen Press, 1989), pp. 110-115. It is only fair to point out that such actions were never approved by official mission policies, and drew sharp reprimands from mission administrators.

18. See my article, "'All Things to All Persons'—The Missionary as a Racist-Imperialist, 1860-1918," in *Missiology: An International Review*, Vol. VIII, No. 3 (July, 1980), pp. 292-293. Henry Drummond, *Tropical Africa* (London: Hodder & Stoughton, 1889).

19. Malcolm Muggeridge, *Chronicles of Wasted Time. Part I. The Green Stick* (London: Collins, 1972), p. 100.

20. The "entitlement" mentality is well depicted by Fyodor Dostoyevsky's description of the miff felt by Kalganov and his rich friends when they visited a monastery: "It was strange that their arrival did not seem expected, and that they were not received with special honour, though one of them had recently made a donation of a thousand roubles, while another was a very wealthy and highly cultured landowner, upon whom all in the monastery were in a sense dependent. . . . Yet no official personage met them" (from Chapter 1 of Book Two, Part One, of *The Brothers Karamazov*, translated by Constance Garnett. New York: Random House, 1950).

21. Stuart Piggin, *Making Evangelical Missionaries 1798-1858: The Social Background, Motives and Training of British Protestant Missionaries to India* (Oxford: The Sutton Courtney Press, 1984), especially pp. 124-155.

22. Henry Knollys, *English Life in China* (London: Smith, Elder & Company, 1885). See also the writings of a long time resident in China, Alexander Michie, especially his *Missionaries in China* (London: Edward Stanford, 1891).

23. Related by Paul Hiebert in his lectures at Overseas Ministries Study Center, Oct. 26-30, 1987. Missionary polygyny was deduced from the presence of single lady missionaries who, if and when a wife died, would take her place as wife of the widower.

24. Shaw to Thompson, March 9, 1885, Urambo, as cited by Bonk, "All Things to All Men," p. 86

25. Jones to Whitehouse, June 24, 1884, Uguha, as cited by Bonk, ibid. p. 86. Missionary correspondence of this period is chequered with similar complaints.

26. Nutt to Thompson, July 25, 1895, Kambole, as cited by Bonk, ibid. p. 87.

27. Draper to Thompson, March 26, 1902, Kawimbe, as cited by Bonk, ibid. p. 88.

28. Griffith John, "North China-Hankow," in *The Chronicle of the London Missionary Society* (July, 1891), p. 166.

29. In my experience, the sort of admission contained in a letter sent to me by a twenty-year veteran missionary from the U.S. to the Philippines is quite rare. Said he: "Betty and I both come from home backgrounds in Canada and the States respectively where we had sufficient to live on, but were far from the affluence seen even in those days in North America. We then joined [the faith mission] and actually felt we had moved up a step financially (even though [our mission] as you know is far from one of the affluent Missions). ... Over the years, we have seen [our mission], including ourselves, move up the economic ladder." See letter of Harrison to Bonk, November 17, 1987, Singapore.

30. *Missionary Service in Asia Today*. A Report on a Consultation Held by the Asia Methodist Advisory Committee, February 18-23, 1971, in cooperation with the Life, Message Unity Committee of the East Asian Christian Conference (Kuala Lumpur: University of Malaya, 1971), p. 132.

31. *Missionary Service in Asia Today*, p. 136.

32. John Kenneth Galbraith, *The Affluent Society*, p. 69.

33. See especially the brilliant study by Helmut Schoeck, *Envy: A Theory of Social Behaviour* (London: Secker & Ward, 1969). Schoeck is Professor of Sociology at the Johannes Gutenberg University, Mainz. His book should be of special interest to missionary theologians, since his sociological model corresponds closely with the Christian doctrine of original sin. For an interesting and open expression of envy, see C. A. Doxiadis, "Three Letters to an American," in *Dædalus: Journal of the American Academy of Arts and Sciences*, Vol. 101, No. 4 (Fall, 1972), pp. 163-183.

34. Marjory Foyle, "Missionary Relationships: Powderkeg or Powerhouse?" *Evangelical Missions Quarterly*, Vol. 21, No. 4 (October, 1985), p. 346.

35. *Missionary Service in Asia Today*, p. 133

36. Edward Hoagland, *African Calliope: A Journey to the Sudan* (Harmondsworth: Penguin Books, 1978), p. 83.

37. Peking Correspondent, "Are You Friend of Foreigner?" *The Economist*, Vol. 295, No. 7395 (May 25, 1985), p. 41.

38. Letter of Peters and Nelson to Bonk, November 1, 1987, Nairobi.

5. COMMUNICATORY AND STRATEGIC CONSEQUENCES OF MISSIONARY AFFLUENCE

1. See, for example, Doris Haley's article, "Ralph and Roberta Winter: A Wartime Lifestyle," in *Family Life Today* (March, 1983), pp. 29-33.

2. A number of the issues dealt with in this chapter are more than simply communications problems. Even more fundamentally, they raise theological and ethical questions which must be addressed by any missionary who would avoid hypocrisy.

3. See Roger William Brown, *Words and Things* (Glencoe: The Free Press, 1958), pp. 321-322.

4. David J. Hesselgrave, *Communicating Christ Cross-Culturally: An Introduction to Missionary Communication* (Grand Rapids: Zondervan, 1978), p. 91.

5. This theme will be more fully elaborated in the concluding chapter. Kosuke Koyama's discussion of the "crucified mind" in his *Waterbuffalo Theology* (Maryknoll, N.Y.: Orbis Books, 1974, pp. 209-224) should be required reading for every North American missiologist and missionary.

6. Canon Isaac Taylor, "The Great Missionary Failure," in *The Fortnightly Review* 44 (July-December, 1888), pp. 496, 499.

7. R. Wardlaw Thompson, *Griffith John: The Story of Fifty Years in China* (London: Religious Tract Society, 1906), p. 414.

8. See Eugene Nida, *Message and Mission* (New York: Harper & Row, 1960), pp. 164-166 especially, for his discussion of the correlation between degrees of identification and levels of communication. The three communication levels outlined below are an adaptation of the four-level model outlined by Nida.

9. Ibid., p. 166.

10. A letter from Jones to Thompson, Uguha, December 2, 1884, see Bonk, "All Things to All Men," p. 75. See also Daniel Johnson Fleming, *Living As Comrades: A Study of Factors Making for "Community"* (New York: Published for the Foreign Missions Conference of North America by Agricultural Missions, Inc., 1950), pp. 23-24.

11. The word *mimeomai* (imitate, follow) is found four times in the New Testament (2 Thes. 3:7, 9; Heb. 13:7; 3 John 11); *mimetes* (Imitator) six times (1 Cor. 4:16; 11:1; Eph. 5:1; 1 Thes. 1:6; 2:14; Heb. 6:12); and *symmimetes* (Fellow imitator) once (Phil. 3:17). In each instance, ethical imperatives associated with a specific kind of Christian conduct are involved. While Christian imitation must ultimately be of Christ, in the New Testament the words are usually applied to actual persons who are obvious living examples of Christlike living. See W. Bauder's article in Vol. I of *Dictionary of New Testament Theology*, edited by Colin Brown, pp. 490-492.

12. A letter from C. Murray Rogers to Dr. Taylor-Jones, in *Missionary Service in Asia Today*. A Report on a Consultation Held by the Asia Methodist Advisory Committee February 18-23, 1971, in cooperation with the Life, Message, Unity Committee of the East Asian Christian Conference. (Kuala Lumpur: University of Malaysia, 1971), p. 126.

13. Ibid., pp. 126-127.

14. Roy Larson, Kinshasa, Zaire, to Trinity Evangelical Free Church, Woodbridge, Connecticut, December, 1987.

15. Thompson to Jones, July 17, 1885, as cited by Bonk, "All Things to All Men," pp. 85-86.

16. David Potter, *People of Plenty: Economic Abundance and the American Character* (Chicago: University of Chicago Press, 1954), pp. 128-141. See also Gail Kennedy, ed., *Democracy and the Gospel of Wealth* (Boston: D.C. Heath and Company, 1949).

17. Erin Kelly, "Mac in the USSR," in *The New Journal*, Vol. 20, No. 2 (October 16, 1987), pp. 6-7.

18. Shaw to Thompson, March 9, 1885, Urambo, as cited by Bonk, "All Things to All Men," p. 86.

19. Jones to Whitehouse, June 24, 1884, Uguha, as cited by Bonk, ibid.

20. Draper to Thompson, March 26, 1902, Kawimbe, as cited by Bonk, ibid., p. 88. Such complaints abound in missionary correspondence of the time.

21. Griffith John, "North China — Hankow," in *The Chronicle of the London Missionary Society* 46 (July 1881), p. 166. See Bonk, ibid., pp. 315-321 for a brief examination of missionary perceptions on non-Western peoples.

22. See George M. Foster, *Traditional Societies and Technological Change* (Second Edition. New York: Harper & Row, 1973). According to Foster, among the most potent universal stimulants to change are (1) the desire for economic gain,

and (2) the desire for prestige. Western missionaries have often been frustrated by native conversions motivated not so much by religious appeal as by a sincere desire to improve economically and socially. Such converts, referred to in missionary literature as "rice Christians," frequently become disillusioned with Christianity's failure to deliver the benefits implicitly implied by the missionaries' lifestyles. "Rice missionaries" produce "rice converts"! The role played by missionary affluence in the generation of modern cargo cults needs to be studied. The fact that cargo cults are essentially concerned with material rewards suggests that there might be a positive link between them and Western missionary activities.

23. See Elmer S. Miller, "The Christian Missionary: Agent of Secularization," in *Missiology: An International Review*, Vol. 1, No. 1 (January 1973), pp. 99-107. See also Arthur H. Cole, "The Relations of Missionary Activity to Economic Development," in *Economic Development and Cultural Change*, Vol. 9, No. 2 (January 1961), pp. 120-127; and Kenneth Scott Latourette, "Christian Missions as Mediators of Western Civilization," pp. 83-95 in *Christian Missions in China: Evangelists of What?*, edited by Jessie G. Lutz (Boston: D. C. Heath and Company, 1965).

24. Jacob Loewen, *Culture and Human Values: Christian Intervention in Anthropological Perspective* (South Pasadena: William Carey Library, 1975), pp. xi-xii.

25. Alexis de Tocqueville, *Democracy in America*. The Henry Reeve text as revised by Francis Bowen now further corrected and edited with introduction, editorial notes, and bibliographies by Phillips Bradley. 2 Volumes (New York: Alfred A. Knopf, 1956), Vol. I, p. 51.

26. Frances Trollope, *Domestic Manners of the Americans*. Edited, with a history of Mrs. Trollope's adventures in America, by Donald Smalley. (New York: Alfred A. Knopf, 1949), p. 301. See also Charles Dickens' book, *Dombey and Son*. More recent studies on the theme of the American preoccupation with mammon are so numerous as to make specific mention of any particular one of them unnecessary.

27. A general appeal sent out on July 31 by Missionary Aviation Fellowship (MAF), Canada, in the wake of the May 25th crash, with tragic loss of life, of a Twin Otter in Irian Jaya.

28. Letter of Hardy to Bonk, Fall, 1987, Mozambique.

29. See Jacques Ellul's book, *The Technological Society*, for a sociological and theological analysis of this phenomenon. More recent is the perceptive study by Louise Bernikow, *Alone in America: The Search for Companionship* (New York: Harper & Row, 1986).

30. See the article by David DeVoss, "The New Breed of Missionary," in *Los Angeles Times Magazine* (January 25, 1987).

31. From a letter of Jones to Whitehouse, June 24, 1884, Uguha, cited by Bonk, "All Things to All Men," p. 85.

32. Kosuke Koyama, *Fifty Meditations* (Maryknoll, N.Y.: Orbis Books, 1975), p. 149. See also his book *Three Mile an Hour God: Biblical Reflections* (Maryknoll, N.Y.: Orbis Books, 1980), especially the first chapter.

33. David B. Barrett, "Annual Statistical Table on Global Mission: 1987," in *International Bulletin of Missionary Research* Vol. 12, No. 1 (January, 1988).

34. Lawrence Keyes, "Third World Missionaries: More and Better," in *Evangelical Missions Quarterly*, Vol. 18, No. 4 (October 1982), pp. 216-224. See also James Wong, ed., with Peter Larson and Edward Pentecost, *Mission from the Third World* (Singapore: Church Growth Study Center, 1972); and Marlin Nelson, *The How and Why of Third World Missions* (South Pasadena: William Carey Library, 1976).

35. Bernard E. Quick, "He Who Pays the Piper . . . A Study of Economic Power and Mission in a Revolutionary World," unpublished Manuscript (Princeton Theological Seminary, n.d., p. 56.

36. As quoted by David J. Bosch, "The Missionary: Exemplar or Victim?" in *Theologia Evangelica*, Vol. XVII, No. 1 (March, 1984), p. 11.

37. Mohandas K. Gandhi, *The Mahatma and the Missionary: Selected Writings of Mohandas K. Gandhi*. Edited by Clifford Manshardt (Chicago: Henry Regnery Company, 1949), p. 125. The quotation is taken from an article appearing in *Harijan* (December 12, 1936).

38. Arthur Judson Brown, "A Serious Problem in Missions: Salaries and the Increased Cost of Living in Asia," in *The Missionary Review of the World* 27 (June 1904), pp. 408-413.

39. See, for example, J. Merle Davis, *The Economic and Social Environment of the Younger Churches: The Report of the Department of Social and Economic Research of the International Missionary Council to the Tambaram Meeting—December 1938* (London: The Edinburgh House, 1939). A partial list of the economic research studies undertaken by the commission is found in the appendix to this volume, pp. 225-227. See also his *Mission Finance and the Younger Churches: A Study for the Tambaram Meeting of the International Missionary Council* (Bangalore: Scripture Literature Press, 1938), and the volume edited by him, *The Economic Basis of the Church: Preparatory Studies and Findings, Meeting of the International Missionary Council, at Tambaram, Madras, India December 12th to 29th, 1938*, Volume V of "The Madras Series" (New York: International Missionary Council, 1939).

40. Frederick Dale Bruner, "The American Missionary Problem: An Essay in Conscience," *The Christian Century*, Vol. LXXXV, No. 23 (June 5, 1968), pp. 751-753.

41. For the official report of the Green Lake Conference, see *Missions in Creative Tension*, edited by Vergil Gerber (South Pasadena: William Carey Library, 1971).

42. See Harvie M. Conn's assessment of this conference in his article, "The Money Barrier Between Sending and Receiving Churches," in *The Evangelical Missions Quarterly*, Vol. 14, No. 4 (October, 1978), pp. 231-239.

43. Viv Grigg, "The Urban Poor: Prime Missionary Target," in *Evangelical Review of Theology*, Vol. 11, No. 3 (July, 1987), p. 261. For a description of his work in Manila, see his book, *Companion to the Poor* (Sutherland, NSW, Australia: Albatross Books, 1984). The Roman Catholic church—with its Biblical stress upon the necessity of Apostolic sharing in the sufferings of Christ, and with its force of missionaries who have taken personal vows of poverty—has not been quite so remiss as has the Protestant. Mother Teresa's "Sisters of Charity" is but an outstanding example of the outworking of a genre of Biblical teaching persistently ignored by Protestants.

44. C. G. Baeta, then President of the International Missionary Council, as quoted by D. T. Niles in his book, *Upon the Earth: The Mission of God and the Missionary Enterprise of the Churches* (New York: McGraw-Hill Book Co., 1962), p. 194.

45. A. F. Walls, "The Voice of One Crying in the Supermarket: the West as the Prime Field for Christian Mission." Unpublished paper received in the Fall of 1984 from A. F. Walls, Director of the Scottish Institute of Missionary Studies, now at New College, the University of Edinburgh, Scotland.

6. THEOLOGICAL, ETHICAL, AND BIBLICAL CONSIDERATIONS ON MISSIONARY AFFLUENCE

1. Philip Slater, *The Pursuit of Loneliness*, p. 1.

2. A letter from Thompson to Hemans, December 24, 1898, as cited by Bonk, "All Things to All Men," p. 84.

3. Lewis Mumford, *The Transformations of Man*, cited by David E. Shi, *The Simple Life: Plain Living and High Thinking in American Culture* (New York: Oxford University Press, 1985), p. 250.

4. The results of a survey of 390 missionaries working in 32 countries and representing 37 different mission societies indicated that 60 percent pray between 11 and 30 minutes daily, while 11 percent pray an average of less than five minutes a day. See Phil Parshall's article, "How Spiritual are Missionaries?" in *Evangelical Missions Quarterly*, Vol. 23, No. 1 (January 1987), p. 10.

5. Jacob Loewen, "Missions and the Problems of Cultural Background," in *The Church In Mission: A Sixtieth Anniversary Tribute to J. B. Toews*, edited by A. J. Klassen (Fresno, California: Board of Christian Literature, Mennonite Brethren Church, 1967), pp. 290-292.

6. The chapter, "The Question of Finance" in Watchman Nee's book, *Concerning our Missions* (Shanghai: The Gospel Book Room, 1939), pp. 192-222 should be read by every missionary, mission executive, and missiologist.

7. Lausanne Committee for World Evangelization, Occasional Paper No. 2, *The Willowbank Report.* Report of a Consultation on Gospel and Culture held at Willowbank, Somerset Bridge, Bermuda, from 6th to 13th January 1978. Sponsored by the Lausanne Theology and Education Group (Wheaton: Lausanne Committee for World Evangelization, 1978), pp. 17-18.

8. Trevor D. Verryn, "Outside the Camp: A Study of Religious Authority and Conversion" (Unpublished D. Th. thesis, University of South Africa, as cited by David Bosch in his article, "The Missionary: Exemplar or Victim?" in *Theologia Evangelica*, Vol. XVII, No. 1 (March 1984), p. 14.

9. Mark 15:31. See Kosuke Koyama's chapter, "Theology of the Cross" in his book, *Mount Fuji and Mount Sinai: A Critique of Idols* (Maryknoll, N.Y.: Orbis Books, 1985), pp. 240-261, for a thought provoking development of this theme. See also the article by Catholic theologian William B. Frazier, "Where Mission Begins: A Foundational Probe" in *International Bulletin of Missionary Research*, Vol. 11, No. 4 (October 1987), pp. 146-156.

10. Hutley to Whitehouse, April 23, 1880, Uguha, as cited by Bonk, "All Things to All Men," p. 86.

11. Jones to Thompson, January 6, 1888, Fwambo, ibid., p. 87.

12. Jones to Thompson, March 26, 1895, Kambole, ibid. Confusion arising from mutual misunderstanding of sharing customs on the part of missionaries and their nonmissionary hosts is a frequent subject in missionary writing. See, for example, the article by Donald E. Douglas, "On Sharing Wealth Philippine Style," in *Readings in Missionary Anthropology II*, enlarged 1978 edition, edited by William A. Smalley (South Pasadena: William Carey Library, 1978), pp. 800-806.

13. Choan-seng Song, giving voice to the frustrations of many non-Western Christians, speaks of "the system called mission boards" as symbolizing injustice in the eyes of many Third World Christians: ". . . a mission board is paying for a foreign

missionary couple the rent for an apartment which is as much, or more, monthly than the wages of twenty Indians who have to support themselves, their wives, their children from their pay. The system has encouraged division among Christians and missionaries." From an unpublished paper, "The System, Missionaries and the Future of the Christian Mission" [ca. 1971] located in the Yale Divinity School Pamphlet Collection, Box 359, Folder 2465. Professor Choan-seng Song, author of *Third-Eye Theology* (Maryknoll, N.Y.: Orbis Books, 1979), was at the time of writing this paper, Secretary for Asian Ministries with the Reformed Church in America. He is currently on the faculty of Pacific School of Religion.

14. A "lay" was a portion of the catch of profits from a whaling expedition. Typically, the cabin boy could fairly expect a lay of at least one five-hundredth.

15. Herman Melville, *Moby Dick or The White Whale.* Illustrated by Mead Schaeffer (New York: Dodd, Mead and Company, 1922), pp. 70-71.

16. I have deliberately organized the Biblical material in outline form to facilitate its use for personal or group study. For the most part, aside from actually classifying and citing the references, my comments are kept to a minimum.

17. My handling of the biblical text is, admittedly, rather simplistic. I am not unaware of the strand of biblical teaching which regards wealth as a sign of divine blessing—especially in Deuteronomy. As Willard Swartley kindly reminded me, the earliest Christian mission was often supported by wealthy patrons (e.g., the women who followed Jesus [Luke 8:1-31]; Gaius, whose hospitality extended to Paul and the whole Corinthian church [Romans 16:23]; etc. The socioeconomic milieu in which the early Church existed was inevitably reflected in the sociology of the Church itself. Some have gone so far as to suggest that Paul's missionary strategy produced churches whose membership was comprised predominantly of urban, middle-class, even wealthy, converts. (Among the many worthy participants in the ongoing discussion, Frederick Noris, Robert H. Smith, George Buchanan, Wolfgang Stegemann, and Claus Westermann are particularly helpful.) I have no quarrel with this, but would argue that the relationship of wealthy converts to their wealth was [ideally] necessarily transformed. Theirs was a wealth sanctified—to God rather than to self.

18. From a 1914 pamphlet quoted by Robert L. Heilbroner in *The Quest for Wealth: A Study of Acquisitive Man* (New York: Simon and Schuster, 1956), p. 238.

19. In the introduction to her translation of volume 2 (Purgatory of Dante's *Divine Comedy*, Dorothy Sayers explains that the "seven deadly sins" of medieval theology are more properly understood as the "Seven Capital Sins" (Latin: *caput* = head; "the head or font of offending"), or as the Seven Roots of Sinfulness. . . . "These," she points out, "are the fundamental bad habits of mind recognized and defined by the Church as the well-heads from which all sinful behaviour ultimately springs" (p. 65).

20. John Kenneth Galbraith, "The 1929 Parallel," *The Atlantic,* Vol. 259, No. 1 (January, 1987), p. 62.

21. Jorgen Lissner speaks to this in his *The Politics of Altruism: A Study of the Political Behaviour of Voluntary Development Agencies* (Geneva: Lutheran World Federation, Department of Studies, 1977), as does Redmond Mullin in his *Present Alms: On the Corruption of Philanthropy* (Birmingham: Phlogiston Publishing Ltd., 1980).

22. This is part of the message of the Report of the Consultation of World Evangelization Mini-Consultation on Reaching the Urban Poor, *The Thailand*

Report on The Urban Poor, held in Pattaya, Thailand, from 16-27 June, 1980 (Wheaton: Lausanne Committee for World Evangelization, 1980).

7. GRAPPLING WITH AFFLUENCE

1. Ivan Illich, *Celebration of Awareness: A Call for Institutional Revolution* (Garden City: Doubleday & Co., 1970), p. 27.

2. David Jonathon East, *Western Africa: Its Condition, and Christianity the Means of its Recovery* (London: Houlston & Stoneman, 1844), p. 243.

3. Allan John Macdonald, *Trade, Politics and Christianity in Africa and the East* (London: Longmans, Green and Co., 1916), p. 54.

4. John Kenneth Galbraith, *The Affluent Society*, 3rd edition (New York: New American Library, 1976), p. 1.

5. See E. J. Hobsbawm, *The Age of Empire, 1875-1914* (New York: Pantheon Books, 1987), p. 15.

6. According to David B. Barrett's "Annual Statistical Table on Global Mission: 1987," in *International Bulletin of Missionary Research*, Vol. 12, No. 1 (January, 1988), pp. 16-17, there are now an estimated 262,000 foreign missionaries and 3,800 foreign mission sending agencies. In addition, there are 3,807,600 national church workers. Most of these, in all cases, are non-Western and, by Western standards, poor.

7. David J. Bosch, "Vision for Mission," *International Review of Mission*, Vol. LXXVI, No. 301 (January, 1987), p. 15.

8. Trevor D. Verryn, "What is Communication? Searching for a Missiological Model," *Missionalia*, Vol. 11, No. 1 (April, 1983), p. 25.

9. W. E. Russell, *Sydney Smith* (London: MacMillan & Co., 1905), p. 107.

10. See Eugene A. Nida, *Message and Mission: the Communication of the Christian Faith* (New York: Harper & Row, 1960), pp. 164-165.

11. *Re-Thinking Missions: A Layman's Inquiry after One Hundred Years.* By The Commission of Appraisal, William Ernest Hocking, Chairman (New York: Harper & Brothers, 1932).

12. Kagawa's ten-point critique of the Report was published under the title "A Significant Word from Asia, Giving Dr. Toyohiko Kagawa's Clarion-call to the Church of Christ" (Bombay: Printed by F. Borton for G. Claridge & Co., published by Bishop B. T. Badley, n.d.). This quotation is from page 8. His thinking on the cross is further developed in his book, *Meditations on the Cross*, translated by Helen F. Topping and Marion R. Draper (Chicago: Willett, Clark & Co., 1935).

13. Asian theologians have long been aware of this lack in Western Christian theology generally and missiology particularly. See, for example, the book by Toyohiko Kagawa, *Meditations on the Cross*, translated by Helen F. Topping and Marion R. Draper (Chicago: Willett, Clark & Co., 1935). The cross is a recurring theme in the writings of Kosuke Koyama. See, for example, *Waterbuffalo Theology* (London: Student Christian Movement Press, 1974), especially chapters 5 and 19. See also chapter 20 of his book, *Mount Fuji and Mount Sinai: A Critique of Idols* (Maryknoll, N.Y.: Orbis Books, 1985).

14. Cf. 1 Cor. 1:18-31; 2:1-5; 4:1-16; 2 Cor. 3:7-11; 4:1-18; 11:7-33; 12:7-10.

15. Kosuke Koyama, *No Handle on the Cross: An Asian Meditation on the Crucified Mind* (London: SCM, 1976), p. 77.

16. John Woolman, *The Journal and Major Essays of John Woolman*, edited by Phillips P. Moulton (New York: Oxford University Press, 1971), p. 198

17. Woolman, p. 212. These words were first published in 1761.

18. See Richard Lovett, *James Gilmour of Mongolia: His Diaries, Letters and Reports* (London: Religious Tract Society, 1893), pp. 211, 203. See also my article, "The Role of Affluence in the Christian Missionary Enterprise from the West," *Missiology: An International Review*, Vol. XIV, No. 4 (October, 1986), p. 444.

19. Letter of McGavran to Bonk, January 26, 1988, Pasadena.

20. See W. E. Russell, *Sydney Smith* (London: MacMillan & Co., 1905), note on p. 85.

21. Conciliar Protestant churches have long led the way in searching for alternatives to the old pattern of "sending church-receiving church" relationships. While independent and even denominational Evangelical agencies have, for a variety of reasons, been slower to move away from the nineteenth century stress of Rufus Anderson, Henry Venn, and Roland Allen on the "indigenous church," there is evidence that this is changing. Overseas Missionary Fellowship (OMF), Communaute Evangelique d'Action Apostolique (CEVAA), Community of Latin American Evangelical Ministries (CLAEM), and Pengutusan Injil dan Pelayanan Kasih (PIPKA) are notable examples. See Wilbert R. Shenk's excellent study, "God's New Economy: Interdependence and Mission" (Elkhart: Mission Focus, 1988).

22. Kosuke Koyama, *Three Mile an Hour God: Biblical Reflections* (Maryknoll, N.Y.: Orbis Books, 1980), p. 53.

23. See, for example, the compendium of the "International Conference on Missionary Kids" held in Manila, Philippines, November 5-9, 1984: *New Directions in Missions: Implications for MKs*, edited by Beth A. Tetzel and Patricia Mortenson (West Battleboro, Vt: International Conference on Missionary Kids [ICMK], 1986). There is absolutely no mention made of the children of poor missionaries. A recent (Dec. 4-5, 1987) Overseas Ministries Study Center (OMSC) sponsored "Study Group on Mission Issues" featuring the topic "Resolving the Crisis in MK Education" manifested a similar myopia, although a Filipino pastor and his wife who had been invited to attend expressed amazement at the notion that the children of Western missionaries were anything but privileged.

24. John Woolman, op. cit., p. 199.

25. *Missionary Service in Asia Today*. A Report on a Consultation Held by the Asia Methodist Advisory Committee, February 18-23, 1971, in cooperation with the Life, Message, Unity Committee of the East Asian Christian Conference (Kuala Lumpur: University of Malaya, 1971), p. 94.

26. Some recently established agencies have avoided the question of the legitimacy of Western missionary affluence, instead encouraging Westerners to support bargain basement "national" missionaries from Western coffers at one thirtieth of the cost of a North American. An example of this approach would include the "Gospel for Asia" organization, whose founding president, K. P. Yohannan, spells out his vision in his book, *The Coming Revolution in World Missions* (Altamonte Springs, Florida: Creation House, 1986). While a very good case can be made for this practice on economic grounds, it does not address the problem of why Western missionaries should not be able, when challenged, to follow their Savior among the poor. Another such agency is the "Christian Nationals Evangelism Commission," founded by Allen Finley. His book (co-authored by Lorry Lutz), *The Family Tie* (Nashville: Thomas Nelson Publishers, 1983), outlines what on the cover is described as "an exciting approach that could revolutionize world missions." Christian Aid Mission (201 Stanton St., Fort Erie, Ontario L2A 3N8) has recently

released the film (available on video) "The Hidden Missionaries" which argues that the need for Western missionaries is past. Recently founded by John and Lynn Samaan, "Servants Among the Poor" is a rare example of a Western evangelical agency committed to serving the urban poor in slums of Third World megacities, "incarnationally and wholistically by covenanting together to live a simple and devotional lifestyle . . ." (From their brochure, available by writing to the organization at: 691 E. Howard St., Pasadena, CA 91104).

27. There are some notable exceptions, of course. The writings of Viv Grigg, Ron Sider, and Harvie Conn are a rich, but missiologically neglected source. Likewise, the Lausanne Committee for World Evangelization's Thailand Report No. 22, *Christian Witness to the Urban Poor*, subtitled "Report of the Consultation of World Evangelization Mini-Consultation on Reaching the Urban Poor," held in Pattaya, Thailand from 16-27 June 1980 is highly commendable. But its recommendations have yet to be acted upon by those responsible for designing and implementing the policies of Western-based missions.

28. From the 1987 syllabus, "Incarnation & Mission Among the World's Urban Poor - MB595." A copy of the syllabus may be obtained from Lingua House, 135 N. Oakland #91, Pasadena, CA 91182.

29. Cyril J. Davey, *Kagawa of Japan* (Nashville: Abingdon Press, 1960), p. 18.

30. An example of what I have in mind is the mimeographed, 176 page book produced in 1985 by Brian Fargher (then a missionary with SIM International), *Philip: An Ethiopian Evangelist.* The book is essentially a transcription of the Ethiopian missionary's recorded autobiography. Philip (not his real name), who has struggled with tuberculosis all his life, played the key role in the planting of numerous churches. A good proportion of his missionary career was spent in prison. He was almost always destitute. What is humbling in this story is the relatively insignificant role played by Western missionaries in the life of the Ethiopian Church. It is good to see ourselves as we are seen, and to humbly serve those who are better able than we to pay the price of effective apostolic ministry. My students have been deeply challenged by this simple story. Would that more of these unsung heroes could tell their story to us!

Select Bibliography

GENERAL REFERENCE WORKS

Aikman, J. Logan. *Cyclopaedia of Christian Missions: Their Rise, Progress, and Present Position*. London: Richard Griffin and Co., 1860.

Beach, Harlan P. and Charles H. Fahs, eds., *World Missionary Atlas; Containing a Directory of Missionary Societies, Classified Summaries of Statistics, Maps Showing the Location of Mission Stations Throughout the World, a Descriptive Account of the Principal Mission Lands, and Comprehensive Indices*. New York: Institute of Social and Religious Research, 1925.

International Schools Services. *The ISS Directory of Overseas Schools*. 1987/88 Edition. Princeton: International Schools Services, 1987.

Jacquet, Constant H., Jr., ed. *Yearbook of American and Canadian Churches, 1987*. Annual. Fifty-fifth Issue. Nashville: Abingdon Press, 1987.

Kravis, Irving B., Alan Heston, Robert Summers. *World Product and Income: International Comparisons of Real Gross Product*. Produced by The Statistical Office of the United Nations and The World Bank. Baltimore: Published for The World Bank by The Johns Hopkins University Press, 1982.

Kravis, Irving B., Zoltan Kenessey, Alan Heston, Robert Summers. *Phase IV: World Comparisons of Purchasing Power and Real Product for 1980*. New York: United Nations, 1986.

McEvedy, Colin and Richard Jones. *Atlas of World Population History*. Harmondsworth: Penguin Books, 1978.

Mission Advanced Research and Communication Center. *Mission Handbook: North American Protestant Ministries Overseas*. 13th edition. Edited by Samuel Wilson and John Siewert. Monrovia, California: Missions Advanced Research and Communication Center, 1986.

United Nations Department of International Economic Affairs. Various Years. *Statistical Yearbook*.

U.S. Census Bureau. *Statistical Abstract of the United States, 1981*. Washington, D.C., U. S. Census Bureau: Government Printing Office, 1981.

U.S. Department of State Indexes of Living Costs Abroad and Quarters Allowances: A Technical Description. Report 568. Washington, D.C.: U.S. Department of Labor, Bureau of Labor Statistics, April 1980.

U.S. Department of State Indexes of Living Costs Abroad, Quarters Allowances, and Hardship Differentials. Washington, D.C.: U.S. Department of Labor, Bureau of Labor Statistics, July 1987.

World Bank. *Poverty and Hunger: Issues and Options for Food Security in Developing Countries*. Washington, D.C: 1986.

World Bank. *World Development Report 1987*. Barriers to Adjustment and Growth in the World Economy; Industrialization and Foreign Trade; World Development Indicators. Published for the World Bank by Oxford University Press, 1987.

World Commission on Environment and Development. *Our Common Future.* New York: Oxford University Press, 1987.

World Resources 1987. A Report by The International Institute for Environment and Development and The World Resources Institute. New York: Basic Books, 1987.

BOOKS

Ahlstrom, Sydney E. *A Religious History of the American People.* New Haven: Yale University Press, 1972.

Allen, Roland. *The Ministry of the Spirit; Selected Writings of Roland Allen.* London: World Dominion Press, 1960.

Allen, Roland. *Missionary Methods: St. Paul's or Ours?* London: World Dominion Press, 1912.

Allen, Roland. *The Spontaneous Expansion of the Church and the Causes Which Hinder it.* London: World Dominion Press, 1927.

Almquist, Arden. *Missionary Come Back!* New York: World Publishing Co., 1970.

Arnott, Neil. *A Survey of Human Progress, from the Savage State to the Highest Civilization yet Attained. A Progress as Little Perceived by the Multitude in any Age, as is the Slow Growing of a Tree by the Children who Play under its Shade — but which is Leading to a New Condition of Mankind on Earth.* London: Longman, Green, Longman, and Roberts, 1861.

Axling, William. *Kagawa.* New York: Harper & Bros., 1932.

Barnett, Mrs. H. O. (R.) *Canon Barnett: His Life, Work, and Friends,* by his wife. London: John Murray, 1918.

Barton, James L. *Human Progress through Missions.* New York: Fleming H. Revell Co., 1912.

Barton, James L. *The Missionary and His Critics.* New York: Fleming H. Revell Co., 1906.

Beaver, R. Pierce. *The Missionary Between the Times.* Garden City: Doubleday & Company, 1968.

Bellah, Robert N. *The Broken Covenant: American Civil Religion in Time of Trial.* New York: Seabury Press, 1975.

Bellah, Robert N., Richard Madsen, William N. Sullivan, Ann Swidler, and Steven M. Tipton. *Habits of the Heart: Individualism and Commitment in American Life.* Berkeley: University of California Press, 1985.

Bendix, Reinhard and Seymour Martin Lipset, eds. *Class, Status, and Power: Social Stratification in Comparative Perspective.* Second Edition. New York: The Free Press, 1966.

van den Berg, Johannes. *Constrained by Jesus' Love: An Inquiry into the Motives of the Missionary Awakening in Great Britain in the Period between 1698 and 1815.* Kampen: J. H. Kok N.V., 1956.

Bernikow, Louise. *Alone in America: The Search for Companionship.* New York: Harper & Row, 1986.

Brewster, E. Thomas, and Brewster, Elizabeth S. *Bonding and the Missionary Task: Establishing a Sense of Belonging.* Pasadena: Lingua House, 1982.

Brown, Robert McAfee. *Unexpected News: Reading the Bible with Third World Eyes.* Philadelphia: Westminster Press, 1984.

Brown, Roger William. *Words and Things*. Glencoe: The Free Press, 1958.

Buchan, James. *The Expendable Mary Slessor*. Edinburgh: The Saint Andrew Press, 1980.

Burke, Kenneth. *A Grammar of Motives and a Rhetoric of Motives*. New York: World Publishing Co., 1962.

Carey, William. *An Enquiry into the Obligations of Christians to Use Means for the Conversion of the Heathen*. London: Hodder & Stoughton, 1891 [reprint of the 1792 edition].

Chirgwin, A. M. *Arthington's Million: The Romance of the Arthington Trust*. Westminster, London: The Livingstone Press, 1935.

Clough, Shepard B. *Basic Values of Western Civilisation*. New York: Columbia University Press, 1960.

Coles. Robert. *Privileged Ones: The Well-Off and the Rich in America*. (Volume V of *Children in Crisis*). An Atlantic Monthly Press Book. Boston: Little, Brown and Company, 1977.

Collins, Marjorie A. *Manual for Today's Missionary: From Recruitment to Retirement*. South Pasadena: William Carey Library, 1986.

Considine, John J., ed. *The Missionary's Role in Socio-Economic Betterment*. Published under the sponsorship of the Fordham University Institute of Mission Studies and the International Rural Life Movement with the aid of the Bruno Benziger Fund of Maryknoll. New York: Newman Press, 1960.

Countryman, L. William. *The Rich Christian in the Church of the Early Empire: Contradictions and Accommodations*. Lewiston, N.Y.: Edwin Mellen Press, 1980.

Cumming, John. "God in History." *Lectures Delivered Before the Young Men's Christian Association 1848-1849*. Vol. IV. London: James Nisbet and Co., 1876.

Cust, Robert Needham. *Essay on the Prevailing Methods of the Evangelization of the Non-Christian World*. London: Luzac & Co., 1894.

Cust, Robert Needham. *Notes on Missionary Subjects*. London: Elliot Stock, 1889.

Davey, Cyril J. *Kagawa of Japan*. Nashville: Abingdon Press, 1960.

David, Paul A., and Melvin Reder, eds. *Nations and Households in Economic Growth*. Stanford University Press.

Davis, J. Merle, ed. *The Economic Basis of the Church*. Preparatory Studies and Findings, Meeting of the International Missionary Council, at Tambaram, Madras, India December 12th to 29th, 1938. The Madras Series, Volume V. New York: International Missionary Council, 1939.

Davis, J. Merle. *The Economic and Social Environment of the Younger Churches*. The Report of the Department of Social and Economic Research of the International Missionary Council to the Tambaram Meeting—December 1938. London: Published for the International Council by the Edinburgh House Press, 1938.

Dennis, James S. *Christian Missions and Social Progress: A Sociological Study of Foreign Missions*. 3 Volumes. Edinburgh: Oliphant, Anderson and Ferrier, 1898.

Dickinson, Richard D. N. *Poor, Yet Making Many Rich: The Poor as Agents of Creative Justice*. Commission on the Churches' Participation in Development. Geneva: World Council of Churches, 1983.

Drummond, Henry. *Tropical Africa*. London: Hodder & Stoughton, 1889.

East, David Jonathon. *Western Africa: Its Condition, and Christianity the Means of its Recovery*. London: Houlston & Stoneman, 1844.

Edmond, Mrs. A. M. *Memoir of Mrs. Sarah D. Comstock, Missionary to Arracan . . .*

Philadelphia: American Baptist Publication Society, [1854].

Ferkiss, Victor C. *Technological Man: The Myth and the Reality*. New York: George Braziller, 1969.

Finley, Allen, and Lutz, Lorry. *The Family Tie*. Nashville: Thomas Nelson Publishers, 1983.

Fleming, Daniel Johnson. *Ethical Issues Confronting World Christians*. Published for The International Missionary Council, New York, by The Rumford Press, Concord, New Hampshire: 1935.

Fleming, Daniel Johnson. *Living as Comrades: A Study of Factors Making for "Community."* Published for the Foreign Missions Conference of North America by Agricultural Missions, Inc., New York: 1950.

Fleming, Daniel Johnson. *Ventures in Simpler Living*. Printed for The International Missionary Council, New York, by the Polygraphic Company of America, New York, 1933.

Foster, George M. *Traditional Societies and Technological Change*. Second Edition. New York: Harper & Row, Publishers, 1973.

Galbraith, John Kenneth. *The Affluent Society*. Third Edition, Revised. New York: New American Library, 1976.

Galbraith, John Kenneth. *The Nature of Mass Poverty*. Cambridge, Massachusetts: Harvard University Press, 1979.

Galton, Francis. *The Art of Travel; or, Shifts and Contrivances Available in Wild Countries*. London: John Murray, 1855.

Gandhi, Mohandas K. *The Mahatma and the Missionary: Selected Writings of Mohandas K. Gandhi*. Edited by Clifford Manshardt. Chicago: Henry Regnery Company, 1949.

Gerber, Vergil, ed. *Missions in Creative Tension*. South Pasadena: William Carey Library, 1971.

Gesch, Patrick F. *Initiative and Initiation: A Cargo Cult-Type Movement in the Sepik Against Its Background in Traditional Village Religion*. St. Augustin, West Germany: Anthropos Institute, 1985.

Goudzwaard, Bob. *Aid for the Overdeveloped West*. Toronto: Wedge Publishing Foundation, 1975.

Grigg, Viv. *Companion to the Poor*. Sutherland, NSW, Australia: Albatross Books, 1984.

Guinness, Mrs. Gratan. *The New World of Central Africa, With a History of the First Christian Mission on the Congo*. London: Hodder & Stoughton, 1890.

Heider, Fritz. *The Psychology of Interpersonal Relations*. New York: John Wiley & Sons, 1958.

Heilbroner, Robert L. *The Quest for Wealth: A Study of Acquisitive Man*. New York: Simon and Schuster, 1956.

Henry, Jules. *Culture Against Man*. New York: Random House, 1963.

Hesselgrave, David J. *Communicating Christ Cross-Culturally: An Introduction to Missionary Communication*. Grand Rapids: Zondervan Publishing House, 1978.

Hoagland, Edward. *African Calliope: A Journey to the Sudan*. Harmondsworth: Penguin Books, 1978.

Hobsbawm, E. J. *The Age of Empire, 1875-1914*. New York: Pantheon Books, 1987.

Horney, Karen. *The Neurotic Personality of our Time*. New York: W. W. Norton & Company, 1937.

Hunter, James Davison. *American Evangelicalism*. New Brunswick, N.J.: Rutgers University Press, 1983.

Hvalkof, Soren, and Aaby, Peter, eds. *Is God an American? An Anthropological Perspective on the Missionary Work of the Summer Institute of Linguistics*. Copenhagen: International Work Group for Indigenous Affairs, and London: Survival International, 1981.

Illich, Ivan D. *Celebration of Awareness: A Call for Institutional Revolution*. New York: Doubleday & Co., 1970.

Illich, Ivan D. *The Church, Change and Development*. Chicago: Urban Training Center Press, 1970.

Jaher, Frederic Cople, ed. *The Rich, the Well Born, and the Powerful: Elites and Upper Classes in History*. Urbana: University of Illinois Press, 1973.

Jencks, Christopher. *Inequality*. New York: Basic Books, 1972.

Jewett, Robert. *The Captain America Complex: The Dilemma of Zealous Nationalism*. Philadelphia: The Westminster Press, 1973.

John, Griffith. *A Voice from China*. London: Religious Tract Society, 1907.

Johnston, Harry H. *A History of the Colonization of Africa by Alien Races*. Cambridge: Cambridge University Press, 1899.

Johnston, James. *A Century of Christian Progress and its Lessons*. London: James Nisbet & Co., 1888.

Jones, Landon Y. *Great Expectations: America and the Baby Boom Generation*. New York: Coward, McCann & Geoghegan, 1980.

Kagawa, Toyohiko. *Brotherhood Economics*. New York: Harper & Bros., 1936.

Kagawa, Toyohiko. *Meditations on the Cross*. Chicago: Willett, Clark, 1935.

Kagawa, Toyohiko. *The Religion of Jesus*. London: SCM Press, 1931.

Kagawa, Toyohiko. *Songs from the Slums*. Nashville: Cokesbury, 1935.

Kennedy, Gail. *Democracy and the Gospel of Wealth*. Problems in American Civilization. Readings Selected by the Department of American Studies, Amherst College. Boston: D. C. Heath and Co., 1949.

Klassen, A. J., ed. *The Church in Mission: A Sixtieth Anniversary Tribute to J. B. Toews*. Fresno: Board of Christian Literature, Mennonite Brethren Church, 1967.

Knollys, Henry. *English Life in China*. London: Smith, Elder & Company, 1885.

Koyama, Kosuke. *Fifty Meditations*. Maryknoll, N.Y.: Orbis Books, 1975.

Koyama, Kosuke. *Mount Fuji and Mount Sinai: A Critique of Idols*. Maryknoll, N.Y.: Orbis Books, 1985.

Koyama, Kosuke. *No Handle on the Cross: An Asian Meditation on the Crucified Mind*. London: SCM Press, 1976.

Koyama, Kosuke. *Theology in Contact*. Madras: The Christian Literature Society, 1975.

Koyama, Kosuke. *Three Mile an Hour God: Biblical Reflections*. Maryknoll, N.Y.: Orbis Books, 1980.

Lapierre, Dominique. *The City of Joy*. Translated from the French by Kathryn Spink. Garden City: Doubleday & Company, 1985.

Latourette, Kenneth Scott. *History of the Expansion of Christianity*. Vol. IV. *The Great Century, A.D. 1800-1914: Europe and the United States of America*. London: Eyre and Spottiswoode, 1941.

Latourette, Kenneth Scott. *The Unquenchable Light*. London: Eyre and Spottiswoode, 1940.

Laurie, Thomas. *The Ely Volume; or, The Contributions of our Foreign Missions to Science and Human Wellbeing*. Boston: American Board of Commissioners for Foreign Missions, 1881.

Lausanne Committee for World Evangelization, Occasional Paper No. 22, *The Thailand Report on the Urban Poor*. Report of the Consultation of World Evangelization Mini-Consultation on Reaching the Urban Poor held in Pattaya, Thailand from 16-27 June 1980. Sponsored by the Lausanne Committee for World Evangelization. Wheaton: Lausanne Committee for World Evangelization, 1980.

Lausanne Committee for World Evangelization, Occasional Paper No. 2, *The Willowbank Report*. Report of a Consultation on Gospel and Culture held at Willowbank, Somerset Bridge, Bermuda, from 6th to 13th January 1978. Sponsored by the Lausanne Theology and Education Group. Wheaton: Lausanne Committee for World Evangelization, 1978.

Lennox, William G. *A Comparative Study of the Health of Missionary Families in Japan and China and a Selected Group in America*. Denver: University of Denver, 1922.

Lennox, William G. *The Health and Turnover of Missionaries*. Published by the Advisory Committee, The Foreign Missions Conference, New York, 1933.

Lennox, William G. *The Health of Missionary Families in China: A Statistical Study*. Denver: University of Denver, 1921.

Liggins, John. *The Great Value and Success of Foreign Missions; Proved by Distinguished Witnesses*. London: James Nisbet & Co., 1889.

Lilly, William Samuel. *Christianity and Modern Civilization. Being Some Chapters in European History with an Introductory Dialogue on the Philosophy of History*. London: Chapman & Hill, 1903.

Lissner, Jorgen. *The Politics of Altruism: A Study of the Political Behaviour of Voluntary Development Agencies*. Geneva: Lutheran World Federation, Dept. of Studies, 1977.

Livingstone, David. *Missionary Travels and Researches in South Africa; Including a Sketch of Sixteen Years Residence in the Interior of Africa*. London: J. Murray, 1857.

Loewen, Jacob A. *Culture and Human Values: Christian Intervention in Anthropological Perspective*. Selections from the writings of Jacob A. Loewen originally appearing in *Practical Anthropology*, 1961-1970. South Pasadena: William Carey Library, 1975.

Lovett, Richard. *James Gilmour of Mongolia: His Diaries, Letters and Reports*. London: Religious Tract Society, 1893.

Lutz, Jessie G. *Christian Missions in China: Evangelists of What?* Boston: D. C. Heath and Company, 1965.

MacDonald, Allan. *Trade, Politics and Christianity in Africa and the East*. London: Longmans, Green and Co., 1916.

McGilvary, Daniel, et al. *Counsel to New Missionaries from Older Missionaries of the Presbyterian Church*. New York: Board of Foreign Missions of the Presbyterian Church in the U. S. A., 1905.

Mackenzie, W. Douglas. *Christianity and the Progress of Man as Illustrated by Modern Missions*. Edinburgh: Oliphant, Anderson and Ferrier, 1898.

Maung She Wa, G. and E. Edwards. *Burma Baptist Chronicle*. Rangoon, 1963.

Michie, Alexander. *Missionaries in China*. London: Edward Stanford, 1891.

Missionary Service in Asia Today. A Report on a Consultation Held by the Asia

Methodist Advisory Committee February 18-23, 1971, in cooperation with the Life, Message Unity Committee of the East Asian Christian Conference. Kuala Lumpur: University of Malaya, 1971.

Moffat, Robert. *A Missionary Prize Essay on the Duty, the Privilege, and Encouragement of Christians to Send the Gospel to the Unenlightened Nations of the Earth*. Newcastle: Pattison and Ross, 1842.

Muggeridge, Malcolm. *Chronicles of Wasted Time. Part I. The Green Stick*. London: Collins, 1972.

Mullin, Redmond. *Present Alms: On the Corruption of Philanthropy*. Birmingham: Phlogiston Publishing Ltd., 1980.

Mullin, Redmond. *The Wealth of Christians*. Maryknoll, N.Y.: Orbis Books, 1983.

Mumford, Lewis. *The Transformations of Man*. Volume seven of World Perspectives series, planned and edited by Ruth Nanda Anshen. New York: Harper & Brothers, 1956.

Nee, Watchman. *Concerning our Missions*. Shanghai: The Gospel Book Room, 1939.

Nelson, Marlin. *The How and Why of Third World Missions*. South Pasadena: William Carey Library, 1976.

Nicgorski, Walter and Ronald Weber, eds. *An Almost Chosen People: The Moral Aspirations of Americans*. Notre Dame: The University of Notre Dame Press, 1976.

Niles, D. T. *Upon the Earth: The Mission of God and the Missionary Enterprise of the Churches*. New York: McGraw-Hill Book Company, 1962.

Nisbet, Robert A. *History of the Idea of Progress*. New York: Basic Books, 1980.

O'Brien, Niall. *Revolution from the Heart*. New York: Oxford University Press, 1987.

Orwell, George. *England Your England: And Other Essays*. London: Secker & Ward, 1953.

Phillips, Keith W. *They Dare to Love the Ghetto*. Los Angeles: World Impact, 1975.

Piggin, Stuart. *Making Evangelical Missionaries 1798-1858: The Social Background, Motives and Training of British Protestant Missionaries to India*. With texts of David Bogue's *Missionary Appeal*, 1794; Charles Buck on *Philanthropic Movements*, 1800; Sydney Smith on *Evangelical Missionaries*, 1808. Number 2 in the *Evangelicals and Society from 1750* series, edited by G. E. Duffield. Oxford: The Sutton Courtney Press, 1984.

Potter, David M. *People of Plenty: Economic Abundance and the American Character*. Chicago: University of Chicago Press, 1954.

Ranulf, Svend. *Moral Indignation and Middle Class Psychology: A Sociological Study*. Copenhagen: Levin & Munksgaard, 1938.

Reade, W. Winwood. *The Martyrdom of Man*. London: Kegan Paul, Trench, 1909 [1872].

Reynolds, Lloyd G. *Economic Growth in the Third World: An Introduction*. New Haven: Yale University Press, 1986.

Riesman, David. *Abundance for What? And Other Essays*. New York: Doubleday & Company, 1964.

Robb, Alexander. *The Heathen World and the Duty of the Church*. Edinburgh: Andrew Elliott, 1863.

Rogers, Stanley, ed. and comp. *Centenary Missionary Hymnal*. London: London Missionary Society, 1895.

Ronsvalle, John and Sylvia. *The Hidden Billions: The Potential of the Church in the U.S.A.* Champaign, Illinois: C-4 Resources, Inc., 1984.

Russell, W. E. *Sydney Smith*. London: MacMillan & Co., 1905.

Ryan, William. *Blaming the Victim*. New York: Pantheon Books, 1971.

Samuel, Vinay, and Sugden, Chris. *Evangelism and the Poor: A Third World Study Guide*. Revised Edition. Bangalore: Partnership In Mission-Asia, 1983.

Sayers, Dorothy. *Letters to a Post-Christian World: A Selection of Essays*. Selected and introduced by Roderick Jellema. Grand Rapids: Wm. B. Eerdmans Publishing Co., 1969.

Schoeck, Helmut. *Envy: A Theory of Social Behaviour*. London: Secker & Ward, 1969.

Sheils, W. J. and Diana Wood, eds. *The Church And Wealth*. Papers Read at the 1986 Summer Meeting and the 1987 Winter Meeting of the Ecclesiastical History Society. (Studies in Church History, Vol. 24). Oxford: Published for The Ecclesiastical History Society by Basil Blackwell, 1987.

Shi, David. *The Simple Life: Plain Living and High Thinking in American Culture*. New York: Oxford University Press, 1985.

Simon, Charlie May. *A Seed Shall Serve: The Story of Toyohiko Kagawa, Spiritual Leader of Modern Japan*. London: Hodder & Stoughton, 1959.

Slater, Philip E. *The Pursuit of Loneliness: American Culture at the Breaking Point*. Boston: Beacon Press, 1970.

Smalley, William A., ed. *Readings in Missionary Anthropology II*. Enlarged 1978 edition. South Pasadena: William Carey Library, 1978.

Stavrianos, L. S. *Global Rift: The Third World Comes of Age*. New York: William Morrow and Company, 1981.

Stoll, David. *Fishers of Men or Founders of Empire? The Wycliffe Bible Translators in Latin America*. London: Zed Press, 1982.

Strong, Josiah. *The New Era; or, The Coming Kingdom*. New York: Baker & Taylor, 1893.

Tetzel, Beth A. and Mortenson, Patricia, eds. *New Directions in Missions — Implication for MKs*. Compendium of International Conference on Missionary Kids, Manila, Philippines, November, 1984. West Battleboro, VT: International Conference on Missionary Kids [ICMK], 1986.

Thompson, R. Wardlaw. *Griffith John: The Story of Fifty Years in China*. London: Religious Tract Society, 1906.

Thornton, A. P. *Doctrines of Imperialism*. New York: John Wiley & Sons, 1965.

Tiberondwa, Ado K. *Missionary Teachers as Agents of Colonialism: A Study of their Activities in Uganda*. Lusaka: National Educational Company of Zambia, 1978.

Tocqueville, Alexis de. *Democracy in America*. 2 volumes. The Henry Reeve text as revised by Francis Bowen now further corrected and edited with introduction, editorial notes, and bibliographies by Phillips Bradley. New York: Alfred A. Knopf, 1956 [1835].

Trollope, Frances. *Domestic Manners of the Americans*. Edited, with a history of Mrs. Trollope's adventures in America, by Donald Smalley. New York: Alfred A. Knopf, 1949 [1832].

Trout, Jessie M., ed. *Kagawa, Japanese Prophet: His Witness in Life and Word* (World Christian Books, no. 30). London: Lutterworth, 1959.

Walsh, Michael and Brian Davies, eds. *Proclaiming Justice & Peace: Documents from John XXIII-John Paul II*. Mystic, Connecticut: Twenty-Third Publications, 1984.

Walsh, William Pakenham. *Christian Missions: Six Discourses Delivered before the*

University of Dublin; being the Donnellan Lectures for 1861. Dublin: George Herbert, 1862.

Warneck, Johannes. *Living Forces of the Gospel: Experiences of a Missionary in Animistic Heathendom*. Authorized translation from the 3rd German edition by Neil Buchanan. London: Oliphant, Anderson & Ferrier, 1909.

Warren, William. *These for Those: Our Indebtedness to Foreign Missions; or, What We Get for What We Give*. Portland: Hoyt, Fogg and Breed, 1870.

Wong, James, ed. with Peter Larson, Edward Pentecost. *Mission from the Third World*. Singapore: Church Growth Study Center, 1972.

Woolman, John. *The Journal and Major Essays of John Woolman*. Edited by Phillips P. Moulton. New York: Oxford University Press, 1971.

Worsley, Peter. *The Trumpet Shall Sound: A Study of "Cargo" Cults in Melanesia*. Second, augmented Edition. New York: Schocken Books, 1968.

Yohannan, K. P. *The Coming Revolution in World Missions*. Altamonte Springs: Creation House, 1986.

Young, Robert. *The Success of Christian Missions: Testimonies to their Beneficent Results*. London: Hodder & Stoughton, 1890.

ARTICLES

"A Prophecy According to Roland Allen." *Laity*, No. 12 (October, 1961), pp. 38-43.

Ahlstrom, Sydney E. *"Annuit Coeptis*: America as the Elect Nation. The Rise and Decline of a Patriotic Tradition." in *Continuity and Discontinuity in Church History: Essays Presented to George Huntston Williams on the Occasion of his 65th Birthday*. Edited by F. Forrester Church and Timothy George. Vol. XIX of *Studies in the History of Christian Thought*, edited by Heiko A. Oberman, et al. Leiden: E. J. Brill, 1979, pp. 315-337.

"An Indictment of the Way in Which Science and Technology Have Become Instruments of a Global Structure of Inequity, Exploitation and Oppression." *International Development Review*, Vol. 21, No. 2 (1979), pp. 13-15.

Barrett, David B. "Annual Statistical Table on Global Mission: 1987." *International Bulletin of Missionary Research*, Vol. 12, No. 1 (January, 1988).

Beidelman, Thomas O. "Contradictions between the Sacred and the Secular Life: The Church Missionary Society in Ukaguru, Tanzania, East Africa, 1876-1914," *Comparative Studies in History: An International Quarterly* , Vol. 23, No. 1 (January, 1981), pp. 73-95.

Blasi, Joseph and Diana L. Murrell. "Adolescence and Community Structure: Research on the Kibbutz of Israel." *Adolescence*, Vol. 12, No. 46 (Summer, 1977), pp. 165-173.

Bleek, Wolf. "Envy and Inequality in Fieldwork: An Example of Ghana." *Human Organization*, Vol. 38, No. 2 (Summer, 1979), pp. 200-205.

Bloom, Leonard. "Psychological Aspects of Wealth in Poorer Societies." *Journal of Psychoanalytic Anthropology*, Vol. 7, No. 2 (Spring, 1984), pp. 189-208.

Bonk, Jon. " 'All Things to All Persons' — The Missionary as a Racist-Imperialist, 1860-1910." *Missiology: An International Review*, Vol. VIII, No. 3 (July, 1980), pp. 285-306.

Bonk, Jon [with responses by Stan Nussbaum and James E. Pluddemann]. "Affluence: The Achilles' Heel of Missions." *Evangelical Missions Quarterly*, Vol. XXI, No. 4 (October, 1985), pp. 382-393.

Bonk, Jon. "The Role of Affluence in the Christian Missionary Enterprise from the West." *Missiology: An International Review*, Vol. XIV, No. 4 (October, 1986), pp. 437-461.

Bosch, David J. "The Missionary: Exemplar or Victim?" *Theologia Evangelica*, Vol. XVII, No. 1 (March, 1984), pp. 9-16.

Bosch, David. "Vision for Mission." *International Review of Mission*, Vol. LXXVI, No. 301 (January, 1987), pp. 8-15.

Bruner, Frederick Dale. "The American Missionary Problem: An Essay in Conscience." *The Christian Century*, Vol. 85, No. 23 (June 5, 1968), pp. 751-753.

Callahan, Daniel. "Doing Well by Doing Good: Garrett Hardin's 'Lifeboat Ethic'." *The Hastings Center Report*, Vol. 4, No. 6 (December, 1974), pp. 1-4.

Cole, Arthur H. "The Relations of Missionary Activity to Economic Development." *Economic Development and Cultural Change*, Vol. 9, No. 2 (January, 1961), pp. 120-27.

Conn, Harvie M. "The Money Barrier Between Sending and Receiving Churches." *Evangelical Missions Quarterly*, Vol. 14, No. 4 (October, 1978), pp. 231-239.

DeVoss, David. "The New Breed of Missionary." *Los Angeles Times Magazine*, (January 25, 1987), pp. 14-23, 34-35.

Dow, James. "The Image of Limited Production: Envy and the Domestic Mode of Production in a Peasant Society." *Human Organization*, Vol. 40, No. 4 (Winter, 1981), pp. 360-363.

Doxiadis, C. A. "Three Letters to an American." *Daedalus: Journal of the American Academy of Arts and Sciences*, Vol. 101, No. 4 (Fall, 1972), pp. 163-183.

Drewnowski, Jan. "The Affluence Line." *Social Indicators Research*, Vol. 5, No. 3 (July, 1978), pp. 263-278.

Feagin, J. R. "We Still Believe that God Helps Those Who Help Themselves." *Psychology Today*, Vol. 6 (November, 1972), pp. 101-129.

Feather, N. T. "Explanations of Poverty in Australian and American Samples: The Person, Society, or Fate?" *Australian Journal of Psychology*, Vol. 24, No. 3 (December, 1974), pp. 199-216.

Foyle, Marjory. "Missionary Relationships: Powderkeg or Powerhouse?" *Evangelical Missions Quarterly*. Vol. 21, No. 4 (October, 1985).

Frazier, William B. "Where Mission Begins: A Foundational Probe." *International Bulletin of Missionary Research*. Vol. 11, No. 4 (October, 1987), pp. 146-156.

Fukada, Robert M. "The Legacy of Toyohiko Kagawa." *International Bulletin of Missionary Research*, Vol. 12, No. 1 (January, 1988), pp. 18-22.

Furnham, Adrian. "Why Are the Poor Always with Us? Explanations for Poverty in Britain." *British Journal of Social Psychology*, Vol. 21, No. 4 (November, 1982), pp. 311-322.

Galbraith, John Kenneth. "The 1929 Parallel." *The Atlantic*, Vol. 259, No. 1 (January, 1987), pp. 62-66.

Grigg, Viv. "The Urban Poor: Prime Missionary Target." *Evangelical Review of Theology*. Vol. 11, No. 3 (July 1987), pp. 261-272. Reprinted from *Urban Mission*, March, 1987.

Haley, Doris. "Ralph and Roberta Winter: A Wartime Lifestyle." *Family Life Today* (March, 1983), pp. 29-33.

Hallowes, J. F. T. "The Expansion of England in Relation to the Propagation of the Gospel." *Chronicle of the London Missionary Society*, Vol. 51 (May, 1886), pp. 197-200.

Hallowes, J. F. T. "Our World-Wide Empire." *Chronicle of the London Missionary Society*, Vol. 59 (October, 1894), pp. 225-226.

Heaps, Richard A. and Stanley G. Morrill. "Comparing the Self-Concepts of Navajo and White High School Students." *Journal of American Indian Education*, Vol. 18, No. 3 (May, 1979), pp. 12-14.

Honeycutt, James M. "Altruism and Social Exchange Theory: The Vicarious Rewards of the Altruist." *Mid-American Review of Sociology*, Vol. 6, No. 1 (Spring, 1981), pp. 93-99.

Horder, W. Garett. "Prophecy of a Positivist." *Chronicle of the London Missionary Society*, Vol. 59 (November, 1886), pp. 455-459.

Jones, Anthony James. "Fascism: The Past and the Future." *Comparative Political Studies*, Vol. 7, No. 1 (April, 1974), pp. 107-133.

Kane, J. Herbert. "My Pilgrimage in Mission." *International Bulletin of Missionary Research*. Vol. 11, No. 3 (July, 1987).

Kelly, Erin. "Mac in the USSR." *The New Journal*. Vol. 20, No. 2 (October 16, 1987), pp. 6-7.

von Keuhnelt Leddihn, Erik. "La Morale du Travail: Un Probleme Mondial." *Cahiers de Sociologie Economique*, Vol. 2, No. 2 (December, 1971), pp. 215-227.

Keyes, Lawrence E. "Third World Missionaries: More and Better." *Evangelical Missions Quarterly*, Vol. 18, No. 4 (October, 1982), pp. 216-224.

Lasch, Christopher. "The Narcissistic Personality of Our Time." *Partisan Review*, Vol. 44, No. 1 (1977), pp. 9-19.

Loewen, Jacob A. "Missionaries: Drivers or Spare Tires?" *International Review of Mission*, Vol. LXXV, No. 299 (July 1986), 253-260.

Lundberg, Isabel Carey. "World Revolution, American Plan," *Harper's Magazine*, CXCVII (December, 1948), pp. 38-46.

McCracken, John. "Underdevelopment in Malawi: The Missionary Contribution." *African Affairs*, Vol. 76, No. 303 (April, 1977), pp. 195-209.

Miller, Elmer S. "The Christian Missionary: Agent of Secularization." *Missiology: An International Review*, Vol. 1, No. 1 (January, 1973), pp. 99-107.

Monroy, Juan Antonio. "Why Do Protestant Missionaries Fail in Spain?" *Milligan Missiogram*, Vol. VI, No. 3 (Spring, 1979), pp. 1-9.

Mouyelo-Katoula, Michel. "Comparison of price levels and economic aggregates in some African Countries," *The Courier: Africa-Caribbean-Pacific - European Community*, No. 94 (November-December, 1985), pp. 51-53.

Mullen, Redmond. "The Roles of Private Funding in the Context of International Voluntary Activity." *International Transnational Associations*, No. 4 (April, 1980), pp. 176-179.

Mutch, W. J. "Adaptation in Missionary Method." *Review of Reviews*, Vol. VI (June, 1897), pp. 324-332.

Parshall, Phil. "How Spiritual are Missionaries?" *Evangelical Missions Quarterly*, Vol. 23, No. 1 (January, 1987), pp. 10-16.

Pate, Larry D. with Lawrence E. Keyes. "Emerging Missions in a Global Church." *International Bulletin of Missionary Research*, Vol. 10, No. 4 (October, 1986), pp. 156-165.

Porter, Andrew. "Cambridge, Keswick, and Late-nineteenth-century Attitudes to Africa." *The Journal of Imperial and Commonwealth History*, Vol. V, No. 1 (October, 1976), pp. 5-34.

Porter, Andrew. "Evangelical Enthusiasm, Missionary Motivation and West Africa in the Late Nineteenth Century: The Career of G. W. Brooke." *The Journal of Imperial and Commonwealth History*, Vol. VI, No. 1 (October, 1977), pp. 23-46.

Rydell, Lars H. and Charlene B. "Poverty: Waning or Waxing?" *Social Praxis*, Vol. 1, No. 4 (1973), pp. 389-397.

Silver, Maury and John P. Sabini. "The Perception of Envy." *Social Psychology*, Vol. 41, No. 2 (June 1978), pp. 105-117.

Silver, Maury and John P. Sabini. "The Social Construction of Envy." *Journal for the Theory of Social Behaviour*, Vol. 8, No. 3 (October, 1978), pp. 313-332.

Smith, Kevin B. "I Made It because of Me: Beliefs about the Causes of Wealth and Poverty." *Sociopolitical Spectrum*, Vol. 5, No. 3 (1985), pp. 255-267.

Smith, Sydney. "Critique." *Edinburgh Review*. (January, 1808 and April, 1809).

Sweeney, Vernon E. "A Note on Classical Economics." *Social Science*, Vol. 52, No. 2 (Spring, 1977), pp. 90-93.

Taylor, Isaac. "The Great Missionary Failure." *The Fortnightly Review*. Vol. 44 (July-December, 1888), pp. 488-500.

Thayer, C. C. "Missionary Economics: Personal Efficiency." *Missionary Review of the World*. Vol. 26 (July, 1903), pp. 516-520.

Thompson, Joseph P. "Christian Missions Necessary to a True Civilization." *Bibliotheca Sacra*, Vol. 14, No. 56 (October, 1857), pp. 818-854.

Townsend, Meredith. "Cheap Missionaries." *The Contemporary Review*, Vol. LVI (July, 1889), pp. 1-9.

Verryn, Trevor D. "What is Communication? Searching for A Missiological Model." *Missionalia*, Vol. 11, No. 1 (April, 1983), pp. 17-25.

Walls, A. F. "Black Europeans, White Africans: Some Missionary Motives in West Africa." *Religious Motivation: Biographical and Sociological Problems of the Church Historian*, edited by D. Baker. Cambridge: Cambridge University Press, 1978, pp. 339-348.

Walls, A. F. "Missionary Vocation and the Ministry: The First Generation." *New Testament Christianity for Africa and the World: Essays in Honor of Harry Sawyerr*. Edited by M. E. Glasswell and E. W. Fashole'-Luke. London: SPCK, 1974, pp. 141-156.

Williamson, H. G. M. "The Old Testament and the Material World." *The Evangelical Quarterly*, Vol. LVII, No. 1 (January, 1985), pp. 5-22.

PAMPHLETS

American Board of Commissioners for Foreign Missions. "Manual for Missionary Candidates, and for Appointed Missionaries before Entering their Fields." Revised Edition. Boston: Printed for the Board, Beacon Press, 1877.

American Board. "Preparations and Outfit. A Letter to New Members Joining the North China Mission of the American Board." Shanghai: American Presbyterian Mission Press, 1886.

Kagawa, Toyohika. "A Significant Word from Asia, Giving Dr. Toyohiko Kagawa's Clarion-call to the Church of Christ." Published by Bishop Brenton Thoburn Badley, Episcopal Residence, Byculla, Bombay, India, n.d.

Makanzu, Mavumilusa. "The Twentieth Century Missionaries and the Murmurs of the Africans," *Apophoreta of African Church History* - 3. Aberdeen: Department of Religious Studies, University of Aberdeen in Association with the Scottish Institute of Missionary Studies, 1974.

"Remarks on the Provision that Should be Made for the Children of Missionaries."
    New York: Anson D. F. Randolph, 1855.
Shenk, Wilbert R. "God's New Economy: Interdependence and Mission." Elkhart:
    Mission Focus, 1988.
Southon, E. J. "Hints for Missionaries Proceeding to Central Africa." London:
    Printed for the Directors [of the London Missionary Society] by Yates & Alex-
    ander, 1880.

UNPUBLISHED SOURCES

Manuscripts

Bonk, Jonathan James. " 'All Things to All Men'? Protestant Missionary Identifi-
    cation in Theory and Practice, 1860-1910, with special reference to the London
    Missionary Society in Central Africa and Central China." Ph. D. Thesis, Uni-
    versity of Aberdeen, 1984.
Moore, Tom. "The Support Role to the Bible Translation Task." A workpaper
    prepared for the November, 1985 S.I.L. branch conference, Pucallpa, Peru.
Quick, Bernard E. "He Who Pays the Piper . . . : A Study of Economic Power and
    Mission in a Revolutionary World." With a forward by Dr. M. Richard Shaull,
    Princeton Theological Seminary. Unpublished manuscript, n.d.
Song, Choan-seng. "The System, Missionaries and the Future of the Christian Mis-
    sion." n.d. [ca. 1971] Yale Divinity School Pamphlet Collection, Box 359, Folder
    2465.
Walls, Andrew F. "The Voice of One Crying in the Supermarket: The West as the
    Prime Field for Christian Mission." University of Aberdeen, n.d.
Williams, Cecil Peter. "The Recruitment and Training of Overseas Missionaries in
    England between 1850 and 1900, with special reference to the records of the
    Church Missionary Society, the Wesleyan Methodist Missionary Society, the
    London Missionary Society and the China Inland Mission." M. Litt. Dissertation,
    University of Bristol, 1976.

CONSULTATIONS

Missionary Service in Asia Today. A Report on a Consultation Held by the Asia
    Methodist Advisory Committee February 18-23, 1971, in cooperation with the
    Life, Message, Unity Committee of the East Asian Christian Conference. Kuala
    Lumpur: University of Malaysia, 1971.
World Council of Churches World Consultation on Resource Sharing. El Escorial,
    Spain, 24-31 October 1987.